THE WELFARE STATE AND ITS AFTERMATH

THE WELFARE STATE
AND ITS AFTERMATH

Edited by
S.N. EISENSTADT and ORA AHIMEIR

BARNES & NOBLE BOOKS
Totowa, New Jersey

240048

© 1985 The Jerusalem Institute for Israel Studies
First published in the USA 1985 by
Barnes & Noble Books
81 Adams Drive
Totowa, New Jersey, 07512

Library of Congress Cataloging in Publication Data
Main entry under title:

The Welfare state and its aftermath.

1. Welfare state — Addresses, essays, lectures.
2. Social policy — Addresses, essays, lectures.
I. Eisenstadt, S.N. (Shmuel Noah), 1923-
II. Ahimeir, Ora.
HV37.W437   1985   361.6'5   84-24409
ISBN 0-389-20529-X

This publication was made possible by funds granted by the Charles H. Revson
Foundation of New York to the Jerusalem Institute for Israel Studies. The
statements made and the views expressed, are solely the responsibility of the
authors.

A Seminar in Memory of Ehud Avriel

Printed and bound in Great Britain

CONTENTS

Part Four: The Experience of the Welfare State in Different Countries

Part Five: The Case of Israel

Part Six: Concluding Remarks

FIGURES

TABLES

INTRODUCTION[1]

S.N. Eisenstadt

It is said that either of two disasters can befall a vision: failure or success. The welfare state has succeeded. Firmly established in some countries, evolving more slowly in others, the welfare state has become a permanent feature in most modern states. Without a doubt, it has transformed most contemporary societies, but not always according to the vision that created it. This, of course, is the nature of human history: transformations that occur do not always follow the original intentions, and, moreover, the very institutionalisation of such vision usually generates new social forces and problems.

The late T.H. Marshall assumed that the welfare state would be the 'apogee' of democracy. It would give citizens not only legal and political rights, but also social equality. The purpose of the welfare state, according to Marshall, was to take away the impediments that prevented full equality. This was the prime visionary impetus behind what was eventually institutionalised as the welfare state. Another very important historical element in the development of the welfare state, was the Bismarckian vision of the 'peaceful', 'anti-socialist' incorporation of new social classes (especially the working classes) into the state, as well as the older philanthropic tradition of the social services for the 'poor'. In the contemporary world, however, it was the democratic view of the welfare state, the vision of the system as the guarantor of social equality, which became prevalent.

The creation of such conditions of social equality became one of the major, if not the primary, objective of the welfare state and from this goal several explicit or implicit assumptions have developed.

One such assumption stipulated that each individual is entitled to a decent standard of living, to education, housing, medical care and welfare services, as well as to relief at time of crisis. Another assumption has been that through universal services, with guaranteed standards and under governmental control, the elimination of

1

poverty, the advancement of underprivileged groups and the narrowing gaps in income, education and employment, would be best achieved.

All of this has been regarded as an expression of justice which would have a moderating influence on social conflicts and would increase involvement of the population in matters of state and society. It was also often assumed that greater participation by larger segments of the population in the political and economic process, in close relation to Keynesian economic policies, would further economic growth and ensure the durability of a prosperous society.

The concrete developments in the welfare states have seemingly borne out these hopes. Thus, indeed, social services in the fields of employment, health, education, welfare, etc. were given an enormous boost and have greatly changed the whole contour of modern society.

The standard of living and life expectancy in the welfare state have both risen considerably. At the same time the notion of poverty has undergone a radical transformation, changing from extreme to relative distress or deprivation. The lower sectors of the society have continuously gained better living conditions, while such ills as hunger, epidemics and pauperism have been greatly reduced.

In recent years, however, it has become apparent that the measures introduced by the welfare state neither lived up to the original expectations of its creators nor have they caught up with the new problems which kept appearing, partly as a result of these very changes but primarily as a result of the institutionalisation of the welfare state, which seemingly, at least, contradicted its own major goals.

First, the emergence of a colossal bureaucracy has become a basic feature of the welfare state. While originally created to offer protection against exploitation, environmental damage, anarchy and the 'ruthlessness' of free market economy, it has often been regarded by its clients as an alien and alienating organ which cramps initiative, creates dependence and, in the end, serves only its own interests and those of its makers.

The gargantuan swelling of the bureaucratic machine has frequently resulted in a feeling of resentment against authority, a growing dependence upon the system of services and benefits offered by the state, which is now expected to solve every problem, and often a feeling of helplessness on the part of the individual client.

A second major problem is that the financing of services has become a gigantic burden. Since the cost, in relative terms, is borne more by middle and upper classes through the instrument of progressive taxation, and since these groups perceive themselves to be less in need of such services, tax evasion has proliferated and, consequently, the weaker groups have, in fact, had to shoulder more of the burden.

Of no less importance is the fact that while the standard of living in welfare states has tended to rise continuously, it has risen unequally among different sectors of the society, favouring the wealthy more than the lower strata, and thus, it seems, often widening the gap between at least some of the groups.

Some more far-reaching structural changes which have altered the whole contour of modern society have developed in close association with the combination of Keynesian and economic policies and the institutionalisation of the welfare state.

In conjunction with these trends, the development of what has often been called the model of the post-industrial society has occurred. Its predominant characteristics include: the importance of services in relation to productive industries; a significant rise in the standard of education and economic well-being; the growing emphasis on technological and theoretical know-how; and the prominence of so-called post-bourgeois values (the quality of life and humanist ideals), in contrast to the Protestant ethics of work and morality.

The development of this model or trend became connected with far-reaching changes in the class structure of modern societies and in the modes of political participation and organisation. The old pattern of high class consciousness and political activity became weaker. Both the working class and the middle class tended to lose some of their old identity. New sectors, the middle class and white-collar workers, emerged, very often closely related to the state as part of the public sector, with more and more diversified and segmented interests. At the same time, great expectations of mobility were kindled, which the actual process of mobility from lower to middle class has often failed to meet, frequently giving rise to great frustration.

A growing shift in the modes of political organisation, participation and protest have also taken place. Political parties, the traditional instruments of political organisation and articulation of interests, have been losing their organisational strength and their ability to inspire identification. Instead, political activity has become punctuated by constant oscillations between pursuance of various discrete interests by pressure or single-issue groups, new protest groups, fighting for their aims with increasingly louder clamour, often far away from the original aims of the welfare state. Ecological pressure groups, groups demanding civil rights or those opposing nuclear armament, demanded changes of policy and a larger share in government and resources. Particularly vehement during the 1960s and 1970s were the protest movements of students, ethnic minorities and feminist groups, all demanding an end to historical injustices by means of affirmative action, injustices which they claimed had not been corrected, despite considerable effort and expense, by the welfare state.

The result of all these tendencies has been, and continues to be, rather complex. On the one hand, those demanding a say in decisions likely to effect their lives and a greater participation in various areas of policy and life, have become very local and the issue of participation has become a very central one. On the other hand, there has also developed an increasing apathy among those who desire to obtain access to the sources of power and government, but who may be deterred by the complexity of the issues and the systems in modern society in general and democratic ones in particular, and in between these forces there developed, as we have seen, continuous eruptions of single-issue groups and new protest movements.

Thus, all of these trends, in class structure and in modes of political organisation and activities, have indeed generated a new social reality which attests to the fact that most of the problems created by the welfare state were in no way dreamed of by those who were the first bearers of its vision. Neither have the problems remained constant. For example, 15 or 20 years ago, the emphasis was on the issues of efficiency; and, while they still exist, the problems of the welfare state under discussion today are primarily social, political and economic, bearing on the different aspects of the transformation of modern societies to which we have briefly alluded above and which are discussed in greater detail in the various papers in this volume.

Criticism of the Welfare State

Small wonder, then, that the welfare state has drawn widespread criticism. Critics can be divided into four major schools: the 'Conservatives', the 'Moderates', the 'Traditional Radicals', and the 'New Radicals'.

The 'Conservative' criticism rests its case on the belief in initiative, decentralisation and free market economy. It maintains that the excessive interference by the welfare state jeopardises individual liberties and leads the state towards a socialist or communist regime. Too much involvement by the state undermines ambition, initiative and creativity; it runs counter to the laws of nature governing the improvement of the species through incessant struggle and adaptation. Attaining the goals of the welfare state might impoverish the country, discourage labour and curtail investment. The effective implementation of welfare state programmes tends to make citizens even more demanding, fans inflation, bloats the bureaucratic system and saps the power of the government.

The second type of criticism, the 'Moderate' school, usually comes from within social-democratic circles. It accepts the principles underlying the welfare state, but condemns their poor implementation in the distribution of resources, the abuse of services earmarked for the weaker groups by the middle class, and the burdening of the weakest segments with the brunt of financing these services. Proponents of this approach do not call for a new social order, but demand improvements in welfare plans and a redistribution of means.

The third school of 'Traditional Radical' criticism is one which is based on the Marxist tradition and accepts the basis of the welfare state, but objects to its organisational pattern, the reliance on private property and the principle of representative democracy. A just and egalitarian distribution of resources, they claim, can be achieved only through a radical reform in the procedures of economic productions, and a complete democratisation of government, through some sort of far-reaching, semi-revolutionary change.

The fourth, the 'New Radical' criticism, most fully articulated by some New Left groups, claims that the welfare state suffers from the wrong definition of its objectives. For one thing, this criticism perceives welfare as it exists as a purely material matter, but that the benefits and services are not enough and that the state should endeavour to fulfill the inner spiritual needs of the individual. Secondly, the welfare state favours a social, bureaucratic hierarchy and a conventional distribution of labour, at the expense of the community. Thirdly, the welfare state has failed to cope with the individual's sense of alienation and with the fact that work is an imposition and therefore not creative. Finally, they claim that the welfare state destroys its physical environment.

The Case of Israel

Israel presents an interesting focus for the examination of the welfare state, where the link between welfare services and social integration is very much in evidence. There is a ramified, unconventionally structured system of services which was set up as waves of immigrants were being absorbed, mainly in the 1950s, and which served as a tool used by the government in carrying out its melting-pot policy. The concept of welfare rested on the assumption that a minimum level of services, universally available, and maximum government control, would accelerate the process of social integration and blunt the differences of origin, culture, language and education. Going beyond the objectives of equality, the eradication of poverty and other goals set by welfare states all over the world, Israel regarded its service systems as a vehicle towards yet another target: national rebirth and the building of a state.

Today, it has become obvious that the existence of a welfare state depends upon an enormous public expenditure, an all-embracing bureaucratic activity and an economy capable of carrying the heavy burden. These conditions have not been fulfilled in Israel's political and economic life. However, the state cannot deny services which it has undertaken to provide and which the population has been accustomed to receiving. Thus, the Israeli government, like others, continues to abide by its commitments, even as the service system has generated many problems, some similar to those of other societies and others, specific or local.

This Volume contains the contributions of 23 scholars and experts from ten countries and sums up a seminar which was held under the auspices of The Jerusalem Institute for Israel Studies in

Jerusalem in May 1983. In it, we attempted to assess the achievements, hopes and criticisms of the welfare state, the calls for re-evaluation of the path of democratic society, and the role of welfare services in shaping social policies in the post-welfare state era. We paid special attention to the case of Israel and to its need to engage in scrupulous self-examination in a time of diminishing resources. It is our hope that the stimulating presentations of the distinguished participants will be of interest to decision-makers in the field of social services and will throw light on areas worthy of research and re-appraisal. Needless to say, the views expressed in this book are those of the authors alone, and the editors only claim that the views presented here are interesting and important for the discussion of the problems of the welfare state.

Notes

1. Based in part on a background paper which was prepared for the International Conference, 'The Welfare State and its Aftermath', held in Jerusalem in May 1983, and on the opening statement of S.N. Eisenstadt at the symposium.

PART ONE

THE WELFARE STATE: HISTORY AND
CONTEMPORARY PERCEPTIONS

1 ON THE HISTORY AND CURRENT PROBLEMS OF THE WELFARE STATE

Peter Flora

In the course of a century the welfare state has become an integral part of the institutional framework of Western society. Public authorities today distribute a large share of the national product to private households in the form of cash transfers, and provide some of the most essential services. The institutions of the welfare state must, therefore, be understood as being entrenched elements of the interest and normative structures of our societies. Any fundamental changes in these institutions would deeply affect all other core institutions.

In recent years there has been much talk of a 'crisis' of the welfare state. Pessimists envisage a possible historical regression, a dismantling of the modern welfare state, under the impact of financial problems and the attack of ideological and political adversaries. Optimists, instead, dream of replacing the centralised bureaucratic 'welfare state' with a more decentralised 'welfare society', on the basis of new technologies and/or a revival of intermediary structures. Whilst pessimism and optimism are important attitudes, they are hardly scientific.

Throughout the long history of their development, the institutions of the welfare state have been in an almost continual, and sometimes drastic state of change. But are we experiencing today, or should we expect to experience in the near future, fundamental *changes*? In dealing with this question I propose to distinguish between:

(1) the *general type of Western welfare state* in terms of its linkages to capitalism and mass democracy;
(2) *levels of development* in terms of the extension of benefits in cash and kind throughout the social structure;
(3) *major variations* in terms of expenditure and financing patterns and institutional structures;
(4) *historical phases* in the growth and transformation of the Western welfare states in terms of changes in the international system, the world economy, and the socio-demographic basis.

11

The development of the welfare states has, to varying degrees, been accompanied by financial difficulties and political controversy. But are we experiencing, or should we expect to experience in the near future, a more fundamental crisis? In dealing with this question I propose to distinguish between:

(1) *problems of system integration* in terms of a maladaptation of various institutional orders, and consequences for the public household;
(2) *problems of social integration (first type)* in terms of the frequency and intensity of class/group conflicts, and eventually a polarisation of larger population groups;
(3) *problems of social integration (second type)* in terms of the integration of individuals into smaller groups fulfilling important social functions.

The Western Type of Democratic and Capitalist Welfare State

The welfare state originated in Europe during the late nineteenth century. In both concept and type it still bears the stamp of its origin insofar as it was closely tied to the development of capitalism and mass democracy from the very beginning. Certainly, with the spread of the industrial mode of production and the dissemination of the nation-state as the predominant form of political organisation, the creation of public education, health and social security systems has become a world-wide phenomenon. In this way the problem of balancing 'accumulation versus legitimation', which O'Connor sees as the fundamental systemic problem of capitalist states, has become universal. It is true, however, that the democratic and capitalist institutional framework of the Western welfare states shapes the problems of 'accumulation' and 'legitimation' in specific ways. This is the main reason for speaking of a 'Western type' of welfare state.

Thesis 1

The development of the Western welfare state is not to be understood as a step on the road towards socialism. It should be interpreted instead as a complementary process in the *evolution of a relatively coherent tripartite structure* consisting of: capitalist market economy, democratic mass polity, and welfare state.

The primary objectives of welfare state development were/are neither a nationalisation of production nor a collectivisation of consumption, but to bring about public intervention in the distribution and stabilisation of individual life chances on the basis of individual rights. This led to the creation of a supplementary system of monetarised benefits and the provision of some essential services in areas such as education and health, where production and consumption are highly fused. The market mechanism with private property and decentralised economic decision-making remained basically unaltered.

This means that the Western welfare state is based on the economic surplus produced in the capitalist market economy and that its structure must be adapted to the basic laws governing this economic system. At the same time, however, the Western welfare state is also based on the political consensus produced in the democratic mass polity, and its structure must reflect the basic nature of this consensus. Founded on the economic surplus and political consensus, and restrained by the logic and functioning of capitalist and democratic institutions, the Western welfare state also has the effect of stabilising them and thus contributing to a reconciliation between capitalism and democracy.

The expansive character of the Western welfare state is largely explained by its close linkages with capitalist and democratic development, the internal dynamic within, and the tensions between these two institutional orders.

Thesis 2

The Western welfare state is intrinsically expansive. It should not be interpreted primarily as an attempt to eradicate poverty or to integrate the industrial working class, but rather as an attempt to influence the *distribution and stability of individual life chances of the total population.*

Certainly, the creation of the welfare state as a distinct institutional order was historically linked to the emergence of the industrial working class. It may also be understood however, as an answer to the more fundamental process of 'expropriation of the means of war, administration and production' (Weber), which started with the soldiers and bureaucrats of the early modern state, and in the course of capitalist industrialisation soon extended beyond the working class. Not only has the employment status of 'dependent worker' become generalised, but 'dependence' has

grown in general, in an increasingly interdependent system of production and reproduction. Given the growth of mass democracy, it
may not be surprising, therefore, that the generalisation of 'social
security interests' on the one hand, and class/group conflicts over
the distribution of life chances on the other, led to an expansion of
the welfare state via the process of institutionalised political
competition.

The extension of social security systems in Europe since the
turn of the century illustrates the expansive character of the welfare state (see Figure 1.1). The timing of this process varied from
one country to another, but on the 'European average' it shows a
surprising continuity: it was not even interrupted by the two World
Wars and the Great Depression, and one finds very few national
examples of a retrenchment in system membership.[1]

What is the impact of the expansive and expanded welfare state
on social structure, capitalist economy and democratic polity?

Thesis 3

The impact of the welfare state on the social structure is ambivalent. It has both *egalitarian and status-preserving tendencies.*

In an historical perspective, the Western welfare state has certainly had an egalitarian objective and impact. The evolution of
mass democracy has led to the institutionalisation of basic social
rights as well as to efforts to diminish the inequality of opportunity
(in education), of income (through taxation and transfer payments), and even of the 'quality of life'. The extent of this egalitarian impact is debatable and debated. What is more important
here is that the extension of the welfare state itself has set limits to
its egalitarian impact and strengthened status-preserving tendencies.

This is not only, or even mainly, due to 'Marshall's paradox'
that a greater 'equality of opportunity' may increase the legitimacy
of the 'inequality of results'. The unequal (but relatively continuous) distribution of market incomes (on the basis of private property, formal education and occupational differentiation), will, in
combination with the majority principle of the democratic polity,
be reflected in a differentiated and unequal benefit structure of the
extended welfare state.

The post-war development of the European old-age pension
schemes may be taken as empirical illustration of these two
counter-tendencies. Countries which started with egalitarian

Figure 1.1: The Growth of Social Insurance Coverage in Western Europe

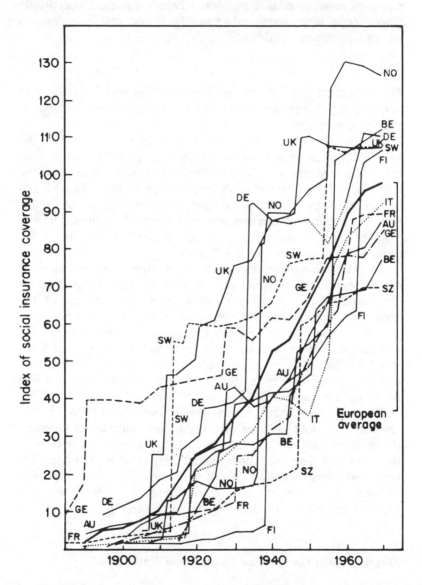

national pension schemes have subsequently added supplementary earnings-related pension benefits, whereas countries with a tradition of earnings-related pension schemes for the economically active population have subsequently introduced elements of national minimum pensions.

Thesis 4

The impact of the welfare state on the capitalist economy and democratic polity is ambivalent. It has both *stabilising and immobilising tendencies.*

The development of the welfare state certainly increases the value of 'human capital' and stabilises aggregate demand; it probably dampens class conflict and thus indirectly could increase the legitimacy of the capitalist economic institutions (or rather, reduce their illegitimacy). At the same time, however, it may also undermine the balance of consumption and saving/investment, immobilise labour, and bureaucratise production, thereby reducing the economic surplus on which it is founded.

The institutionalisation of basic social rights, the extension of social security, and the reduction of (certain) social inequalities by the welfare state, certainly contributes to the stability of the democratic mass policy. At the same time, however, it may also immobilise the political process by institutionalising a variety of new vested interests, and may damage fiscal stability by a tendency to solve these new interest conflicts by an extension of benefits. In this way it may undermine the political consensus on which it is based and thereby lose its liberal character.

To summarise: the Western type of welfare state is characterised by its close linkages with capitalism and mass democracy. Its fundamentally dynamic and ambivalent character derives from these linkages. The institutional variations of this general type over time, and across countries, are of course great, and the respective mixture of egalitarian and status-preserving, stabilising and immobilising tendencies derives from these variations.

Developmental Levels and Institutional Variations

European governments had been active in education, health and poor relief for a relatively long period by the time the real 'take-off' of the modern welfare state took place at the end of the nineteenth century. This occurred with the creation of the new institution of 'social insurance', which provided cover, first against industrial accidents, sickness and old-age, and much later against unemployment. The relative growth of the state (as measured by public expenditure as a percentage of national product) started at that time, after having largely stagnated during the nineteenth century. The general increase of the 'state's share' greatly accelerated during the two World Wars which produced the well-known 'displacement effect' in many countries. In 1950 the average share in Western Europe was around 25 per cent. By the mid-1970s it had almost doubled to more than 45 per cent, and this in a period of rapid economic growth.

This development was almost completely due to the increase in social expenditure, above all for education, health and income maintenance. Table 1.1 gives some figures for the growth of 'social security expenditure' (which includes social insurance, social assistance, family allowances, public health, social benefits for war victims and public employees, but excludes education, housing, and welfare services.[2]

The figures demonstrate the continuous growth from one-tenth in the early 1950s to more than one-fifth in the mid-1970s (and this still excludes major categories of 'social expenditure' such as education). They furthermore demonstrate that the rate of relative growth has accelerated over the period, if one takes the annual average increase in percentage points.

Social security expenditure is dominated by two categories, health and pensions, each of which today amounts to approximately one-third of total expenditure, with a tendency to increase this proportion. Other items usually amount to less than one-tenth. Family allowances steadily declined in relative terms, and up to 1977 unemployment benefits were not a major category, in comparison to the inter-war period.[3]

When analysing causes and components of this growth, one has to distinguish between growth factors within a given institutional framework and those generated by institutional changes. Among the first, cost inflation and population changes are the most important. But they have not been the only, or even the main, factors contributing to the post-war growth of the welfare state. Its 'coverage' has enormously expanded, i.e. social services and transfers have been extended to new and larger population groups, and

Table 1.1: The Relative Growth of Social Security Expenditure (as a percentage of GDP/GNP)

	AU	BE	DE	FI	FR	GE	IR	IT	NE	NO	SW	SZ	UK	Average
1950	12.4	11.6	7.9	7.4	11.5	14.8	7.2	8.4	8.0	6.2	9.7	5.9	9.6	9.3
1955	12.8	13.0	9.8	8.3	10.7	14.3	8.9	10.8	8.3	7.5	11.1	6.8	9.6	10.2
1960	15.4	15.3	11.7	8.8	13.2	15.5	9.3	11.6	11.0	9.4	10.9	7.6	10.8	11.6
1965	17.6	16.1	12.2	10.6	15.6	16.5	10.2	14.8	15.5	10.9	13.6	8.8	11.7	13.4
1970	18.8	18.1	16.6	13.1	15.3	16.8	11.4	16.3	20.0	15.5	18.8	10.6	13.8	15.8
1974	18.2	20.9	21.0	15.4	21.6	20.3	15.8	21.4	24.8	17.8	24.4	13.9	14.6	19.2
1977	21.1	25.5	24.0	19.3	25.6	23.4	18.3	22.8	27.6	19.6	30.5	16.1	17.3	22.4

Table 1.2: Average Growth Rates of Social Security Expenditure (in percentage points, average of 13 countries)

1950-1955	0.18
1955-1960	0.28
1960-1965	0.35
1965-1970	0.48
1970-1974	0.85
1974-1977	1.07

Table 1.3: Major Categories of Social Security Expenditure (as percentage of total social security expenditure, average of 13 countries)

	Pensions	Health	Family allowance	Unemployment
1954	24.4	25.0	11.8	3.9
1960	31.1	27.8	9.6	2.8
1966	34.0	29.9	8.6	2.3
1971	34.5	30.4	7.3	3.2
1974	35.6	31.0	6.1	3.3

benefit levels have been raised not only in absolute but also in relative terms (i.e. as percentages of average wages).

Table 1.4 presents figures on the extension of coverage in terms of the percentage of the labour force covered by the four main social security schemes.[4] The figures demonstrate the continuous extension of coverage in all four schemes but they conceal the qualitative change: since the Second World War, social security has ceased to be an institution which only benefits the dependent labour force, and has increasingly been extended to cover the self-employed and to persons outside the labour force. Given this general process of extension throughout the social structure, most European welfare states today can be called 'mature' in this (limited) respect. They are 'mature' also in the sense that the extension of coverage was accompanied by a substantial increase of the major cash benefits not only in absolute terms (i.e. at constant prices) but also in relative terms (i.e. in relation to average earnings).

Table 1.4: Social Security Coverage (average of 13 countries)

	Industrial accidents	Sickness	Old age	Unemployment	Average
1950	60	67	76	34	60
1955	66	71	81	41	65
1960	72	72	90	47	70
1965	74	87	92	51	76
1970	79	89	92	56	79
1975	83	91	93	63	83

Beyond these common growth tendencies, however, important institutional variations persist. They are reflected first of all in the great differences of expenditure levels (see Table 1.1). Thus, in 1950 social security expenditure varied from 5.9 per cent of GDP (Switzerland) to 14.8 per cent (Germany), and in 1977 from 16.1 per cent (Switzerland) to 30.5 per cent (Sweden). Curiously, among those countries traditionally identified with the welfare state, only Sweden and Denmark had expenditure levels above the European average, and then only since the late 1960s.

Institutional differences are furthermore reflected in expenditure patterns (see Figure 1.2).[5] In the period from 1949 to 1974 Britain and Scandinavian countries spent relatively more on health, whereas the continental countries (with the notable exceptions of France and Belgium) spent more on pensions. Differences in family allowances, to take another example, still reflect the varying impact of Catholic social philosophy.

Even more revealing are the differences in the structure of financing (see Figure 1.3).[6] On average in Britain, Ireland and Scandinavia almost 60 per cent of social security expenditure was financed from general revenues, whereas the respective share was below 25 per cent for the remaining countries. In this second group the contributions by the insured are higher. Even more important, however, are the employers' contributions, especially in Italy and France where they amounted to over 60 per cent.

There is a bewildering variety of institutional differences which hardly form clear-cut empirical patterns. One may say nevertheless that the Scandinavian countries and Britain come close to the ideal type of the 'Nordic welfare state' which could be defined by the following characteristics:

Figure 1.2: Shares in the Financing of Social Security (country averages 1949-77)

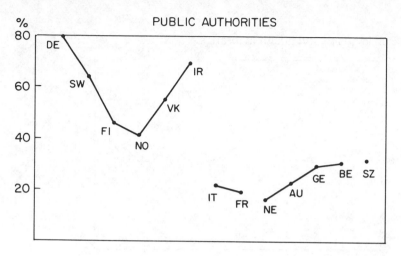

PUBLIC AUTHORITIES

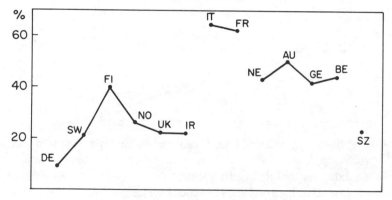

EMPLOYERS

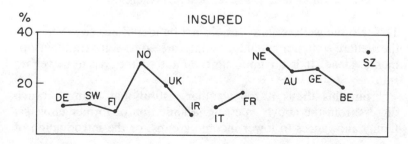

INSURED

Figure 1.3: Expenditure Patterns as a Percentage of Total Social Security Expenditure (country averages 1949-74)

Public health and health insurance

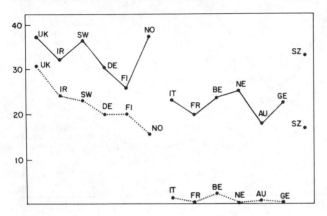

Family allowances

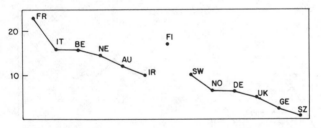

— emphasis on universal and egalitarian income maintenance schemes;
— an extended public health sector;
— an extended comprehensive school system;
— reliance on general tax revenues in financing.

This 'Nordic welfare state' should not be identified, however, with the welfare state nor should it be interpreted as a general developmental stage. It is an important variant of the Western welfare state.

From this thesis it follows that institutional changes which digress from the above type (e.g. a limitation of former universal family allowances to lower income groups, or the introduction of

Figure 1.4: Expenditure Categories as a Percentage of Total Social Security Expenditure (country averages 1949-74)

Pensions

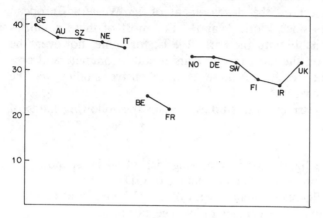

Social assistance

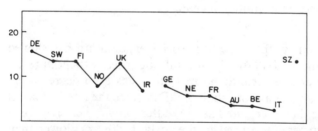

some social insurance elements) are not to be interpreted as a 'regression' but as shifts from one subtype to another within the group of 'mature' welfare states.

If we now take developmental levels and/or institutional subtypes as points of reference, can we observe any basic changes since the mid-1970s?

Thesis 5

The period since the mid-1970s has not (yet) been characterised by a dismantling of the welfare state but rather by attempts to limit its further expansion in a period of economic restraints.

It is very difficult to prove this thesis in a systematic and empirical way, as no survey has yet examined either all or the most important changes. Furthermore, most European governments seem to have reacted towards the new economic situation with a delay of several years. Thus, there are very few examples of major cuts or institutional changes prior to 1979–80.

In my assessment, I can rely on results of an international research project on the development of 13 Western European welfare states since World War II.[7] For most of these countries data are available until the early 1980s; for some, however, the information on the most recent years is still incomplete and preliminary. The results of these comprehensive studies will be published elsewhere.[8]

For an assessment, the studies contain the following kinds of information:

(a) aggregate figures for major categories of social spending, at constant prices and as a percentage of GDP;
(b) average figures on major types of social benefits, at constant prices and as a percentage of average earnings;
(c) some indicators on social services;
(d) information on institutional changes.

Not surprisingly, the growth of social expenditure has slowed down since the mid-1970s. In several countries, expenditure on income maintenance, health and education has even decreased in relative terms, i.e. as a proportion of GDP, since the late 1970s. At the same time, however, one has to see that only in very few cases the relative expenditure level in the early 1980s was lower than before the onset of the economic recession in 1974, and in no case was it lower in real terms. In most cases it was substantially higher.

The same observation can be made with respect to average benefits (at constant prices) which in general have further increased. Major exceptions were child allowances, because they lacked indexation in a period of high inflation, and unemployment benefits, probably more because of the changing structure of unemployment, and less because of lowered earnings-replacement ratios.

In general, the available data seem to support the above thesis. The mature welfare state has become an entrenched element of our societies which is very difficult to change and has established, through the extension of welfare clienteles, a solid basis of political support. This general conclusion, however, needs some qualification.

(a) There are significant differences between the Western European countries with respect to the problems they encounter and the ways in which they react to them (Norway, Sweden and Finland, for example, have hardly known any cuts, whereas Belgium and the Netherlands seem to have undergone a thorough change of their welfare programmes).

(b) In some countries more important changes may be made in the near future, at least partially enforced by increasing problems in balancing the public household and in financing social security, as in Italy for example.

(c) The essential meaning of the changes since the mid-1970s may be found much less in the threat of an 'historical regression' of the European welfare state, and much more in the break of the past 'growth pattern' which will require a readjustment of major institutions.

System and Social Integration in a Changed Macro-constellation

Consideration of the 'logic' of the general type of Western welfare state may enable us to gain some insight into its basic features, though at a highly abstract level only. Mapping important variations in the development and structure of the Western welfare states, we may be able to find some explanations by relating them to major political, economic and other changes, or differences among the Western societies. In the same way a definition of 'problems' could be sought with reference to the basic type and/or to developmental levels/institutional patterns. This will not be sufficient, however, for an understanding of the present situation and the current problems of the welfare states (as it would not have been sufficient in the past). For such an understanding I propose to use the concept of 'historical macro-constellation' as a coincidence of major and relatively independent development of the world economy, the international system, and the socio-demographic basis. Historical phases (in contrast to developmental levels) of the Western welfare states have been closely linked to their long-term or/and dramatic changes.

Thesis 6

The current (and probably future) difficulties of the Western welfare states lie in a changed historical macro-constellation and are not the result of a 'necessary' system development.

Thesis 7

The current (and probably future) difficulties of the Western welfare states do not arise from a resurgence of class conflict, but from problems of system integration produced by this new macro-constellation.

In an analysis of the current difficulties one should distinguish between problems of social integration (i.e. the social control of individual and group behaviour) and system integration (i.e. the harmonisation of institutional orders). A prominent example combining both aspects is Marx's theory of the internal contradictions of the capitalist mode of production (system integration) and class conflict (social integration). In contrast to this tradition (as well as to the modifications suggested, for example, by Lockwood), I assume:

— that it can be misleading to explain social disintegration primarily as a consequence of system disintegration; it may have different origins and may also create or at least aggravate problems of system integration;
— that one should draw a clear distinction between problems of interest conflicts/mediation and problems of social integration in a stricter sense ('moral integration' in Durkheim's terminology);
— that the general problem of system integration lies in a 'harmonisation' of the elements of the macro-constellation (internal structures/international environment; relationships between institutional orders);
— that the core of system integration lies in the political order, because 'system breakdown' can only be defined in terms of the internal order or external independence of the state.

Thesis 8

The current problems of the Western welfare states manifest themselves most clearly in a structural imbalance of the public households. An enduring 'fiscal crisis' of the welfare state poses the most severe problem.

Rostow has suggested to 'operationalise' political stability, with some qualifications, in terms of the public household. A political system is equilibrated, according to him, if mobilised resources roughly correspond to expenditure, and if the level and allocation of expenditure solve the politically articulated problems to an extent that dissatisfaction and opposition remain within the existing constitutional order.

In this sense we are confronted with a situation of declining stability as a consequence of the following developments:

— the structural problems of the world economy since the mid-1970s: not only do they set limits to the growth of public revenues, but they simultaneously require increased public transfers and subsidies to facilitate the structural adaptation and to master the unemployment problem;
— the changing external security situation because of increasing East-West and South-North tensions which are only partially a consequence of the world economic crisis: the trend since the Korean war of relatively declining military expenditure has been stopped;
— the independently changing age structure of the Western population which, even if it does not greatly change the 'dependency ratio', leads to a shift of resources in favour of private households (fewer children), to the disadvantage of public households (more old people);
— the continuing dynamic of social expenditure: since the 1960s it has been the fastest growing expenditure category, and for several reasons (such as cost inflation, unemployment, the above demographic changes) it seems to remain, without institutional changes, inherently dynamic;
— the political and economic limits to further taxation: never since the First World War, has the tax burden (including social security contributions) increased so rapidly as since the mid-1960s.

Thesis 9

The structural imbalance of the public household reflects the fact that the Western welfare state in the present historical macro-constellation has probably reached its 'limits to growth' beyond which it would undermine its own bases: market economy and mass democracy.

For more than a decade the development of the Western welfare states has been accompanied by a shift of resources from private and public investment to private and public consumption and probably also by an immobilisation of the labour market. In this way the welfare state has lost revenue because of slackening growth. In addition, however, it seems to lose revenue through the relative growth of production outside the market or of hidden market transactions. To secure the necessary revenue in such a situation, without institutional changes, necessarily implies increasing state control and repression, which would, if exercised, entail the loss of much of the liberal character of the welfare state.

The imbalance of the public household reflects a maladjustment of institutions. An obvious example lies in the change of reproductive behaviour and the way in which old age pensions are financed. A new equilibrium will have to be sought by strengthening family policy (a fairly neglected policy field until the mid-1970s), by re-introducing elements of capital accumulation into the insurance schemes, and probably by increasing again the age of retirement. Another example may be found in the relationships between the labour market and the financing of social security in general. High unemployment rates have tended to undermine the earnings-related contribution basis of social security. On the other hand, the employment-related way of financing has increased the costs of labour over-proportionally and has made demand and supply of labour less flexible.

Problems like these will be solved by institutional adaptation, if the political support can be found. In most European countries this process of institutional adaptation seems well under way. A more difficult problem, at least in the middle range, may lie in a 'blockade of structural mobility'.

Thesis 10

At least for a decade, the Western European welfare states will face the problem of a 'blocked structural mobility' produced by the historical coincidence of the extension in higher education and a demographic wave with the fiscal problems of the state.

Upward social mobility to a large extent has always been the consequence of structural changes. This is especially true with respect to the growth of the service sector and the increase of qualified positions after the Second World War. The 'revolution in higher education' since the early-1960s went closely hand in hand with the most rapid expansion of state activities from the mid-1960s to the mid-1970s, creating an equilibrium in the supply and demand of positions with higher qualifications.

As a consequence of the enduring fiscal problems of the public household — and as a result of the pace of expansion in the past — this equilibrium has become imbalanced and 'structural' social mobility has tended to become 'blocked'. The imbalance is further aggravated by the fact that relatively large age cohorts (from the late-1950s to the mid-1960s birth rates were relatively high across Western Europe) pass the system of higher education and enter a labour market characterised by a stagnating public sector and high unemployment in the private sector.

The declining birth rates (since the mid-1960s) will bring some relief to this problem, and economic recovery will ease many of the financial problems, but it will not bring back past growth rates. The European welfare states will have to face a prolonged period of relative stagnation (in terms of public expenditure and public employment) and of institutional adaptation. However, the very success of the welfare state — in its own terms — makes it unlikely that stagnation and adjustment will lead to historical regression.

Notes

1. The 'index of social insurance coverage' is designed to facilitate a comparison of the growth of social security systems across the Western European countries. It consists of a weighted average of the population covered in all four systems (measured as a percentage of the economically active population). The four percentages are weighted as follows: old age insurance 1.5, health and unemployment insurance 1.0, industrial accident insurance 0.5. In the case of subsidised voluntary insurance, the corresponding percentages were halved. The bold line represents the 'European average', i.e. the average of the index values of 13 European countries. For a more extensive analysis of the index see Peter Flora, Jens Alber and Jürgen Kohl, 'Zur Entwicklung der westeuropäischen Wohlfahrtsstaaten', *Politische Vierteljahresschrift*, vol. 18, no. 4 (1977). AU = Austria, BE = Belgium, DE = Denmark, FI = Finland, FR = France, GE = West Germany, IR = Ireland (Republic), IT = Italy, NE = Netherlands, NO = Norway, SW = Sweden, SZ = Switzerland, UK = United Kingdom, GB = Great Britain.

2. Peter Flora *et al.*, *State, Economy and Society in Western Europe 1815-1975*, vol. I, Frankfurt, Campus, 1983.

3. Flora, *State, Economy and Society*. The countries included are those of Table 1.

4. Flora, *State, Economy and Society*. The countries included are those of Table 1.

5. Flora, *State, Economy and Society*. In principle, country figures represent the averages for the 25 years period 1949-74.

6. Flora, *State, Economy and Society*. In principle, country figures represent averages of the years 1949, 1954, 1957, 1960, 1963, 1966, 1971, 1974, 1977.

7. This project was started in spring 1980. It is directed by Peter Flora and involves a group of 18 social scientists from 13 different European countries. Until 1983, it was financed by the European Community and was scheduled for completion in summer 1984.

8. Peter Flora (ed.), *Growth to Limits. The Western European Welfare States 1950-1980*, 5 vols., Berlin, De Gruyter, 1984 and 1985.

2 THE MAJOR PROBLEMS OF THE WELFARE STATE: DEFINING THE ISSUES

Brian Abel-Smith

Throughout the industrialised countries, the welfare state is under attack. The attack comes from both 'the left' and 'the right' — though the arguments used in the debate vary considerably among different societies. The strongest consensus is about the cost. The point seems to be reached in all societies when the majority insist on being left with more of their money to spend in their own way. The political process reacts to these demands by trying to curtail or check the constantly rising bill for welfare. Debates about the level of welfare spending have now moved to the centre of political debate and underly the instability of many governments throughout the Western world.

Less noticed is the trend in those developing countries which are rapidly advancing to make the creation of a welfare state the centre of political aspiration. Countries still want to advance welfare when resources are available to do so in a relatively painless way. It is when fewer extra resources become available that welfare comes under attack. And it is in this respect that the scenario of the 1970s and 1980s differs so much from the scenario of the 1950s and 1960s.

A much longer paper than this would be needed to define all the issues in the debate. The approach of this paper is to try to distinguish between problems which are relatively minor and those which are of major significance. Inevitably a number of questions are dealt with rather superficially. But at least it may be the basis for a discussion of what are and what are not the really important questions.

The Polarised Debate

From the right, the welfare state is accused, if not of creating, at least of exacerbating the current world economic crisis. The high taxes and contributions needed to finance it are said to cause inflation,

31

low rates of saving and investment, poor labour productivity because of reduced incentives to work and thus to contribute to the stagnation of exports and low rates of economic growth. High employers' contributions come in for particular criticism for reducing international competitiveness. The benefits provided are said to create dependence and also damage incentives of work. On top of all this the welfare state is accused of scooping the talent out of the labour market and 'crowding out' the capacity for industrial growth. On the basis of all these arguments, the solution advocated is nothing less than the dismantling of the whole apparatus, leaving people to buy such services as they choose and restricting welfare to a residual service for the poorest or a redistribution of income via a negative income tax. The argument that in our richer societies most people can afford to buy their security is pressed with greater vehemence.

From the left, the welfare state is attacked for failing to eradicate poverty and create a more equal society. Social services are said to be manipulated by the more affluent to strengthen the inequality of life chances through education and the distribution of health care, to reinforce the subjection of women and strengthen capitalism by reinforcing the work ethic. The solution advocated is a radical redistribution of power in society.

The Real Achievements

In assessing the contribution which the 'welfare state' has made to our societies, it is important to be clear about what it was originally intended to do — on how the consensus which created it and extended it was built. It is very doubtful whether the architects of our welfare states ever envisaged them as great engines of equality. The objectives of Roosevelt in the USA, Beveridge in Britain or Laroque in France were much more modest. Their aims were no more than to provide a minimum of security, defined in somewhat different ways. They did not intend to try to create a more equal society but to establish a floor of protection at the bottom. And it is because the proposals were to establish no more than minimum rights, in some countries specifically excluding the higher income groups, that they found favour with successive legislatures who voted the funds to establish and steadily develop these systems. Of course, there were radicals supporting the legislators who hoped for much more. But the original aim which won such broad support was to establish a floor of rights upon which individuals could build further social protection on an individual basis. Only the extremes of discontent were to be squashed by the welfare state.

Judged in these narrow terms, the welfare state has real achievements to its credit. It has provided a minimum of security — a right of access to free or nearly free health and welfare services, to a minimum number of years of free education, to minimum income in defined contingencies, and in many countries to subsidised housing. To a considerable extent all this is paid for by the transfer of income within income groups rather than between income groups, using property taxes, indirect taxes and social security contributions. The device of making employers pay contributions make systems seem more redistributive and thus more acceptable than would otherwise have been the case. Workers did not realise that they were likely to pay their employer's contribution themselves, in addition to the employee's contribution.

Thus, to a large extent, the welfare state is a mechanism which redistributes income over life. But it also redistributes from those with no children to those with more than the average number, from those with secure employment to those with insecure employment, from those with short lives to those with long lives, from those with good health to those with poor health. While the lower income groups may have large families and less secure employment, it tends to be the higher income groups whose children continue longest in education and who retire earliest and draw their pensions for the greatest number of years.

While people see much of what they pay for this security, the value of what they receive is much less visible. And this cost has been steadily rising over the years for a number of main reasons. First has been the extension in the number of years of education, with particular costly provision in the later years. Second has been the ageing of the population: more elderly people retiring early, drawing their pensions longer and generally receiving better pensions as schemes have steadily matured. Third has been the growing cost of health care due to technical progress in medicine, the changing age structure of the population for which care has to be provided and the general expansion of supply, mainly in response to the demands of providers. Fourth has been the growth of one-parent families. Fifth, and most important of all, has been the recent formidable cost of growing unemployment which both reduces the income as well as expanding the expenditure of social security schemes.

The Need for Security in Affluent Societies

It is because of these and other reasons that the cost of welfare has risen faster than domestic product; and that it is not convincing to argue that as societies get richer, people can be left individually to buy their own security. Moreover, in an age of continuing inflation, pension security simply cannot be bought on the private market. People of working age would be posed with impossible problems if they were to be expected to pay for the upbringing and education of their children and at the same time to help support their parents and contribute to the cost of health and welfare care for their grandparents. 'Social security', as Winston Churchill once said, 'brings the magic of averages to the service of millions.' Because of longer schooling, earlier retirement, heavy unemployment and the rising cost of health and social care, this service is needed now more than ever before.

The evidence to support the conclusion that welfare is not only needed but wanted comes from observation of the choices made by the higher income groups and the interpretations of these choices made by private employers. The higher income groups are not content with the minimum of welfare guaranteed by the state. The major development of the last thirty years has been in the supplementation of the minimum by a variety of private arrangements — for pensions, for life insurance, for sick pay, for supplementary health insurance, for redundancy, for the financing of private education, and so on. So, far from making private saving unnecessary, the development of the welfare state has been accompanied by a massive expansion of private saving in a variety of complex institutional forms.

The Economic Case against the Welfare State

Nor is it possible to find convincing support for the argument that the welfare state has harmed economic growth or generated unemployment. The welfare state has been most extensively developed in countries which have been among the most successful in terms

Table 2 1: Percentage of GNP Devoted to Social Protection (EEC, excluding Greece, 1980)

The Netherlands	30.7
F.R. Germany	28.3
Denmark	28.0
Belgium	27.7
Luxembourg	26.5
France	25.8
Italy	22.8
Ireland	22.0
United Kingdom	21.4

of economic growth over the past thirty years. Japan is often quoted to prove the contrary, but in Japan welfare is extensively developed within the firm rather than by the state. Among the EEC countries the high spenders on social protection (the definition excludes education) are the Netherlands, F.R. Germany and Denmark (see Table 2.1). The United Kingdom is often quoted as a country which has ruined itself by high spending on its welfare state. But in 1980 it was the lowest spender among the nine EEC countries (excluding Greece for which data are not available).

Nor is there much in the argument that high social security contributions falling on employers are bad for economic growth or employment — for example by favouring capital intensive industries at the expense of labour intensive industries. It is total labour costs that matter and employers' social security contributions fall on firms making capital goods as well as on firms making consumer goods. Moreover, the relative economic success of some European countries since the Second World War compared, for example, with that of the USA may have been partly due to their high capital investment.

What is certainly true, however, is that it has been those countries which have enjoyed the most rapid economic growth which have expanded their welfare spending most rapidly. People could be given more public welfare and still enjoy a considerable growth of real cash income at the same time. In recent years this has no longer been possible, hence the major discussions of levels of public spending throughout nearly all EEC countries.

The argument that the welfare state destroys the will to work or makes people prefer benefit to work also seems to have little real credibility. There were few who took this position when levels of employment were high and when Europe was recruiting 'guest workers' and immigrants to man the less desirable jobs in their societies. It is only in recent years when employment levels have been low that more people have started to blame the generosity of provisions for those without work for part of the growth of unemployment.

The Persistence of Poverty

The welfare state provides strictly limited benefits and services. Granting these limited rights to defined categories has inevitably led to demands to extend rights to others and broaden definitions. Traditional social security systems have been built on a contributory basis and thus exclude or treat less favourably those who do not contribute — particularly women caring for children and disabled dependants, or women whose marriages have broken up; those disabled before entering working life; and those who, given present employment prospects, have never had a regular job. Inevitably the contributory basis of social security comes under attack from those excluded from it, as they see it, through no fault of their own, and adaptations are made to meet some of these demands. But the full adjustment needed, for example, to give fair treatment to women is far from complete. On the other hand, those who support themselves on low-paid work, irregular work or part-time work and live below the minimum look enviously or grudgingly on those who are given a minimum income without doing any work to earn it. Thus the provision of minimum income for some leads to the demand for an absolute right to a minimum income for all — a call for an end to poverty, or at least for its prevention.

While the welfare state has on the whole abolished hunger and extreme deprivation, it has not abolished relative poverty. Using as a bench mark half the average net income per person adjusted for household size, a recent EEC study found at least 30 million persons (11.4 per cent) of the EEC population (excluding Greece) in poverty in the mid-1970s (Commission of the European Communities, *Final Report from the Commission to the Council on the First Programme of Pilot Schemes and Studies to Combat Poverty*, Com (81) 769 Final, Brussels 1981). The percentage of those in poverty in each of the nine countries is shown in Table 2.2. Among the reasons were benefit and social assistance levels below the bench mark, a failure to claim social assistance and means tested benefits, and inadequate provision to protect the low earner and larger family. The commission recommended the introduction of a minimum income at an early date and ways of achieving this are being studied.

The possibilities of using tax credits and reverse income tax has been extensively studied in Canada, the United States and the United Kingdom. The use of a tax credit scheme to achieve this objective would be very expensive and involve a number of administrative problems which are not easily resolved. A negative income tax would either involve payment substantially later than the need had arisen or a system of claiming that would be different in little more than name from social assistance and thus would be likely to involve problems of take-up. In theory modern information technology could be used to resolve some of these problems but the enforcement of requirements to provide all the necessary information would be likely to be regarded as a further major invasion of privacy and confidentiality. Moreover in some countries there is simply no room to impose yet another means tested scheme on top of other means tested schemes. Already the loss of benefits from earning more involves, in theory at least, a poverty trap already unacceptably high. It is partly because there is no administratively easy and relatively cheap solution which preserves incentives to work that it remains unresolved. Those who argue that the whole social insurance system can be swept away and a reverse income tax established at lower cost have not come to grips with all these difficulties.

Table 2.2: The Incidence of Relative Income Poverty of Private Households (EEC, excluding Greece)

	Percentages
The Netherlands (1979)	4.8
United Kingdom (1975)	6.3
Belgium	6.6
F.R. Germany	6.6
Denmark	13.0
Luxembourg	14.6
France	14.8
Italy	21.8
Ireland	23.1

Greater Equality?

As pointed out above, social insurance schemes do not do much to equalise incomes between vertical income groups. This is one of the features which make them acceptable and might well make a large system of reverse income tax unacceptable even if ways could be found of administering it effectively. People pay social insurance contributions more readily than taxes because they believe that they are paying towards their own pensions and other benefits. As a result, whereas a bill to raise social security contributions hurries through the British parliament in a matter of hours with poor attendance, a bill to raise taxes always involves a long and highly contested debate.

But what about health and education? There were many who argued that the provision of free education would do much to equalise life chances. This has certainly not been the case in Britain. The sons and daughters of manual workers are now more likely to end up with middle-class jobs than in the past. But this is entirely because more such jobs are available. Their *relative* chances have not improved. In this sense we have made no progress in equalising the outcome of the educational process. It is still the children of the higher socio-economic groups who are most likely to receive costly higher education.

There were some who assumed that removing money barriers and providing health care free to all at time of use would go much of the way towards equalising health standards. But there is no evidence that the gap in health standards between socio-economic groups has been narrowing. And that gap can be large. For example, in Britain the daughters of manual workers are four times more likely to die aged one month to one year than the daughters of the managerial and professional classes. For sons the incidence of death is five times greater. Partly to blame are patterns of professional behaviour and partly the failure of the lower social groups to take problems to the health service to the extent needed. But the more fundamental problem is that health standards are mainly the product of the wider social and economic environment and of behaviour patterns within it.

In short, the welfare state provides rights of access: it does little or nothing to promote greater equality in terms of outcome. It is nevertheless virtually certain that there would be even more inequality in many different senses if the welfare state were 'abolished'. In one sense the welfare state has clearly contributed to greater equality. It has created a much higher proportion of high status jobs for women than are offered in industry or in other service occupations. Moreover, it has been to a considerable extent responsible for the general improvement of job opportunities for women — particularly married women. The two-earner family has in part been created by the 'welfare state'.

But the fact that so many jobs depend upon the welfare state has its disadvantages as well as its advantages. In many countries, an excess of hospital beds has come to be provided. With shorter lengths of stay and improved facilities for care at home, they are no longer needed. But there is formidable local political opposition to the closure of a hospital because of the loss of jobs. Similarly with a falling birth rate, fewer school places are required, but again there is formidable opposition to closing a local school.

Public Relations and the Problem of Bureaucracy

There are some who argue that formidable bureaucratic problems are an inevitable feature of a welfare state, as if private insurance schemes never presented any problems in understanding, interpreting and disputing the meaning of the small print defining risks covered. Any system of insurance inevitably involves problems of understanding and interpretation. These types of problems are avoided in the national health service where, until recent legislation to exclude foreigners, everyone could turn up at any hospital or register with any general practitioner willing to take them. There are more complaints about bureaucracy with national health insurance schemes in continental Europe than with service schemes such as in Britain or Denmark. Indeed, regular surveys show over 70 per cent of the population satisfied or very satisfied with the national health service.

Complaints about bureaucracy and delay are greatest in Western Europe where there are a large number of different funds covering different risks or different occupational groups each operating on a centralised basis. This means that there is no local office where people can discuss their grievances face-to-face and have their problems sorted out. A multiplicity of schemes inevitably leads to borderline problems of entitlement so that the insured person can find himself referred backwards and forwards between different agencies alleging that responsibility lies elsewhere. In this respect a unified scheme of social security, as in Britain, has advantages: it is economic to staff local offices with the intention that they should sort out problems on the spot and explain how benefits are calculated.

But in general social security institutions, whether autonomous or governmental, tend to be poor at public relations. While large firms spend lavishly to inform the public about their activities, social security spends relatively little, though the messages it needs to convey are inevitably much more complex. Often there is a cheese-paring attitude to public relations — leaflets and forms packed with close print on poor quality paper, a limited budget for advertising and gross understaffing and undergrading of staff in local offices leading to queues, and an inefficient system of information retrieval leading to delays and further queues. Attempts to improve efficiency by computerisation can lead to further depersonalisation of service.

If greater public support for the welfare state is to be generated, much greater attention is needed to public relations. Citizens should have the right to general information about social security in a form which they can readily absorb. They should also have had any questions asked about their own personal rights answered promptly either in writing or in person. There should be rights of appeal to an independent body and all communications about benefits should include a statement about how to use the appeal machinery and obtain skilled help in doing so. Citizens should have access to their own files and rights to confidentiality. These and other questions are currently under active discussion in the European Community. Some have suggested that there should be a legal code to enforce the rights of citizens against social security institutions.

Ways can be found to overcome some of the problems of bureaucracy if there is political will to make this happen. But the running of any large service is inevitably complex and where scarce resources have to be rationed, rules have to be established for priorities of entitlement. Inevitably those who do not get what they want when they want it become dissatisfied. Moreover, there is always a risk that the more articulate will receive more than their strict entitlement. This would happen on a larger scale if purchasing power were used to distribute services. It is not, however, necessarily the case in all societies that regulating agencies become taken over by those they are intended to regulate. Imperfect regulation may be better than no regulation. Problems of rationing arise because of lack of resources to meet demands and the need to develop systems to define relative needs. The fact that assessments of need can be challenged and appealed against is a clear sign of the healthy working of democracy. Again it is likely to be the more articulate who press complaints through every available channel. But the victory of one complainant may lead to changes which benefit all users thereafter.

There are constant pressures to centralise services so that resources are evenly distributed and citizens everywhere have the same opportunities to use a similar level of services. But this search for territorial justice has its dangers. Where major decisions are taken by vast centralised bureaucracies, it leads to a sense of impotence and remoteness in the minds of ordinary citizens who cease to take a lively interest in public affairs because they feel unable to exercise any effective influence. This is part of the reason for the growth in apathy, indifference and scepticism, and lack of involvement in political parties. Decentralisation of power to the lowest possible level of government may be worth considerable losses of efficiency and territorial equality if it leads to a greater degree of active involvement in public affairs.

The Underlying Tensions

There were some who imagined that the re-establishment of minimum rights to welfare would lead to a more harmonious society in which everyone would willingly pay out to help the less fortunate, in which there would be more social cohesion and a greater sense of brotherhood and participation. Instead there seems to be continuing acrimony as each group seeks to maximise its cash spending power — its rights to exercise command over consumer goods. Groups who see themselves as less favoured than others press for improvements in their rights and become organised in or represented by pressure groups — for old age pensioners, the disabled, one-parent families and so on. There are continual accusations from those who see themselves as payers rather than receivers, that people are cheating the system by working while receiving unemployment benefit, by becoming pregnant to obtain better benefits, or avoiding payment of contributions and taxes in the black economy. Such abuses undoubtedly exist, but their extent tends to be exaggerated by the media out of all proportion. The reaction of successive governments in Britain has been to increase year by year the manpower employed to detect abuse and fraud among social security claimants. Much more strenuous efforts are taken to detect social security fraud than the evasion of liability to tax.

Where the higher income groups have obtained, normally through employers' schemes, generous supplementary rights to welfare, they come to see these rights as their main source of security and no longer identify with the main national scheme, which they see as designed not for them but for those lower in the income scale. They ignore the enormous extent to which this supplementary welfare is subsidised by concessions in income tax. They press for improvements in their own occupational benefits and criticise the heavy deductions from their pay which go to finance the main schemes. Politically their interest may be in newer causes such as the environment, animal welfare or nuclear energy.

But those who see themselves as payers rather than receivers are not all to be found in the higher income groups. The most punitive attitudes to those receiving cash benefits can be found among manual workers with steady employment and, as yet, good health. They underestimate their own risks, know little about where the money goes which is deducted from their wages and want more of their money to spend on themselves, so that they also can enjoy more of the advantages of a middle-class style of consumption. They are the crucial voters in the election of governments pledged to cut public expenditure. In societies where consumer goods are lavishly promoted and their acquisition regarded as the sole purpose of work, and where public goods are not promoted and only dimly understood, such attitudes are inevitable.

All these pressures are part of the democratic process as everyone scrambles for a better share of the national cake. But they have come to the forefront of politics because of low economic growth or nil growth and heavy unemployment. They were much less evident when people could be given both more welfare and more real income. The largest single factor has been the growth of unemployment which has depleted the tax and contribution base of the welfare state while at the same time imposing massive increases in the cost of cash benefits for the unemployed. These costs of unemployment in Britain could finance about half another national health service. It is as if the cost of a thirty-year growth in the number of pensioners has had to be absorbed within the span of only a few years. The tensions are inevitable. The main problem is not the welfare state but the high level of unemployment.

Any attempt to make the better-off pay more of the cost so that the lower-paid could pay less would be strongly resisted. The pecking order of real net earnings levels seems to be a feature of our societies most resistant to change. And the unionisation of white-collar workers has strengthened this resistance. In a materialist society when most people see work simply as a means for acquiring rights to consumption, the battle for pay is fought long and hard. Nevertheless, in some countries of Northern Europe it has proved possible to create a measure of greater equality in earnings from public employment.

Conclusion

To describe some of the forces in our societies which maintain inequality, obstruct policies to eradicate poverty, keep many public services under-financed and social security to a limited role is not to admit defeat. The more these forces are understood, the greater the chance of finding ways round them. Moreover, it is important to distinguish the real problems of the welfare state from those which are exaggerated to justify cuts in welfare spending. Understanding why particular policies have not had the effects which some hoped for, helps in devising policies which will be more effective in the future.

3 MAJOR PROBLEMS AND DIMENSIONS OF THE WELFARE STATE

Franz-Xaver Kaufmann

> It is important to distinguish the real problems of the Welfare State from those which are exaggerated to justify cuts in welfare spending.
>
> B. Abel-Smith

In spite of a rather general agreement that Western democracies can be labelled as welfare states — at least for the period from the end of the Second World War to the 1970s — the attempts to define the properties of welfare states are rather loose, various and depend on national traditions. Moreover, this task proves to be particularly difficult because the concept of the welfare state is considered to be both empirical and normative. If one wants to speak of a 'crisis of the welfare state'[1] or if one asks for what is 'beyond the welfare state' it is assumed that there are common properties that constitute a welfare state and that may now be in a crisis or a period of transition. In this paper propositions are made that challenge some basic assumptions about the welfare state and oppose to them alternative assumptions that may contribute to a better understanding about our actual problems.

Problems of Definition

As the work of various research groups shows[2] it is very difficult to ascertain a common pattern of the development of welfare states or to explain the genesis by single or even compound factor theories that prove to be valid on a comparative basis. This contrasts with the evidence that modern welfare states show in fact common properties despite certain variations in scope and institutional embodiment. This can be explained by the theoretical assumption that the welfare aspects of modern states are emergent properties that have developed in a process of trial and error. In an evolutionary perspective one may consider various historical

44

situations, socio-political movements and conflicts as challenges, and the responses of the already institutionalised forms of political power (in terms of, e.g., social legislation, repression or migration policies) as variations. The emergence of common properties calls then for explanation. If Western societies have adopted rather similar ideas and institutions for promoting what is called the welfare state there must be also common properties in the challenges that have acted in a selective way upon the variations in political responses. That is, we have to identify not only the answers that constitute the properties of welfare states but also the problems that were solved by these answers in order to understand what may be in crisis or transition now. From an ideological or programmatic point of view — and this is predominant in the current literature — one may summarise the dominant perceptions of welfare states as follows:

(a) a state that provides economic security and social services for certain categories (or all) of its citizens;
(b) a state that takes care of a substantial redistribution of resources from the wealthier to the poor;
(c) a state that has instituted social rights, as part of citizenship;
(d) a state that aims at security for and equality among its citizens;
(e) a state that is assumed to be explicitly responsible for the basic well-being of all of its members.

If one considers the institutional counterparts to these programmatic definitions, one sees of course a multiple overlapping, as many institutions serve various of these goals. But there is also evidence that, in choosing one or another approach, one is led to different results with respect to the scope and the problems of welfare state activities. These definitions have in common that they do not define the properties of a state, but only of the welfare aspects of a state. If one speaks about Western democracies as welfare states additional properties of modern states are implied, e.g. democratic government, civil and political rights, constitutionalism, etc. These preconditions are not necessary for all of the above mentioned properties. From a constitutional point of view definition (c) deserves particular attention. It is incompatible with an absolutistic or totalitarian conception of the welfare state.

From an institutional point of view one finds in the Anglo-Saxon discussion a common understanding — that the welfare state may be identified with the social services. In the German discussion the 'Sozialstaat' (a comparable, but already slightly different term) is identified with 'Sozialpolitik'. These assumptions are of course not wrong but superficial. They consider particular aspects as the whole thing. The whole thing we have to consider is the modern state performing not only functions of welfare but of, for example, defence, maintaining internal order, and political integration, too. There do not exist two separate entities: one called welfare state (Sozialstaat) and the other called constitutional state (Rechtsstaat), but it is the same government that decides about pollution control, full employment policy, defence and social security. Speakers and writers about the welfare state concentrate on an idea and the corresponding particular institutions as if they were isolated from the rest of the policies. *The services, however, do not or seldom constitute an integrated specific system, and the welfare functions of the state cannot be reduced to the operation of the social services.* Therefore I propose to speak not about the welfare state, as if one could take for granted that modern states are concerned primarily with the welfare of its citizens, but about the welfare properties or policies of modern states that may be differentiated in various dimensions. Thus a state can be said to have welfare properties to the extent that

— it takes explicit responsibility for certain aspects of the basic well-being of its members,
— this responsibility is not only a political declaration but institutionalised in the form of social rights that can be claimed by every individual entitled to,
— this responsibility materialises also in certain forms of political activities to improve the realisation of these rights.[3]

This definition tries to emphasize the *political* quality of state interventions that are legitimised by expected improvements of social welfare. It does neither assume that particular interventions are benevolent and beneficiary *per se* nor that social welfare can be maintained or maximised only by political action. However, the normative content of the welfare state concept is incorporated by assuming that social rights are essential correlates of state activities. Measures that may be retracted by governments or other public agencies without violation of individual rights do not exhibit the full quality of welfare *state* interventions.

Concrete states may differ with regard to their welfare aspects,

(a) in the *ideological* dimension: as to the scope and limits of state responsibility for individual and collective welfare (there is some empirical evidence that in spite of sometimes hard conflicts about political preferences there is a rather high normative consensus about the dimensions of basic welfare or quality of life, on an international as well as on a comparative basis);

(b) in the *institutional* dimension: as to the degree of state influence on the provision of services, the redistribution of wealth and the control of semi-public or private relationships (there is some evidence that this dimension transcends the welfare sector and that basic properties of various national societies have a strong impact here);

(c) in the *organisational* dimension: as to the organised forms and the degree of centralisation/decentralisation by which certain social problems are treated (there is some evidence that the kind of state organisation has an impact on that dimension);

(d) in the *performance* dimension: as to the kind and amount of resources allotted to different public programmes and the impact of public action upon changes in the life situation of various social groups (there is some empirical evidence that state intervention may have quite different impacts depending on the kind of social problem and on the kind of political intervention as well as on the kind and relationship of non-state organisations that are involved).

The Ambivalence of Welfare Politics and Policies

Theories about the welfare state normally assume that policies or services — that are said to be delivered in order to promote welfare — are motivated in fact mainly for that or similar altruistic reasons. It is a well-known source of grief that Bismarck promoted social security mainly to control the labour movement. Though this argument underestimates the real concern, even of Bismarck, with the 'social question', it is nevertheless correct that *political motives are operating as strongly as moral ones do when politicians make decisions on social reforms.* In the theory of fiscal policy, social services are called meritory goods, i.e. they are delivered not only for the satisfaction of individual needs (that could be operated by market mechanisms, too). If there is any public provision of goods one has to assume that they have additional merits, i.e. they satisfy also collective needs. The expansion of educational services in the 1960s was motivated by the human capital theory and the 'sputnik-shock'. Moral arguments alone do not suffice to promote or to fight against cut-back of welfare expenditures. The collective utility of social services is an issue in social policy as well as the individual utility.

Another but related issue in welfare politics concerns the traditional assumption, that welfare measures always have benevolent effects. The argument against this assumption is twofold:

(1) *Individual and collective utilities may become opposite.* If, for example, childcare services are not accepted by foreign immigrants it is questionable that they produce utility to them. But it may be nevertheless of collective interest to assimilate the children as early as possible to the country they are living in.

(2) Even if the *ex ante* estimation of the overall effects of some measure of welfare is quite positive, *there is no guarantee that the real outcomes and impacts operate correctly in the way anticipated by the men who decided about it.* This is shown by the growing evidence of implementation and impact research in the social sciences. I propose therefore to substitute the assumption that the welfare measures of the state aim at promoting welfare by the assumption that they operate as an *intervention* which is *legitimised* by the promotion of welfare. Our starting point for analysing the welfare state is therefore not the concept of social services, but that of political and social intervention.

In the United States 'social services' designates the five main domains of welfare institutions — namely, education, health, income maintenance, housing and employment. In the English classifications the last domain seems to be regularly excluded. In the German context the literally corresponding term 'Soziale Dienste' is restricted to what is called sometimes the personal social services (cf. Kaufmann, 1980: 35). Books about the welfare state or about social policy normally differentiate along the lines of the mentioned five (or perhaps also four or six) domains of welfare institutions. This, however, obscures the fact that the operation of these institutions — e.g. of income maintenance and personal services — produces quite *different* problems. To speak of 'social services' as if they were a homogeneous kind of public intervention makes a reasonable discussion of the conditions of effective public intervention impossible. For analytic purposes — and we need more analytic knowledge if we want to overcome actual inconsistencies in reasoning about the welfare state — I have proposed elsewhere the following classification of welfare policies (cf. Kaufmann, 1982):

- public interventions granting and protecting social rights (legal form of intervention);
- public interventions influencing the income situation (economic form of intervention);
- public interventions to improve the material and social environment (ecological form of intervention);
- public interventions to improve directly the competence of individuals (educational/advisory form of intervention).

Each of these forms of intervention (that may be found in reality often combined) shows particular conditions of effectivity and needs different forms of organisation. I can not go deeper in that issue now but I want to emphasise that, if there should be a crisis of the welfare state, the arguments advanced do not fit with all policies and their parts. We need therefore more analytical concepts for understanding what is going on in different domains of social policy.

Understanding welfare policies as part of government, or state activities, that are ambivalent interventions in already constituted social relationships unveils of course the simplicity of most arguments about the welfare state. Even if these policies are formulated by scientists, their intentions are mainly political and not analytical. The welfare state is until now more a political and moral than a scientific issue.

But what is gained by analytical sophistication? I think that it enables us to overcome the great words of pros and cons, of crisis and welfare, and to ascertain the domains where particular critics are applicable, without denying the success and enduring impact of social policy for the life situation of the underprivileged parts of society.

Let me explain that point by a few examples. In Germany critics of the welfare state crystallise in five concepts:

— *juridification,* i.e. the fact that human miseries and their treatments are regulated and hence altered by the forms of law;

— *bureaucratisation and centralisation,* i.e. the tendencies toward more influence of the central state and more inter-organisational controls and hence more rigid standard setting, loss of initiative and empathy, etc.;

— *economisation,* i.e. the tendency to consider social services under the aspect of costs only and not of their utility;

— *professionalisation,* i.e. the fact that social services are administered more and more by professionals cultivating their particular vision of life and social problems, thus degrading and deteriorating the knowledge of everyday man to meaninglessness.

Instead of bureaucratic and professional interventions, these critics call for self-help and mutual aid of non-professionals, for the reactivation of families and neighbourhoods or — to name it shortly — for a new solidarity. Relationships to the alternative movement are obvious. But there are also conservatives and liberals (in the German sense) that may be attracted by these critics.

Sociologists dealing with social policy in Germany have picked up that issue, and with financial help of two research foundations they co-operate since 1978 in exploring the inter-relationships of social policy and non-professional social systems.

One can show that the criticisms are of quite limited scope and demonstrate a manifest misunderstanding of the most important forms of socio-political intervention. They exhibit, however, some truth in the realm of the personal social services, e.g. in chronic diseases or in drug and youth problems (cf. Badura/von Ferber, 1981; Kaufmann, 1982a). Moreover, one can observe forms of mutual adaptation of both self-help movements and political bodies operating at the local level. A growing emphasis on the conditions of ecological and educational/advisory intervention results from that research, whereas legal and economic forms of intervention are bound necessarily (and without major inconvenience for their effectivity) to juridification and bureaucratisation.

The Public Production of Welfare in the Context of State and Society

If one speaks about a welfare state that, for example, provides services, one considers the state or the government as a single actor that acts in favour of the welfare of any part of the population. This perspective disguises the fact that only a variable part of the services regulated or financed by the state is administered by boards placed under direct governmental control. *Governments prefer to create semi-autonomous bodies or to subsidise and regulate already existing private bodies in order to promote the delivery of social services.* The names and the structures are quite different in various countries, but there is growing evidence on an international level that the welfare sector is one area where the newly defined species of political animal called 'Quango' (quasi-non-government-organisation; cf. Hood, 1983) is proliferating most actively. Moreover, insofar as the provision of welfare presupposes a personal contact between the service delivering agencies and the clients, a nation-wide decentralisation of these services is needed, which would make centralised control virtually impossible. If we want to understand the operation of what is called the welfare state, we should use a broader perspective.

Whereas the 'classical' functions of the modern state were centred around the problem of political order under the conditions of individual freedom, the welfare functions are related to problems that are not essentially state-related in character. German thinkers have therefore tried to conceive the problem of 'Social-Politik' as the mediation of 'state' and 'society' (cf. Pankoke, 1970). This refers to the famous distinction of Hegel (1821) between the state as the constitution of self-containing power, and the family and 'civil society' as the network of new economic opportunities. For Beveridge, full employment policy formed an integral part of the political welfare concept. Thus the concept of the welfare state has to include also assumptions about its relation to structures and processes of society if one really wants to conceive it as an entity that may be in crisis or in transition. Welfare state then becomes a kind of symbol for a pattern of societal integration by the means of the state that is assumed to operate, for example, as a kind of exchange between mass loyalty and increase in social welfare.

Effective intervention needs, therefore, new links between state and civil society, *a mingling of public and private operations and issues.* In order to change the operations of existing social structures the state had to interfere in those operations and, hence, lost its autonomy. New corporatism is a school of thinking that tries to account for that fact. Instead of the state as a singular actor we have to consider, therefore, the production of welfare as a (partially contingent) result of networks of both governmental and non-governmental, formally public and private corporate actors (cf. Kaufmann/Majone/Ostrom, forthcoming).

Crisis of the Welfare State

From a more general point of view the emergence of the welfare properties of modern states is related to two paramount sets of problems:

(a) the problem of providing goods and services for the satisfaction of basic needs, especially in the fields of medical treatment, care, education, housing and income;
(b) the control of power relationships within society that emerge from differences of economic and social status (e.g. worker and consumer protection, lowering the differences of social groups/classes in terms of education and income).

These sets of problems have been named from a normative point of view as problems of security and equality. From a historical point of view most of the challenges that account for progress in social legislation stemmed from consequences of the development of a capitalist market economy. This development was the moving factor for the social changes which led to a deterioration in older forms of communal life. The emergence of the welfare aspects of modern states has thus to do not only with the immediate challenges of market economy but also with the more encompassing problem of *inclusion,* i.e. the problem of participation for everybody in every functional area of society. In this perspective the emergence of the welfare aspects of modern states is a consequent pursuit of the enlightenment programme, based on the experience that a strong separation of state and free economy would lead to social consequences threatening the maintenance of an existing political order.

Whereas the promises of the welfare state for social inclusion and internal peace have bound political interests for three decades after the Second World War, recently we have experienced growing tensions in welfare policies and disillusionment about the power and potential of the welfare state to perform its programme. We exclude from our considerations new challenges that may superimpose the welfare issues on politics, and concentrate upon new challenges within the welfare area:

(a) *Rising aspirations*: In democratic systems there seems to be a strong trend towards improvements of social benefits without respect to their efficiency, bearing on the assumption that people vote for parties or governments because they want more welfare.

(b) *Fiscal shortages*: The past expansion of social benefits correlated with a never before experienced period of overall economic growth. Economic stagnation restricts the fiscal realm of action and reinforces the propensity of individuals to withdraw from taxation or to exploit public provision in order to maintain an attained standard of living. Thus cut-backs in social benefits are probable and in general the struggle for distribution of the national income becomes sharper.

(c) *Efficiency gaps*: There is growing criticism of the performance of social services and a questioning of their impact for furthering inclusion and improving the life situation of the underprivileged groups. The main arguments are:

— services serve the middle classes more than they do the poor;
— state intervention furthers the bureaucratisation of services and renders them ineffective;
— new forms of social deprivation have emerged that will not be improved by existing forms of state intervention.

(d) *Side-effects*: Numerous critiques maintain that the expansion of the welfare function of the state has led to unanticipated and undesirable consequences, for example:

— the emergence of a 'distributive elite' and new power structures that are beyond democratic or judicial control;
— the lowering of motivation to work;

— a constant tendency to inflation, and thus to a decline in economic growth as well as to an increase in unemployment;
— a decline in political loyalty of growing segments of the population that feel (for rising aspirations and/or for political
reasons) in opposition to the existing modes of production and
political action.

Whereas fiscal shortages are quite evident at the present time and
are impinging on nearly the whole field of welfare activities, the
other points mentioned deserve scrutiny as to what extent they are
dominated by, and are necessary consequences of, welfare policies
or they are only specific reversible tendencies. Insofar as the maintained side-effects are concerned, one may question the predominant causal relationships to welfare functions of the state.
Several issues seem to depend more upon other factors of social
change.

We maintain that the high variability of national solutions to the
problems of social welfare and inclusion shows no uniform tendency to a 'crisis of the welfare state'. If there is any crisis in
modern society (and I believe there has been crisis since its beginning!) its core is not the welfare sector. However, this may be
affected by strains in other sectors of society, and it certainly shows
weaknesses in some respects. Thinking 'beyond the welfare state'
does not mean questioning the achievements of public responsibility for social rights, but, on the one hand, one must explore in
more detail the necessary functions and operative limits of the
state in providing social welfare, and, on the other hand, one must
ask about the potential of political systems to find adequate
responses to new challenges outside the problems of inclusion and
individual welfare.

I shall close with an attempt to define the actual situation of
Western societies with respect to their developed political welfare
function. As already stated, I doubt if most of the charges against
the welfare state — if true at all — stem from governments performing the welfare function, or from other developments within
modern states and societies. Nevertheless it seems that the limits of
problem solving of welfare politics and policies have become more
apparent today. There are, first, limits in income redistribution,
resistance to pay contributions and taxes (e.g. tax evasion seems to
be growing). Second, problems of guidance, control and performance evaluation emerge, insofar as the welfare properties of the

state become systemic structures. The growing inter-dependence of entitlements and interventions may lead to counter-intuitive effects, impact of which is widely unknown. Third, some side-effects of administrative problem-solving become more apparent, as the already mentioned concepts of juridification and bureaucratisation show. Fourth, new social problems emerge as consequences of overall modernisation (e.g. drug addiction, loneliness of old people, failures in education or family disorganisation), and it seems that these problems are more resistant to classical forms of political-administrative problem-solving. Finally, some political measures that have proved to be quite successful in the past (e.g. full employment policy) seem to lose a part of their efficiency or effectivity. It is, however, quite an open question to what extent this argument is true. The main challenges to the state's welfare function actually stem from fiscal shortages due to decreased economic growth and growing unemployment. The latter is related also to the impact of demographic irregularities that act as strong, but often neglected, strains upon employment, as well as upon the needed size and costs of services (cf. Kaufmann/Leisering, 1984).

If these limits of socio-political problem-solving become more apparent, this will lead to a disillusionment about the welfare state. The so-called crisis of the welfare state seems to be not primarily an institutional, but an ideological crisis. If one considers the welfare state as a kind of civil religion, as the basis of truce between the big socio-political groups and as a basis of trust of the population in the legitimacy of political power, it may well be that these hopes for internal peace and eternal well-being are again waning, as so often in history. Economic and demographic challenges will doubtless lead to political strain and to an acerbity in the relations between various socio-political groups. The collective utility of welfare measures, then, may be assessed to be lower than in the past, and this may lower the support of the 'well-offs' to the services. These tensions may lead in some countries to changes in the institutional structure of welfare. Some minor changes may even improve the efficiency of welfare policy, but I doubt strongly that major cut-backs would be a very effective medicine for the illnesses of our time. I suspect that the withdrawal of support to the welfare functions of the state would lead to a deterioration of the regulating power of the state as such, and I confess that I can hardly imagine such a situation as progress, but only as a renewed outburst of human passions.

Notes

1. A crisis that was — by the way — voiced by *The Times* as early as 1962, Cf. Marshall, 1965: 92
2. Cf. especially Heclo, 1974; Flora Heidenheimer, 1981; Mommsen, 1981; Köhler/Zacher, 1981; Alber, 1982.
3. Cf. also the general Declaration of Human Rights by the United Nations, art. 22-7.

References

Alber, J., 1982: *Vom Armenhaus zum Wohlfahrtsstaat. Analysen zur Entwicklung der Sozialversicherung in Westeuropa*, Frankfurt/New York (Campus).

Badura, E. and von Ferber, C. (Hrsg.), 1981: *Selbsthilfe und Selbstorganisation im Gesundheitswesen*, München/Wien (Oldenburg).

Flora, P. and Heidenheimer, A.J. (eds.), 1981: *The Development of Welfare States in Europe and America*, New Brunswik (Transaction Inc.)

Hegel, G.W.F., 1821: *Grundlinien der Philosophie des Rechts oder Naturrechts und Staatswissenschaft im Grundrisse*, Berlin.

Heclo, H., 1974: *Modern Social Politics in Britain and Sweden*, New Haven/London (Yale University Press).

Hood, C., 1983: 'The Hidden Public Sector: The "Quangocratization" of the World?', to be published in: Kaufmann, F.-X., Majone, G. and Ostrom, V. (eds.), *Guidance, Control and Performance Evaluation in the Public Sector*, Berlin/New York (De Gruyter).

Kaufmann, F.-X., 1980: 'Social Policy and Social Services: Some Problems of Policy Formation, Program Implementation, and Impact Evaluation', in: Grunow, D. and Hegner, F. (eds.), *Welfare or Bureaucracy. Problems of Matching Social Services to Client's Needs*, Cambridge/Massachusetts (Oelgeschlager, Gunn & Hain) and Königstein/Ts. (Hain, pp. 29-43).

Kaufmann, F.-X., 1982: *Towards a Sociological Theory of Political Intervention*, University of Bielefeld, Center for Interdisciplinary Research, Research Group 'Guidance, Control and Performance Evaluation in the Public Sector', reprint no. 2.

Kaufmann, F.-X. (Hrsg.), 1982a: *Staatliche Sozialpolitik und Familie*, München/Wien (Oldenburg).

Kaufmann, F.-X. and Leisering, L., 1984: 'Demographic Challenges in the Welfare State', to be published in: Øyen, E. (ed.), *The Future of the Welfare State*, London (Heinemann).

Köhler, P.A. and Zache, H.F. (eds.), 1981: *Ein Jahrhundert Sozialversicherung in der Bundesrepublik Deutschland, Frankreich, Großbritannien, Österreich und der Schweiz*, Berlin (Dunker & Humblodt).

Marshall, T.H., 1965: *Social Policy*, London (Hutchinson).

Mommsen, W.J. (ed.), 1981: *The Emergence of the Welfare State in Britain and Germany: 1850-1950*, London (Croom Helm).

Pankoke, E., 1970: *Sociale Bewegung — Sociale Frage — Sociale Politik. Grundfragen der deutschen 'Socialwissenschaft' im 19. Jahrhundert*, Stuttgart (Klett).

PART TWO

THE CONTROVERSIES OVER THE WELFARE STATE

4 THE IDEA OF THE WELFARE STATE AND ITS CONSEQUENCES

Arthur Seldon

The welfare state was conceived in Germany but nurtured mainly by Britain; the country which pioneered its successive stages, was earliest in seeing the consequences, and is now catching up with the United States in leading the search for new solutions and reform.

This paper considers the aftermath of a long social experiment that is ending in Britain and in Western Europe — for as it tried to remove deficiencies in education, public health, housing, income and social security, it did so with politically-decided techniques whose long-run, or even medium-run, consequences and 'externalities' it did not pause to take into account. The experiment is now gradually withering away because the policy cannot keep pace with the changing economy and society. It will not even have to be 'dismantled' because it is yielding to market forces, mainly *embourgeoisement* on the side of demand and technical innovation on the side of supply.

The Plausible Reasons for a Welfare State and the Wrong Solutions

I discern ten main reasons for state welfare throughout the past century. However, in all cases the solution was ineffective or damaging, as we can now see.

(1) In the case of primary poverty, the problem is best tackled by redistribution in cash that allows for indirect as well as direct taxes, and not by services in kind that advantage the culturally stronger in bargaining with officialdom.

(2) As to secondary poverty, this is best handled by earmarked purchasing power — such as vouchers with which the USA experimented in the field of education and Australia in housing. In Britain, however, such a solution is being obstructed by the bureaucracy.

59

(3) The problem of inequality is also best removed by redistributing purchasing power, generalised or earmarked. Nothing can create equality in income or wealth, but the levelling of purchasing power can create the substance of equality of status.

(4) Similarly resolved could be the issue of parity of esteem; otherwise, the workers of the world will continue to be outwitted by the middle-class professionals, such as academics, who deploy their accents, family connections, character, temperament, knowledge of Latin tags or biblical texts, and political influence. As it happens, the state, not least the welfare state, responds to pressure group decibels, not polling booth numbers.

(5) The issue of retirement or disability pensions paid by the state — the welfare state's obligations — will before long, in the so-called representative democracies in the USA, Australia, the UK, Sweden, and no doubt before long in Israel, have to be curbed by raising pensionable ages, by higher insurance contributions; or as Dr David Owen is saying currently, by relating them not only to fading inflation or to crude national average incomes, but, much more importantly for the individual, to his own other means. Government reneging on its so-called obligations is not new. Even the Social-Democratic Sweden has had to reduce its state pension.

(6) There was a better way to liberate the people from local or regional private monopoly in the supply of or in the insurance financing of welfare. It was not by state monopoly but by private competition between a wider range and variety of sources of supply. Even the disabled can escape from monopoly by what a British economist calls 'service credits' as a passport to alternative services.

(7) The state welfare services in kind were not the best way to generalise the so-called external benefits of universal literacy, good health, wholesome housing, or assurance of income in emergency — except where the state had to supply them because they were public goods. Even here mainly privately-produced drugs are reducing communicable disease, and the narrow-sighted solution of favouring generic rather than brand drugs would reduce expenditure on research and development. Even where the state can produce beneficial externalities, they can be countered with detrimental externalities.

(8) The welfare state was urged in more recent years to reduce social costs of industry, such as smoke pollution, noise, or congestion, and to ensure better conservation of heritage. But the state

is not only more politically motivated and therefore myopic, it is more ruthless and less accountable for its actions than private, relatively small-scale transgressors. The solution is not more state regulation, but more modern techniques of charging the sources of damage to prevent or inhibit their harmfulness.

(9) The more recent rationale of the welfare state is that the large income it appropriated through national insurance, and other forms of taxation, could, in macro-economic theory, be dispensed in order to moderate the amplitude of economic fluctuations by generating budget deficits and surpluses. Such use of insurance funds might help to achieve this purpose but only by frustrating or distorting its original purpose as insurance. But Aneurin Bevan had long before recognised the myth of national insurance that welfare states turn into windfall general taxation and misuse to the disadvantage of the working classes who think their pensions or other benefits are guaranteed by this national insurance.

(10) Finally, had we known then what we know now, we could have prevented the welfare state from being turned from an engine of mercy into an instrument and producer of vested interests. Its misuse by the administrative bureaucrats and trade unions have turned many in both the new British coalitions — the liberal Conservatives and the Social Democrats–Liberal Alliance — away from what was to be the second most unsordid act in history after the Marshall Plan.

To summarise, the tendency of the welfare state is to politicise its centralised decisions, even if it conceals them by empowering fashionable technocrats, educational sociologists, hospital architects, town planners, pensioneering actuaries and others, with brainwaves, or brainstorms to run amok. (They ride roughshod over the ordinary people by locking them in 2,000-child schools, 2,000-bed hospitals — a British medical vice-chancellor allowed his technical euphoria to run to 5,000 beds, and to hell with the long-distance staff, patients, families or suppliers — or 2,000-tenant tower blocks.)

The Neglected Externalities

The welfare state is being increasingly condemned not only by intellectuals disappointed by its results. It is not only questioned by students of public opinion. The British journal, *New Society* (14 April 1983), had the grace to say that a 1981 survey had largely vindicated the main findings of an Institute of Economic Affairs (IEA) survey in 1978, the latest of four begun in 1963. Even then the journal did not grasp the essential uniqueness of the IEA surveys: that they elicited preferences based on *price* — the absence of which is the source of continuing error in opinion sampling. The welfare state is not only being queried by British politicians who recognise the inherent defects of centralisation and its inability to ascertain preferences and respond to them. (I shall argue later that *political* decentralisation will not suffice because it will not correct differences in cultural bargaining power that depress the masses.)

The welfare state is under attack not only from its intellectual sponsors, its observers, and its former political controllers. It is also, less consciously but more effectively, under attack from its supposed beneficiaries. And this because of the gradual realisation over the years that it unavoidably carries long ignored side-effects or penalties and costs. For example, in the welfare state, taxes are higher than they otherwise would be. The effects on incentives, investment and output are incalculable, and they are the same whether taxes are levied for purposes generally approved by the tax-payers, such as retirement pensions (though not for the non-poor), or not approved, such as subsidies for non-poor council house tenants. International comparisons which show that other countries have even higher *average* taxes are unhelpful: the demands for income in terms of effort are related more to *marginal* tax rates in a previous year than to whether the Dane or Italian or Spaniard is suffering even more in total tax deductions.

Moreover, the costs of tax collection are understated in official statistics because the costs passed to industry and the tax-payer are ignored. Nor has any welfare state calculated the billions of man-hours spent in calculating or evading taxes that could have been translated into welfare. The welfare state cooks its books.

The opportunity cost of minimising tax 'avoision' (the tax rejection that degenerates, or graduates, from legal avoidance to illegal evasion) must be horrendous, not least because it is increasingly subconscious. Without a doubt, the distortions in economic resources must be damaging. Decisions in industry — from Italy to Sweden, which Gunnar Myrdal condemned as 'a nation of cheats' — are often made not to maximise production or earnings but to minimise taxes. Tax evasion in Britain now exceeds government borrowing.

The high costs of the welfare state requires taxes on the low-paid, many of whom can earn more without taxes in the economic underground. The welfare state creates law-breakers. In Britain, perhaps one million of our three million officially unemployed are happily hard at work. An unknown but growing form of tax avoision begins with innocent swapping of objects or services and ends with international tax rejection by barter at high values.

Needless to say, the ignored 'moral' cost of state welfare is the diminishing respect for law of any kind because taxes are an archetypal impost that represent a resented *deduction* from disposable income and become a symbol of repression. National accounts allow for 2.5-3.5 per cent of income that escapes taxes; a semi-official estimate allows 7.5 per cent; an independent estimate is 15 per cent; with barter, I put it at 20 per cent. The ultimate effect is the dangerous rejection of democracy as unrepresentative of people with little to say in how much 'take-home' pay they are left with and no say in how their taxes are spent on 'the social wage' (not least by the less articulate, activist or adroit, and especially in education and medicine, the two largest state welfare services in kind). From that sense of frustration it is not a long step to cynicism about representative democracy and parliamentary government.

Another side effect of the welfare state is that the administrative cost of the welfare bureaucracy is understated. The official statistic of 6 per cent for the National Health Service is dismissed by doctors, traders and industrialists who incur accounting costs, patients who lose earnings while waiting for treatment, families who incur costs visiting relatives in hospitals placed where it suits the system. Our children's future taxes (if they pay them) will have to restore the neglected fabric on which too little was spent because of spectacular surgeries, which win more votes, rather than on renewal of routine equipment.

A distinguishing weakness of government services which are supplied at nil or nominal price is that the output is measured by *quantity*. Yet the consumer is interested in *quality*. On these grounds alone international comparisons, in which even definitions of terms vary, are mischievous. In the escalation of medical costs accompanying third-party payment under health insurance, it is claimed that the National Health Service is better able to contain costs (at some 5.75 per cent of GNP), than the mixed social/ private insurance systems of Europe (at 7-8 per cent). This is a characteristically fallacious defence of the NHS. Third-party pay-ment inflates costs through the 'agency relationship' or by doctor/ patient collusion. But the implication that the NHS keeps costs at an optimum is insupportable. It uses its monopoly (in the case of Israel it is the Histadrut that fulfills the role) to depress costs *below* the amounts that patients would willingly have paid for the quality of service they wanted. The choice is between too high a cost and too much service under insurance, or too low a cost but too little service in the NHS. (In a democracy of intelligent citizens the Israelis were able to make the choice; the British still prefer too much service to too little.)

Moreover, people would want to pay more for welfare if the method of payment produced visibly improved service. This is a proposition in public choice economics — that consumers will demand more at nil or nominal price than they will pay for in taxes — that was virtually accepted and confirmed by two Labour social service ministers in the 1960s and 1970s, R.H.S. Crossman and Douglas Houghton.

The denial of choice is a self-evident 'externality'. The notion (voiced by a former Labour junior minister) that 95 per cent of parents receive their first preference in school places for their children is another error: parents do not list their first preferences for fear of losing their second or third choices.

Another major side-effect is that the welfare state is becoming increasingly regressive in that it transfers income from the poor to the rich. The effect, analysed in two recent books by Labour sym-pathisers, Julian Le Grand of the London School of Economics and Frank Field of the House of Commons, is not accidental. The fundamental reason is the difference in cultural power in its various forms.

At the same time, the monopoly in state welfare inflates costs and retards innovation which is inhibited by the millions of employees, from professionals to caretakers, whose first concern is preserving their jobs. 'Job creation' and 'job preservation' have become the most infamous corruptions in the litany of state wel-fare. (Labour in Britain has become the *public-sector* Labour Party.) In addition, welfare employees can subject the community to dislocation of services by the *threat* of strike; it is not necessary to strike, its potential suffices.

Fundamentally the more grievous 'opportunity' cost of the welfare state is the loss of development of the variegated private services, commercial or co-operative, that were virtually suppressed but which are now returning.

The large number of employed in labour-intensive education and medicine (and local government) services have replaced consumer sovereignty by syndicalism which, as in Yugoslavia, puts immediate improvement in pay and conditions of work before long-term investment in advancing technology for consumer services.

Since the kind and direction of some state welfare is determined largely by the majority, individuals or small groups are made impotent in decision-making. (Insofar as the majority in Northern Ireland is Protestant, the Catholics are projected into social conflict which they can resolve only by emigration or outnumbering the majority, which would, in turn, create a similar grievance.)

Another major side-effect is the problem of corruption, which is no less, and probably more prevalent, in welfare than in other state services or large undertakings of any kind.

Last, but not the least side-effect, is that a *national* welfare state operates in a *world* market. Thus, Britain has lost 5,000 British-trained doctors to English-speaking countries. Israel has lost young doctors who may (or may not) return in national crises. A national welfare state is no more feasible in a world economy than is socialist Britain in the EEC.

The Withering State Marx did not Prophesy

With such massed interests intent to defend it at all costs, the welfare state looks impregnable. And no doubt it can keep itself going for some time yet, by coercion, suppression and exclusion. A British Conservative health minister has advised the prime minister to claim 'the NHS is safe with us', although the motivation was electoral as much as medical. But they may be out of office in five years. And economists must take a longer view of the prospects.

I cannot see the NHS continuing for much longer as it was originally designed — centralised, comprehensive, 'free' at the time of service, with public ownership of its physical assets, and providing equal access for all ailments to all (or aiming to provide, for in reality it fails).

Strains have been appearing for some years. The NHS is 35 years old. During that period real incomes have risen, social habits and aspirations have been transformed, technology has advanced and is progressing with unpredictable rapidity.

The system today cannot respond to personal feelings and it cannot respond to the requirements of industry. Its autocratic 'Don't call us, we'll call you' (when we have a doctor, an X-ray machine, or a bed), explains why the electrical workers have been followed by railwaymen in being offered private health insurance so that they can be examined when it suits the industry, not the hospital. The NHS will gradually succumb to market forces, at least four on the side of demand and six on the side of supply. The former include:

(1) Rising incomes, which will enable more people further down the income scale to be able to pay through insurance (not least the long-established working man's Hospital Savings Associations) for better services. The NHS cannot stretch itself from the eleemosynary service it provides for the poor, old and chronically sick, to a luxury service for the younger, busier, bustling, family.

(2) Demand for better services, as the family will assert itself against the state which treats it relatively as supplicants in education and medicine (and housing and much else) when it is treated by the private market like lords in its everyday and household purchasing.

(3) The continuing emancipation of women which will strengthen the family against the state, not only because of maternal assertion but because women in their everyday shopping know the trap of monopoly and the liberation of competition.

(4) The growing sense among the quiet people who realise that the government often reacts to rowdy noise rather than to democratic numbers. The (welfare) state has in effect induced the people who prefer to go home rather than to committee rooms to reconsider their democratic 'rights'.

In the realm of education, British families will escape to private schools which may be simpler, unsophisticated, but at least more under their watch, supervision and ultimate control. That is why the education voucher, espoused so far in principle by the liberal Conservatives, some Liberals and even two Labour (now SDP) intellectuals, is an instrument for equating the power of the inarticulate working classes with that of the middle-classes in asserting their voices.

Social reforms aimed at facilitating 'participation' and 'involvement' acquiesce in unequal voices, the weaker voices will not be heard unless they are reinforced by potential exits. *Political* decentralisation must be a first stage to *economic* decentralisation — as market socialists like Professor Alec Nove have finally accepted, even for fully socialised societies, now unlikely in Britain.

On the side of supply, the market forces to which the NHS is slowly yielding include:

(1) Technical innovations, too numerous and complex to list, which will, in time, enable education and medicine to be conducted in small units, with more individual tuition or attention. Small units will be financed locally more easily, on a small, private scale.

(2) Local suppliers — small, co-operative schools or hospitals, mutual aid groups — which will be able to serve local clients better than distant officials can.

(3) Small local units, which will reduce industrial strife and strikes by better co-operation with staff.

(4) Regional, sectarian, ethnic, and other homogeneous minority groups, which will demand small, local, private services, perhaps with a return of their taxes they have paid for services they rejected, like Pakistani families that want their daughters in single-sex schools. And that demand will spread to jews and catholics. There will no 'bussing' in Britain.

(5) Tax 'avoision', as described earlier, which will deny funds required by government to continue, still less improve, state welfare. Government in its demand to provide more revenue for unwanted services is increasingly seen not as friend but as foe.

(6) And finally, the international pull of the EEC, or even larger groupings, which will undermine *national* welfare systems.

The Consequences

In discerning the aftermath of the welfare state, its intellectual architects and their political pupils have tended to treat symptoms rather than causes; their tendency has been to over-concentrate on income effects and to ignore or understate price (distribution, efficiency) effects, and to almost overlook feedback supply side-effects. They not only face errors in their new prescriptions for what they hope will save the familiar welfare state in new decentralised forms. They also ignore most of the elements in the 'new economics' that have a direct bearing on thought and policy in welfare and on the new institutions that will accompany non-state welfare. And their neglect causes them to repeat proposals in a form that leaves them still vulnerable to the weaknesses that have wasted decades of effort, institutions, manpower and money.

I would like to summarise the main developments in the economics of the welfare state:

— Micro-economics, the analysis of *small* institutions, is overtaking, supplementing, and in time could dominate macro-economics, the analysis of *large* (national or international) institutions. The macro-economists since Keynes tended to emphasise demand and to ignore supply. The micro-economists are emphasising the 'supply side' to redress the imbalance. A macro-econometric Nobel Laureate, Professor Lawrence Klein has a new book, *The Economics of Supply and Demand* (Blackwell, London), which is a significant retreat from the dominance of Keynesian macro-economics and a renewed recognition of classical market supply-and-demand economics. The welfare state is a macro-artefact that ignores micro-economic reactions by suppressing or distorting price.

— The welfare state was (is) advocated largely by social scientists on the ground that only the state could alleviate or remove the poverty (Marx's 'immiseration') originating allegedly in late-eighteenth- and early-nineteenth-century capitalism. Two fallacies continue to be ignored. First, initial ·inequality may be wider in a market economy than in a coercive planned society but final poverty is lesser because the prodigious productivity generated by the market can be redistributed *outside* the market in order to maintain its internal incentives for production. Second, redistribution is better made in cash so that its recipients can re-enter the market and share in its (efficient) productivity. 'The welfare state' does not require state-owned (or local government) schools, state (or regional board) hospitals or local authority (council) housing. It can do better for minimising inequality and poverty by redistributing money.

— Advocacy of reformed welfare statism still rests on the political unrealism of government, against which Knut Wicksell the Swedish economist and Alfred Marshall the British economist warned economists a century ago. Professor J.M. Buchanan, one of the American founding fathers of 'public choice' theory, tirelessly tells us we shall get nowhere if we suppose that government comprises 'benevolent despots' (or, I would add, that bureaucrats are disinterested eunuchs). The school of public choice is attracting political scientists, historians, lawyers and sociologists who see its analysis of government — run by people with self-interested aims that may conflict with those of the public — as a much more fruitful approach that is yielding more realistic predictions. In particular the notion of a social welfare function, which was an implicit intellectual support for the welfare state, is nowhere considered even as a working hypothesis.

— The welfare state expressed collectivised charity: socialised selfless giving. But if it is socialised, unless it is a public good in which none will join unless all join, it is not giving but coercive yielding. Professor Gordon Tullock, Professor Buchanan's close collaborator, calculates that people are charitable with some 5 per cent of their income, and even that is only a half of the biblical tithe. There is more giving where some incomes are very large — as Israel knows to her benefit — than when they are equalised. There are also, as several American economists have analysed, reasons for giving that are not charitable but self-regarding, yet no less effective if the interests of the recipients are the desideratum. The welfare state has not maximised selfless, benign giving.

— The welfare state rests, through taxes, on productivity. Re-examination of 1,000 years of history by Professors Douglas North and Robert Thomas indicate that private ownership, typified by agricultural enclosure of common land (now to be decided in the sea-beds), and for long experienced by the communist countries, especially where private ownership is most tolerated, is more productive than 'public' ownership. Advocates of the welfare state should divorce it from public ownership and bolster it by advocating private property, in schools, hospitals, housing, land and private funded pensions, not least because it reduces the transaction costs of rearranging property into its most productive holdings.

— The welfare state has been condemned for stimulating infla-

by inducing government to tax, borrow and print money. But the welfare state would not continue if inflation ran out of control. The new economists have three antidotes. Professor Milton Friedman has proposed a rule for the control of money supply to master inflation. Professors Buchanan and Richard Wagner have proposed a constitutional discipline over the power of government to issue money. Most radically, Professor F.A. Hayek has lately argued that money is not a function of government but that it should be supplied by competing issuers, each of which would limit the supply of its money in order to maintain its value. Thus would inflation be nipped in the bud. British economists, Professors Patrick Minford (based on an earlier work by Professor Robert Lucas of Carnegie-Mellon), C.K. Rowley, Michael Beenstock and Alan Budd have also proposed market restraints on inflation.

Proposals to master inflation may be defective. But the advocates of welfare state reform offer nothing to stop inflation except compacts, concordats or other agreements with trade unions on 'incomes policies' for which no history anywhere offers much theoretical or empirical support that they can resist market forces for long without delayed inflation.

— The welfare reforms that require continued state regulation ignore the evidence analysed by Professor George Stigler that state regulation simply does not achieve its objectives. Yet British reforms hitherto by both Conservative and Labour parties have proposed regulative reorganisation that leave the structure of financial incentives for success and penalties for failure unchanged: they reshuffle the old pack of cards with a new joker or two in the hope — no more than a conjecture — that new tricks will fall out. The sociologists, especially of Britain, have become devotees of a new cult of theology: 'capitalism *has* failed; the state *must* work; perhaps this new gimmick will do the trick.'

— Economists are analysing *all* human action: government as well as industry; the family as well as the firm; mutual aid as well as exchange; giving (charity) as well as selling. The welfare of the family depends on its economic efficiency as a partnership with division of labour, the complementarity of the spouses' talents, and so on. Families make up society. Investment in human capital in children through education, medicine and other services requires sacrifices and opportunity costs that parents can know, or can learn, with advice, guidance, pooling of local experience, and financial supplementation, better than officials, social workers or politicians. These analyses are more revealing than the notion of the welfare state as a huge firm producing welfare without knowledge of costs, consumer preferences, or returns on capital in alternative employments. All the failures of large-scale, centralised socialism are repeated in the welfare state. The welfare of the family rests on its ability to act as a coherent social unit with knowledge of its requirements and potentialities in exchange with other families.

— The plausible case for the welfare state was that it comprised largely public goods, which economists from Adam Smith to Keynes had designated as necessarily produced by government. A radical element in the new economics, deployed most persistently by Professors Murray Rothbard and David Friedman, and originating from the Austrian school of Carl Menger to F.A. Hayek, is that technical change is reducing the range of public goods in welfare. Professor E.G. West (of Britain, now in Canada) has long questioned the external benefit of state education in reducing crime and spreading literacy. Little comfort for such claims can be drawn from some recent experience in Britain. And technology has reduced the diseases communicable by contagion or infection. The externalities of state welfare have been exaggerated.

— Not least, representative government is not representative, certainly not equally representative, of the citizenry. In Britain it has degenerated under both Conservative and Labour parties into government of the activist, by the activist, for the activist: in its worst form, government of the busy, by the bossy, for the bully.

My conclusions for the aftermath are that private, voluntary welfare will return in the market or by mutual aid, with the advantage of 60 years or more of technological innovation and social advance, and with the lessons or warnings to be drawn from the centralised welfare state. The wide variety of welfare organisations and methods of financing that were developing in embryo in Britain in the 1870s and earlier in education, medical insurance, housing (including ownership by artisans) and saving for sickness, unemployment, old age and other emergencies, described by Lord Beveridge in *Voluntary Action as a Means of Social Advance*, will be resumed after a century of induced inaction. Its main features will probably be:

(1) The state will gradually do much less.

(2) What remains will be devolved to regional and local authorities or governments.

(3) It will farm out the parts of welfare service that can be performed more efficiently by competing private suppliers.

(4) The range of relationship will vary from pure giving through mutual aid to pure exchange in the market.

(5) The family will be allowed and encouraged to learn more authority.

(6) Non-profit organisations will not be encouraged more (or less) than profit-making organisations because the sense of mission that is the strength of the provident, co-operative or mutual association requires to be complemented by the sense of urgency of the profit-making organisation. (In my childhood Achei Brit and B'nai Brith were kept on their toes by Prudential Insurance — despite its higher administrative costs.)

(7) A single social cash benefit, varying with individual or family circumstance, will gradually replace a widening range of cash grants and allowances and of benefits in kind. Dr David Owen, the probable leader of the alternative government, has recently suggested it could cover the family income supplement (which tops up low earnings), rent and rate (local property tax) rebates, and ('free') school meals. It could be extended to cover more services that consume wasteful manpower, create bureaucratic organisation, and deny choice.

(8) The cash benefit could in some instances be ear-marked to ensure expenditure on education and medical care. There would be more room for experimental action in a decentralised structure.

(9) *Political* decentralisation might suffice in some services but would be inadequate where cultural differences were difficult to remove as determinants of access or choice. *Economic* decentralisation to the market would then be indispensable to complement or replace it by generalising buying status.

(10) Monopoly of supply will be less of an obstruction from private suppliers than from the state. But it will persist. The power of the suppliers of state education, medicine, housing and insurance will have to be tempered and disciplined by competition.

Such a decentralised structure would be more sensitive, more efficient, more in harmony with the requirements of a society that tolerates individual idiosyncracy, values the family, respects ethnic diversity, disrespects benevolent despots. But we, intellectuals, administrators, public officials, politicians, shall not have the decisive authority in shaping the aftermath. If even Russian women no longer fear to voice dissatisfaction with rejected state services, demand for individualised, tailored welfare will have more influence in the advanced West than the post-war designers of state supply foresaw.

5 THE REAL CRISES: UNATTAINABLE GOALS AND MORAL VAGUENESS

Raphaella Bilski Ben-Hur

When dealing with the broad subject of the welfare state and its aftermath, the political scientist is confronted by a crucial issue: how to reconcile the following two contradictory phenomena. First, the feeling of crisis concerning the future of the welfare state; second, an analysis of the welfare policies of Western democracies over the last few years clearly shows that, despite economic difficulties, welfare activities have increased, or, at worst, have undergone only minor cuts.

If indeed the welfare state survived economic crises and in many cases continued to grow, one can reach the conclusion that in Western democracies the welfare state has become an inseparable part of life. Why, then, the feeling of crisis accompanied by thinking about alternatives to the existing welfare state, as expressed by both social scientists and politicians?[1] On the one hand it is possible that the feeling of crisis is artificial, created by the mass media and intellectual cliques, whereas in reality, for the majority of the people, the welfare state has become an integral part of modern life to such an extent that it is impossible not only to dismantle it but even to change it drastically. On the other hand it is possible that a real fundamental crisis, which has nothing to do with the economic recession and the growing cost of welfare services, does exist.

It is my assumption that a real crisis does exist, and that understanding it and coping with it is essential for the future of the welfare state.

The Unattainable Goals

The welfare state in all its variations, as we know it today in the Western world, has expanded far beyond the original intent. In many instances the growth of the welfare state was not based upon constant assessment and systematic thinking by social scientists.

74

Neither was it accompanied by normative and ideological thinking. Because the welfare state succeeded, at least partly, in achieving its initial goals,[2] more goals were added. The major additional goals are: abolishing poverty, substantially diminishing inequality, increasing social integration, and finally, intensifying the participation of the population. As a result, expectations of the welfare state grew accordingly.

This trend toward expansion was indirectly encouraged by social scientists. We find broad definitions of the goals of the welfare state in various works. These definitions are not merely descriptive, they carry positive connotations. True, they substitute the term social policy for welfare policy, but it is not clear in what way this social policy differs from what is conceived as welfare policy.[3]

Indeed, it seems that many, both on the theoretical and political levels, think that the welfare state is able and should accomplish the additional goals mentioned. Yet, when occasionally the achievements of the welfare state are seriously evaluated, it emerges that, as far as the four additional goals are concerned, the welfare state is not a success story. Poverty has not been abolished, socio-economic gaps have not been meaningfully affected by welfare measures, and neither were integration and participation.[4]

Facing these findings, it is possible to reach three different conclusions which at first glance seem logical. The first is that the gap between expectations and attainments can be accounted for by the lack of resources available for welfare, and that, if adequate resources were available, the additional goals could — at least to a certain degree — be achieved.

The second conclusion could be termed the 'reform approach': according to this, little is achieved because of some deficiencies inherent in the welfare institutions themselves. For example, the alienating huge bureaucracy which has developed, the centralisation of welfare policies, the highly professionalised workers, also constituting a pressure group — developments which increase costs but not necessarily the standard of services. These and other defects within the welfare system itself are, according to this argument, responsible for the lack of achievements in certain areas. If, therefore, the necessary reforms in the welfare services were implemented, the welfare state would be able to attain the additional goals as well.

The third conclusion, as logical as the first two, is that the welfare state *in toto* is a failure. If the welfare state failed in increasing integration, participation and equality and in abolishing poverty — despite the fact that for years it had ample resources at its disposal, then the whole welfare system is a failure. Moreover, the welfare state has many negative side-effects, such as creating a culture of dependency and demands. One should therefore dismantle the welfare state and look for an entirely different alternative.

Is any one of these conclusions more correct than the other? It is my opinion that all three are wrong, as they are based on the erroneous assumption that the welfare state, through its various services and policies, can and should abolish poverty, reduce inequality substantially and increase integration and participation.

The four additional goals have become the criteria according to which the welfare state is judged. The real question, whether the welfare state, given optimal conditions, can achieve these goals, has not been dealt with. Indeed, implicitly and explicitly it is assumed that these goals can be attained. Failure to achieve them means, as stated before, either lack of resources, need for reform, or the complete failure of the welfare state.

Yet, the existing evaluation and research point at least to one other possibility: that the four additional goals are unattainable in terms of the welfare state. If this is true, then we ought to come to entirely different conclusions.

We can take Israel as an example where no distinction is made between the attainable and unattainable goals. At the end of the 1960s, as a result of the nation-wide social uprising of the Black Panthers, a new era began. For the first time the government appointed a public committee that was to look closely into the problems of social and economic distress. The findings of the committee and the awakened awareness not merely of the needs of the distressed population but of the close correlation between distress and country of origin (Muslim countries) made the government add new goals to its welfare policy: greater equality by narrowing socio-economic gaps, increased integration and later also increased participation. This is to say that the 'unattainable goals' were added.

The expectations of the social sectors concerned were raised accordingly. The inability of the welfare state to attain these goals, even when adequate resources were allocated, aroused frustration and anger. This had clear political consequences, as these feelings were aimed directly at the Labour Party which had been the ruling party ever since the establishment of the state.

In 1977, despite the fact that under Labour leadership a welfare state was established in Israel, which provides minimum income, security and free (or almost free) access to health and social services and housing subsidies, a large part of the distressed population and Sephardic Jews voted against Labour. This vote against Labour can be partially explained by the fact that Labour was blamed for the insufficient integration, for the continuing existence of poverty and socio-economic gaps, and for the scant upward mobility of Sephardic Jews. This trend persisted and even became stronger in the 1981 elections, despite the fact that Labour had already been four years in opposition. Labour continued to be associated with the old establishment which had not delivered the 'unattainable' goals. In other words, the fact that Labour had tried to accomplish the 'unattainable' goals through welfare policies and not by employing other measures, resulting in only minor achievements, created frustration and contributed its share to Labour's defeats in 1977 and 1981.

In Israel there has not yet been a backlash against the welfare state, though sceptic voices can already be heard. Still, unless the attainable goals are distinguished from the unattainable ones, and unless the moral basis of the welfare state becomes clear to all and a real consensus is reached, there will be dangers in store for the welfare services. The main immediate danger is that, in case of economic difficulties (a situation which seems inevitable), retrenchment will affect precisely the successful welfare policies oriented towards the attainable goals. The paradox is that the 'unattainable' goals, because of their political importance and due to the unawareness of the fact that they cannot really be achieved through welfare policies, will remain practically intact.

To sum up, the first real crisis of the welfare state lies in the fact that, despite our vast experience and knowledge of welfare policies, no distinction has been made between attainable and unattainable goals.

The Moral and Ideological Vagueness

The absence of systematic thinking was exacerbated by moral and ideological vagueness. The expansion of goals, and therefore of expectations, as well as the failure to achieve unattainable goals through welfare policies, contributed to normative and ideological confusion. The consesus of the political right and left about the welfare state in the 1960s and 1970s also contributed to the normative vagueness. The discussion concerning the welfare state focused on ways and means. Indeed, when the values which a policy is meant to pursue become unclear, they are excluded from the discussion, and the debate centres on more technical issues, such as cost and efficiency. Eventually ways and means take the place of the normative values, and goals become technical. Of course, the technical issues are important, and it is necessary to know how policies are and should be carried out. Yet, dealing only with ways and means leads us nowhere in regard to the fundamental question: what should be done, and why?

The lack of a normative and ideological discussion explains an interesting phenomenon. Newly awakened ideological groups from all over the political spectrum — neo-marxist, neo-liberal, neo-conservative — have one thing in common: they are attacking the welfare state. What they attack is a major institution in modern Western democracy which lacks a normative basis. Thus, for instance, three different approaches to the welfare state, those of Michael Novak, Martin Larnoy, and George and Wilding, criticise the ideological vacuum surrounding the welfare state. Michael Novak, who wants to reassert democratic capitalism, stresses the importance of a known moral foundation for any policy: 'Moral ignorance will bring moral paralysis. Necessary reform and advances cannot be attempted when individuals within the system have lost sight of its proper ideals.'[5]

George and Wilding, who are on the other side of the ideological fence and carry the flag of radical democratic socialism, share the view on the importance of values: 'The thrust of welfare policy has been hopelessly weakened because of the absence of a set of values which support and legitimize welfare policy.'[6]

Both of these views presents a different alternative to the welfare state. What they have in common is the close tie between the social policy they propose and a value system. Indeed, the lack of a moral basis is the second real crisis of the welfare state.

In Israel, for example, the moral basis of the welfare state became vague after the unattainable goals were added. The ideological consensus was no longer based on mutually agreed goals, and this consensus became possible only because the different parties interpreted the additional goals in different ways. Vagueness became a political necessity in order to maintain the artificial consensus. No party could say in public that it was against the additional (unattainable) goals, even when these goals were contrary to its ideology, due to public sensitivity and for electoral reasons.

How to Confront the Crises

What, then, can be done by social scientists to fight these crises? On the basis of experience accumulated in Western welfare states it is possible to distinguish and define:

(a) The attainable goals, i.e. those goals which the welfare state can achieve provided appropriate resources are allocated and right policies pursued.
(b) The unattainable goals, i.e. those goals which cannot be achieved through welfare policy.

Among the attainable goals, those which are of the greatest importance are:

— a certain standard of security;
— access to free or almost free health and welfare services;
— free education up to a certain age;
— a minimum income;
— housing subsidies.

It should be emphasised that this does not mean a return to the beginnings of the welfare state, as the above-mentioned goals go far beyond the initial minimal goals of the welfare state.

As for the goals added in the last 15 years — abolishing poverty, substantially diminishing inequality, increasing integration and participation — our present state of knowledge suffices at least to question the ability of the welfare state to achieve them.

When the attainable goals are separated from the unattainable ones, future welfare policies can concentrate on the attainable goals. If thought is applied and resources are channelled accordingly, it is reasonable to assume that the degree of success will be higher within the attainable areas. Expectations will be changed and criteria for judging the welfare state will change accordingly. Moreover, once goals are clearly defined, a moral basis for the welfare state will more easily develop. Thereafter it will be legitimate and helpful to discuss ways and means and to think about reforms in order to improve the services.

As to the negative side-effects of welfare policies, the major ones being dependency and demands, these can only partly be dealt with by introducing reforms within the welfare system. In this manner it is, however, impossible to deal fundamentally with those side-effects, just as in the field of medicine the negative side-effects of a drug can only partly be eliminated by changing the dose — for real treatment, different means are required.

The key is to acknowledge that welfare policies constitute only one major way of dealing with social, economic and political problems. The real crisis of the welfare state was caused by the conviction that it could solve most, or even all, problems.

If the welfare state would limit itself to the attainable goals, it may be reasonably expected that in most Western democracies a real broad ideological consensus on welfare policies will be reached. This assumption seems realistic, since the moral basis underlying the attainable goals is, in a nutshell, humanitarianism. It is the humanitarianism based upon Judeo-Christian ideas and adapted to the realities of the 1980s. It differs from the humanitarianism of the early twentieth century in that it recognises more clearly the collective duty of society (through the state) to its members, and in the fact that the social rights have become broader.

As for the goals defined in this paper as 'unattainable', they are such only insofar as welfare policies are concerned. Each individual society has to decide whether it believes in greater equality, integration and participation. This decision, which is a normative one, can be reached after an ideological debate between the parties, mainly concerning social justice. Needless to say that such a discussion can contribute a lot to revive Western democracies, and the ideological debate will not be the prerogative of extreme groups. In the theoretical sphere, interest in social justice has already awakened,[7] and it is about time that public interest in social justice was rekindled.

It is my contention that it is impossible to put forward a single theory of social justice. Needless to say that this is true not only in the realm of theory but of ideology as well. The importance of the concept of social justice, which is central to organised human life, is the continuous search for it. It is the quest which is important, as it stimulates a normative debate on the crucial issues facing society.

Those who fear ideological politics because of the effects of radical ideologies and who prefer the so-called pragmatic politics, forget the price democracy may have to pay for non-ideological politics, viz. the loss of a moral basis. As John Stewart Mill pointed out in his *On Liberty*,[8] opinions and beliefs become stagnant unless debated, and put to the test, constantly.

After a normative debate about the desirability of equality, integration, participation, and the abolishment of poverty has taken place and a decision is reached, then comes the stage of implementation. For example, if a party which advocates equality comes to power, it can strive to reach it through various economic, social and political measures. Welfare policies have a certain equalising effect, and by improving living conditions they help distressed populations to shift their interest to the fight for participation and integration. Yet the necessary means for increasing equality, integration and participation, do not belong to welfare policies.

Conclusion

In order to forestall a general attack on the welfare state and to channel its future development into the right directions, a discussion of its goals is essential now. In the past, academe played a poor role in directing the development of the welfare state and in some instances even encouraged wrong tendencies. Yet it is precisely the academic community that has to reopen this discussion which at present cannot be initiated by the political parties, due to their vested interests and lack of knowledge. It can only be hoped that, once the academics open the debate, it will have some impact upon party ideologies and party policy-makers. The direction the influence suggested here should take is from theory to ideology and from ideology to policy. This is a familiar process, and in the case of the future of the welfare state it has an additional importance; a discussion of goals can eventually help to build a new moral basis for the welfare state.

Notes

1. For example: (a) the discussion of a possible alternative by Nathan Glazer 'Toward a self-service society?', *The Public Interest*, Fall, 1982; (b) The alternative of a decentralised, flexible, participatory welfare state, which can be made possible

by new technologies, as outlined in a paper prepared for this conference by Shirley Williams, 'Welfare Politics in Western Democracies'.

2. For initial goals defined by Brian Abel-Smith in his paper presented at this conference are: 'to establish a floor of protection at the bottom ...', 'a minimum of security — a right of access to free or nearly free health and welfare services, to a minimum number of years of free education, to minimum income in defined contingencies ...' entitled: 'The Major Problems of the Welfare State: Defining the Issues'.

3. See for example D.G. Gil, *Unravelling Social Policy*, Schenkman Publishing Company, Cambridge, Massachusetts, 1976. Gil devoted a whole chapter to the issue of the broader definition of social policy.

4. See, e.g., Peter Townsend, *Poverty in the United Kingdom*, Pelican Books, 1979; Y. Peres, *Ethnic Relations in Israel*, Sifriat Hapoalim, 1976, Ch. 5.

5. Michael Novak, *The Spirit of Democratic Capitalism*, Simon and Schuster, New York, 1982, p. 335.

6. Vic. George and Paul Wilding, *Ideology and Social Welfare*, Routledge and Kegan Paul, London, 1976, p. 129.

7. The two major works which revived the discussion on social justice are J. Rawls, *A Theory of Justice*, Harvard, 1971; and Robert Nozick, *Anarchy, State and Utopia*, Basic Books, New York, 1974.

8. John Stewart Mill, *On Liberty*, Hackett Publ., Indianapolis, 1978, Ch. 2.

6 WELFARE POLITICS IN WESTERN DEMOCRACIES

Shirley Williams

The welfare state of Western Europe, the most remarkable contribution to the political and social stability of these countries in the thirty years after the Second World War, is now under attack from several directions. Indeed, so fierce is the criticism in some quarters that the real achievements in terms of a better educated, healthier population, protected at least in part from the exigencies of unemployment and injury, and able to live with dignity in old age, are in danger of being forgotten.

There are two major themes of attack on the welfare state: the first is that it is too expensive, the second that it is too bureaucratic. As we shall see, there is some evidence for both charges. The 1960s and early 1970s were years of very rapid expansion in state pensions and benefits, linking them to the cost of living, so that there could be no loss of value as a result of inflation. Other countries, like the Netherlands, Sweden and, for a brief period, Britain, went further, indexing pensions to the rise in earnings also, so that pensioners would enjoy the general rise in the standard of life, while being protected against inflation. Free secondary education up to the age of sixteen or even eighteen, became universal in Western Europe, and was complemented by a doubling or trebling of higher education in many countries. Few doubted that formal education was a good of which there could not be too much. Indeed, for those of liberal and progressive views, the desirability of an increase in the quantity and quality of formal education was the ark of the covenant, the badge of being an enlightened citizen. Health care became more sophisticated as new medical techniques were tried out and then incorporated in the treatment available to all insured people, or through public health services. But the techniques were not only more sophisticated, they were notably more expensive.

By the mid-1970s, public expenditure as a share of gross national product was averaging 43.7 per cent in the OECD countries, with the Netherlands, Norway and Sweden exceeding 50 per cent. Of this total, transfer payments (pensions, benefits, etc.)

83

accounted for about two-fifths, and the services themselves (expenditure on schools, hospitals, community services and so on) for a similar proportion. The social services were, in short, taking an ever larger share of an ever increasing gross national product. Furthermore, if the expenditure per head were to be maintained, there was no avoiding such a development. For population patterns in the 1960s and 1970s increased the ratio of dependants to those sustaining them. In most European countries birth rates rose rapidly in the late 1950s and early 1960s. The so-called bulge of children born in this period worked their way through the educational system compelling expansions at every stage, in school building programmes, teacher training and recruitment, administrative staff and so on. The dramatic decline in the death rate due to the conquest of common infectious diseases like diphtheria and tuberculosis led to a longer expectation of life. Today, the fastest-growing section of the population is the over-eighties, the very people who make the greatest demands on the medical services. Medical advances also enabled many people with serious handicaps to survive, including some severely handicapped at birth, for example with spina bifida. Their survival again carried permanent consequences for the social services, since many needed lifelong care.

The welfare state has paradoxically become the victim of its own success, creating from that success fresh demands that it cannot easily meet. But that is not the sum of the problems of financing it. The most serious problem of all is the end of the era of economic growth, combined with a growing resentment against the burden of taxation in all its forms. Against the background of constant, or even declining gross national product, the competition between private demands and public needs for each person's pocket becomes acute. People resist a fall in their material standard of life; and they become more conscious of the demands made by government through taxation. It is difficult to find any way of financing the social services that is not highly sensitive. National insurance contributions which finance a large part of Western European expenditure on pensions and on health, are now so high as to be a substantial disincentive to employing labour. It is instructive that Italy has moved in the direction of waiving insurance contributions for the first year of a new job for a young worker; the burden of this tax on labour nearly doubles the cost to the employer of each person employed. Direct taxes are no more popular. Indeed, the level of direct taxation was a significant factor in the 1976 defeat of Sweden's semi-permanent Social Democratic government. Taxes on property, known as rates in Britain, and imposed by local or state government, arouse the most resentment of all. It was skillful exploitation of this resentment that led to the passage of Proposition 13 in California in 1978. Resentment at high levels of taxation has been a major strand in the crucial shift of public sympathy away from the neo-Keynesian paternalism of the liberal and social democratic political parties in the West.

But not the only one. Bureaucracy and professionalisation of the public services are the others. The welfare state has become remote from the people it serves, and heavily administered. It is staffed by professionals, whose qualifications have become more demanding, and whose pay has therefore had to be higher. The institutions themselves have become larger, more centralised and more expensive. The one- or two-teacher village school is vanishing. The big regional or district hospital with its gleaming and expensive equipment replaces the local cottage hospital, and every non-routine case is referred to a specialist. In an OECD paper, one expert on social policy, Rudolf Klein, declared that 'the implicit ideal of Welfare State services is the professionalisation of everyone' working in them. It is now rare to find non-professionals except in such lowly jobs as home-helps or unskilled hospital work, and there are occasional drives to professionalise these too. In parallel with professionalisation itself, the qualifications required to become professional have been driven up. In Britain, for example, no unqualified teacher can any longer teach in maintained schools, and the minimum length of training has risen from two years to four. Professionalisation has been accompanied by bureaucracy. The proportion of administrators to those undertaking the actual work of teaching or nursing has grown steadily in recent years. Yet neither this adoption of higher standards of qualification, nor the replacement of amateurs or the unqualified by professionals, has improved people's perception of the services. If anything, they have become more resentful of their status as 'client' or patient — passive recipients of services determined for them by others.

Professionalisation has a significance also in the wider political context. The public service has become a very large employer, and its staff is now an important pressure group. Half the members of the trade unions affiliated to the Trades Union Congress in Britain are public service workers, substantially more than all the private sector blue-collar trade union members. The horny-handed son of toil has become a teacher or a laboratory technician. Parties of the left are therefore under great pressure to sustain the welfare state as it is, and indeed to expand it, in its present, highly institutionalised form. This phenomenon is not new. For many years, teachers were a dominant force in the SFIO, forerunner to the present French socialist party. It is, however, becoming even more important.

Demography, professionalisation, the growing sophistication of equipment and technique all add to the cost of the welfare state; so, paradoxically, does unemployment. In Britain transfer payments to the unemployed have led to an increase in the share of gross national product taken by public expenditure, despite all the protestations of a determinedly monetarist government. Yet the political and public resistance to any further taxation to pay for it is now very strong. In Britain, the government has not lost much ground with public opinion in its long and bitter battle with the health service unions. The nurses alone command public sympathy.

The future of the welfare state could be one of disablement by a thousand cuts, each fought by the organisations representing staff, each diminishing the quality of the service, while those who can afford it opt out into private education or private medical treatment. Gradually, the welfare state would shrivel to what it once was, a publicly financed, low-level system used by the poor.

There is, however, an alternative future, making use of new technologies, and involving people in maintaining their own health, teaching themselves and looking after each other, an enabling state, rather than a welfare state.

The new technologies — by which I mean particular information technologies — will alter the pattern both of demand and of supply. Demand will become more flexible; for example, people will need periods of re-training and new education throughout their lives, but formal education may yield to a mixture of learning and practical experience. Some of the learning will be distance learning, using teaching machines, computers and visual display units, a further development of the ideas embodied in the Open University. In health, computerised records make it easy for people to be notified of the need for immunisation or vaccination at the appropriate age, and comparisons between large numbers of medical records will make diagnosis easier; indeed individuals will be able to feed in information to a computer and get their symptoms diagnosed. Side-effects of new drugs should be picked up more rapidly, and hospitals should save money on stocks of expensive drugs. The problem still to be resolved is of course, that of the confidentiality of medical records.

In the personal social services too, the new technologies could revolutionise the service. Many elderly people will be able to continue to live at home, since shopping, entertainment, financial transactions and ultimately chats with friends or with a social worker will all be accessible through two-way communications systems such as teletext and citizens' band radio. Social workers will be able to monitor a group of people for whom they are responsible, visiting only those who need assistance. The pattern of supply of staff is likely to be altered too. Many older people are likely to opt for partial retirement, and will be available as volunteers or family members to undertake more personal social work. It is easy to forget that 85 per cent of the housework and shopping needed by house-bound elderly people is provided by family members, friends and neighbours, as are 88 per cent of their meals. The contribution of the unofficial economy to the welfare of the elderly and the sick is still much greater than that of the statutory services.

The new technologies imply a decentralised, flexible participatory welfare state, in which the professionals are called upon where needed for advice or help, but are no longer the front line of the welfare state. In such a new structure, health maintenance and health education would take precedence over curative medicine. Greater emphasis would be placed on diet, on avoiding smoking or excessive drinking, on cutting down road accidents. Institutional care would be a last resort. Mobile crisis management teams dealing with patients suffering heart attacks who are nursed at home already show at least as good results as intensive care in hospital. And for those afflicted by chronic illness, mutual help groups of fellow-sufferers are more supportive than professionals without first-hand experience.

The prospects are exciting; but the institutions are conservative and find it hard to change. A responsive, accountable welfare state offering people choices is now feasible. If the opportunity is not grasped, the traditional welfare state will wither away, and millions of deprived people will be the losers.

7 OBSERVATIONS ON SOME SORE SPOTS OF SOCIAL WELFARE INSTITUTIONS

Francois Bourricaud

Let us consider the cultural component which formed the threads of the institutions of the welfare state. Professor Flora has said that he considers welfare institutions to have started at the beginning of the nineteenth century. I suggest we look back even earlier and analyse the value components of the welfare institutions. To do this we must enter the religious domain and also that of the history of ideas. For example, I would like to comment on the traditional obligation of charity in Judaism and Christianity. It would be interesting to go deep into value analysis but also into the history of the actual social services. Hospitals were once manned, managed and kept in my country by the church, and that explains conflicts in the creation of institutions by the modern state such as those in which the church wished to maintain control.

Another component of our welfare institutions stems from the rationalist concept of *bonheur*, happiness, meaning the feelings of satisfaction and usefulness that accrue in any one of us when we behave as decent and sensible persons. This term is very vague — how can one define exactly what this happiness is? — but it is an important aspect of the modern concept of welfare. In the same context and related to welfare is the notion of an extra income, not earned by sheer effort or merit. This is obviously ambiguous and reminds me of something in Montesquieu's diary. He saw the opening of the House of Lords and was amazed by the splendour and pageantry of the event. 'How fortunate we are,' he heard some people saying, 'to have such powerful and wealthy lords.' As an example of 'externality', the splendour of the prince, enters too into the welfare 'bundle'.

One more idea here: not only the happiness of the greatest number of people is considered but also the happiness of every single person who belongs to those people. The necessity for using a criterion encourages us to refer to the welfare system by looking at the consequences of welfare on the individual; here we also come to the relationship between the general choice and individual satisfaction. We would be reminded here of interesting discussions of utility in relation to specific individuals and from what do they benefit, and who gains that benefit.

There are three or four obvious difficulties facing the welfare state today, and one especially worth discussing. We have all mentioned the less satisfactory procedures of welfare institutions, the importance of the aspect of voluntarism, the inefficiency of the state and centrally managed agencies, the problems of their financing, the possible conflict between the recipients of the various benefits. We have not discussed the effect of the expansion of welfare on the status of doctors, lawyers, educators, etc. In this context, I define the 'professions' as a large complex of activities and people who, despite their differences, share a set of common attitudes towards privacy. I assume that the professionals constitute a sensitive and central group in all modern societies. The prerequisite for the functioning of the professional complex is some sort of independence in relation to the source of their income and in relation to any hierarchal (political or bureaucratic) authority.

Now suppose the financing of the system becomes a political problem. 'Intervention' then takes place between the client and professional by the 'paying party', i.e. government, which gets itself involved by wishing to define programmes, by desiring to determine factors such as the number of doctors, etc. This raises interesting questions on how to deal with such institutional arrangements in their relation to the hard core of our value system.

I would like to offer a few final comments that I hope will not sound too much like a prediction. If you take welfare institutions as they appear, they seem like a complex set of loosely connected institutions. At the end of the Second World War there was a wish to 'integrate' these various institutions. Today, in most countries, we can see that this attempt did not really work too well. Despite the relative inefficiency of these institutions, the various opinion polls offer evidence of their being deeply institutionalised — in the way sociologists use that word. Many complain about the high expense of the system but most would complain if they were deprived of any of its benefits.

My feelings are that these institutions benefit from a large consensus, not for what they are but because of the purpose they are meant to perform. Nevertheless in spite of the consensual basis upon which these institutions were built, they will become more and more a source of conflict, and a target for attacks. There are problems in financing, allocation of funds, competition between various beneficiaries. Professor Seldon has pointed how much these programmes have cost not only in money terms, but also in all sorts of social costs. May I suggest that we are saddled with the system and will go on living with it, although with qualms and difficulties.

PART THREE

INSTITUTIONAL ASPECTS OF THE WELFARE STATE

8 YOUTH AND THE WELFARE STATE IN THE UNITED STATES

Morris Janowitz

There is a growing body of literature seeking to explain why the welfare state of democratic nations has failed to reach its long-debated goals. I want to discuss one aspect of the dilemmas of the welfare state — namely the position of youth — in the benefits and costs of the welfare state. I want to explore the potentials of national service for dealing with our immense youth problems. Although I speak of the United States, these difficulties are present in varying degrees in other Western political democracies.

First, it is obvious that one cannot discuss the welfare state's impact on young people without simultaneously examining the consequences of the educational system we have created. In fact, I follow the unorthodox approach in my analysis, at various points, of lumping together expenditures for welfare with those for education. Many issues in social policy which political leaders face focus directly on linkages between the education and welfare systems.

Second, it is equally obvious that the analysis of youth and welfare state require close attention to the pattern of personnel in the armed forces. In the United States under the all-volunteer system, more than 400,000 new personnel must be recruited every year. The system of welfare in the armed forces is extensive. However, because of the high turnover in personnel, and because of pressures of service in a large active duty force with world-wide responsibilities, there is constant debate about how to meet the welfare needs of the armed forces.

Third, the system of social welfare in the US is deeply influenced by the nation's pattern of social stratification, and the reverse is also operative. Welfare influences the social stratification system. However, it makes little sense to utilise an overly simple conception of social stratification in examining the welfare system of the US or any other advanced industrial society. Research into welfare, for example, can start with a three 'class' configuration based on socio-economic indicators. However, it is well known that in an advanced industrial society, the citizenry is just as likely, or even more likely, to think of themselves as members of an occupation group than to consider themselves as belonging to a socio-economic class. But the issue of social stratification is much more complex and subtle. There are a number of other social dimensions which must be incorporated. In advanced industrial society, social stratification does not produce a simple hierarchy of a limited number of society-wide strata. Social stratification does not parallel the pattern of geological strata.[1] The pattern of social stratification includes the population dimensions of age, sex, length and type of education, and ethnic-racial-religious groupings, for example. These variables interact and produce complex and diffuse patterns of social stratification. It makes sense to call these variegated group structures, which are generated by urbanisation and industrialism, 'ordered social segments', or just social segments.[2]

The distinction between socio-economic class categories and ordered social segments is not a mere academic exercise. A realistic view of social stratification is required if the analysis of the welfare state is to be meaningful. In the historical development of the welfare state, the social structure has become more and more differentiated. The trend can best be described not in socio-economic categories, but instead by the terminology of social segmentation. With the development of urbanisation and industrialisation, clients of the welfare state encompass a larger and larger proportion of the nation's population. Increased segmentation of society also means that there is growth in the number and visibility of these social segments. In turn, this trend has led welfare states to believe that they can only do their job and 'survive' if they specialise their welfare agencies. But efforts to solve questions of organisational performance by specialisation of tasks to be accomplished have, in general, failed or been counter-productive.

Efforts of the welfare state to deal with the needs and demands of increasing numbers and greater specialisation of social segments has not been conspicuously successful. Failure to improve the performance of youth programmes has been especially visible. Despite the good will of top administrators, the interaction between the welfare agency personnel and their particular population segments leads to much personal resentment on the part of clients and to a fierce bureaucratisation on the part of the social service agents. Social welfare managers seek higher levels of performance and more rapid performance by rationalising the process through internal specialisation. But, paradoxically, the more the specialisation, the greater the resentment by immediate clients. To handle social welfare problems requires an overall and holistic approach, difficult, if not impossible, to achieve in terms of our present conceptions of social administration. To be effective, welfare agencies must have flexibility and an important element of discretion. The emphasis on specialisation is self-defeating; the human problems which social welfare confront require some concern with the totality of the person. This is especially the case with youth problems.

Such tensions are wide-spread throughout welfare agencies and serve as powerful barriers to increased effectiveness and efficiency, especially in agencies which serve youth. Troubled young persons do not see themselves as a collection of different problems, but as persons who are frustrated, under-employed and unhappy.

Obviously, young people in a nation such as the United States are highly diverse and constitute a variety of ordered social segments. By youth or young people, I mean males and females roughly 16 to 26 years of age. The bulk of American youth make a relatively successful transition to adulthood without having a seriously troubled adolescence. Such an assertion should not lead one to overlook the marked instability of marriage for this group. However, one does not have to be utopian to believe that in an advanced industrial society, current rates of criminality and delinquency are much too high and collective action is required to bring them under control. Realists and idealists differ on tactics for dealing with wayward youth; both are convinced that current levels of youthful crime are unacceptable. The vast writing on youth problems in the welfare state should have produced more concrete results. But the gap between scholarship and viable social welfare action is indeed large. Among top administrators are men of insight and compassion for the fate of troubled youth. In fact, we have had a period of interesting experimentation. But these experiments have had little discernible effect. Instead, as public intolerance of youthful crime has grown, the result has been greater acceptance of tough sentences and tough imprisonment.

It must be remembered that troubled youth is a category which is, in essence, broader than criminal behaviour. It includes a range of social segments. For example, it encompasses those who are drifting away from school and from the agencies of welfare. In this social segment I would include those young people who are drifting through school and whose talents and energy are not mobilised by the school and its teachers. One must include the teenage mother who is raising her family without the benefit of a husband. And the list can readily be extended.

Have no fear, I shall not review the causes of crime among young people. Instead, my goal is to examine the realities and possibilities of the welfare state in dealing with various social segments of the youthful population — both the troubled and the well-adjusted. My approach is to examine the linkages, and the lack of linkages, between the youthful social segments and the welfare state. I shall emphasise a limited number of central institutions. Linkages, of course, include fiscal benefits, social welfare service, and self-images. But we shall not overlook the mass media, political parties and various voluntary associations.

The welfare state acts out the expression of a political ideology that the state should act to bring the lowest social segments up to a minimally acceptable standard of living. This means that where economic institutions fail to supply suitable employment, or where the person is unable to be employed, the state will act to redistribute income and offer appropriate social welfare services to eliminate 'poverty' and the associated hardships. Over the last two to three decades, the welfare state has failed to significantly reduce inequalities in income in an advanced industrial society. This does not mean that the quality of life has not been significantly improved. The improvement in the quality of life has included the situation of the lowest income segments.

One reason for the failure to improve more effectively the quality of life for the lowest segments and more equal distribution of income is that benefits of the welfare state extend upward into middle level segments of the United States. In fact the phrase 'middle-class welfare' is an important aspect of advanced industrial nations. Middle-class welfare includes grants and loans for middle-class children to attend college, ensure loans to develop single- and multi-family housing, and various but important expenditures for medical treatment. I am interested primarily in how the welfare state affects the quality of life of young people. At this point, it is necessary to examine at the same time, the impact of both welfare and educational allocations for young people.

Political leaders and intellectuals who pressed for development of a welfare state never anticipated the actual development of educational and social welfare benefits. The federal government has rapidly developed various systems of assistance to young men and women to attend college-level and professional training institutions. This assistance for youth pays educational fees and living expenses. The support to the student is separate from the extensive grants by state governments and the federal government to operate the massive system of higher education.

The striking aspect of these programmes is the loose means test involved. Such financial assistance flows strongly toward the middle class. Students who obtain such assistance have a strong linkage to the welfare state. It makes it possible for the middle class to have a higher proportion of offspring in college and enables many with limited income to attend more prestigious institutions. In fact, it appears that such assistance works in the opposite fashion from that which advocates of the welfare state expect. These programmes are large scale.

From the late 1970s on, the federal government spent more than five billion dollars each year for such assistance. The amount is scheduled to be increased. In fact, in current years, federal expenditures have increased and further increases are projected. The conservatives in Congress have not been able to reverse the amount allocated. Some programmes are available to students whose family may earn up to $30,000 per year; under certain conditions, families can earn up to $60,000 per year and remain eligible.

The US sends a high proportion of its young people to college, and movement from a low income family to a first rank college or university is possible. Nevertheless, the educational benefits programme works in the opposite direction. In fact, the system of educational grants to middle-class students and the decline in the vitality of the inner-city comprehensive high school have meant that the American high school has become more Europeanised; that is, there exist earlier selection and preparation for college and separation between the college-oriented stream and the vocational stream. It is difficult to analyse the trends in national education budgets because of lack of uniformity in budgeting and the large number of separate school systems. However, it does appear that special grants to low strata schools for assisting low income areas to improve their instructional programme have declined in recent years.

A central programme of the welfare state in the United States is

Aid to Families with Dependent Children (AFDC). It extends cash payments to families with low or no income. While it serves as a crucial source of benefits for poor families with children under 21, it can hardly be viewed as a success from the point of view of social impact. This scheme of welfare is closely linked to public housing, with its large high rise living complexes. The two programmes operate simultaneously to isolate recipients and their offspring from the larger community. In effect, these programmes serve to undermine potential linkages which might help youth make a successful transition to adult society.

I have described federal expenditures for education of the middle class, which gives middle-class offspring crucial assistance in the transition to adult society. By contrast, the extensive pro-grammes of family welfare (AFDC) have the opposite effect. The negative effects are especially felt by young males from minority groups.

Originally, AFDC was designed to assist children in families whose wage-earning parent or parents died or became disabled before the children reached the age of 21. When the programme of aid to dependent children had this specific goal, it was relatively successful. With the passage of time, it became a US version of the European system of family allowances. It became a system of family welfare payments to the lowest social segments of society; these welfare payments were almost automatically extended to families with low or no income.

The dynamics of the AFDC family have been extensively described — powerful social disorganisation and frustration. The life style which could be supported is meagre indeed. The striking aspect of the economics of this type of welfare is the large over-head costs involved. It has been estimated that at least one-third of the operating budget of AFDC and public housing are for administrative overheads. In addition, a dramatic and destructive aspect of the 'welfare' family is that the programme is so structured that a 'family' without a 'father in residence' makes out better financially than one with a father at home. The AFDC-housing project syndrome is both highly disruptive and repressive for the young people who live in these complexes. Barriers to a successful transition from adolescence to adulthood are immense. The school sysem is ineffective. Neither basic skills such as reading, writing and speaking are effectively taught, nor is there meaningful oppor-tunity for young males to learn responsible orientations toward work. Social work agencies which serve the resident population are mainly engaged in dealing with immediate acute problems, and are generally without linkage to the school system. It does not require extensive research to understand why the 'gang' and the life of the gang is rewarding to its participants.

It is striking to observe those offspring who 'make it' despite extensive social disorganisation and disarticulation of social institutions. Adequate statistics are not available. One can point to the substantial numbers who graduate from high school and enter the labour market. The most dramatic aspect is that a surprising number attend local community colleges and metropolitan-based four-year colleges. Moreover, it is striking to note that the male offspring in their twenties start to depart from the gang culture. The bulk of young males slowly enter the labour force, first in marginal jobs, gradually into more regularised employment. Some get a measure of training on the job, others enroll in programmes designed to develop minimum skills. Others move from job to job and find themselves in dead-end employment. Many live at the margins of the underground economy where odd jobs and even full-time employment is organised outside the regulations governing payment of wages and taxes. But the important observation is that the drift from gang life is not usually the result of intervention of social work agencies. We have no explanation for this pattern, but if it did not occur, the problems of minority youth would be almost unmanageable. Clearly, delinquency during the ages 16 to 26 constitutes the core problem.

The system of aid to families with dependent children is so defective and far removed from the original goals that it is difficult to explain why it has remained unreconstructed for such a long time. Obviously, there are owners and managers of the local stores who profit from the crowded residents of public housing. But these entrepreneurs hardly constitute a political bloc with power to maintain the existing pattern. It appears that sheer administrative inertia in good measure is a partial though incomplete explanation.

One set of bureaucratic rules helps to explain the failure of the welfare state in the United States to handle the problems of the bottom of the social stratum. The rent structure in housing projects is based on family income. If the family income rises, residents must move. In essence, the system punishes those with a measure of initiative. Residents are encouraged to hide their extra earning, rather than to feel rewarded. Of central importance is this long-term trend to eliminate successful families. Those left behind have few if any indigenous leaders; successive generations are raised in a setting composed mainly of defeat. The US ethic is such that the housing project is defined as an agency to serve the very poor. Elimination of relatively successful residents reinforces that ethic with most undesirable consequences. The policy of removing more economically successful families is not followed in welfare states such as Great Britain, where 'council' housing is more successful than in the United States. In other words, extensive segregation lies at the root of the failure of the welfare-public housing syndrome.

Various experimental programmes to improve 'welfare' programmes have been suggested and some have been installed on a trial basis. These experiments have not been applied with sufficient vitality and over a long enough time to make any judgements of actual and potential effectiveness. However, by the time the sons of the 'underclass' reach the ages of 24 to 26, except for those who have become hardened criminals with police records, the typical response is to leave gang culture and settle down to a job and seek to construct elements of family life.

The consequences of the welfare state on the youth of the United States is, of course, much wider than on the lowest segments of society. The system of welfare state benefits penetrates very widely through the social structure of the nation. The impact of youth on the vast scheme of taxation and benefits has not only direct economic impact. The system also has a social-psychological impact with powerful political consequences. For example, the mass media give extensive coverage of the crisis of the 'social security' system. The system of social security was designed not only for economic benefits for the various strata of society. It was also developed with the expectation of contributing to a sense of security in the population; that is, to reduce concerns about the quality of life in the years after retirement. But this has hardly been the outcome of this welfare state programme. There is instead a sense of insecurity about the viability of the system. The youth of the nation are not as concerned as old people are, yet segments of the young population, especially the better educated young people, see social security not as a source of stability and effective government, but rather another source of insecurity and one about which they have a lack of confidence. This is similar to youth attitudes to a variety of governmental institutions. In varying degrees the better educated young people are aware that the later one enters the system, the greater the economic burden on that person and the more uncertain are the expectations about the future of the social security system. Moreover, segments of the young population, especially those attending higher education, are fully aware that the old-age segment of society is growing at a rate faster than that of young people. They are aware that the burdens of the social security system will be greater for young people than for older persons.

These observations make it possible to think of the youth population and old-age segment as two different minority groups. Minority groups get differential monetary and psychic rewards. There is no question that, relatively speaking, old folks do have a 'better deal' than young people. Political leaders are fully aware of the relative size of these two minorities, and respond more extensively to old-age groups as an organised pressure. Youth is not only a smaller group, but one which has weak spokesmen and is very poorly organised as a pressure group. Currently, federal legislation makes 70 years the minimum age for mandatory retirement in public and private sectors. Legislation to abolish any form of age basis for retirement is very likely to be passed in the United States. This is the strongest imbalance against youth. Thus, even while there is absence of adequate data, one should not underestimate the awareness of young people of the weak political position which they occupy.

Because of the position of young people in the US welfare state, it would be important to examine the consequences of military service on American youth. Even a brief examination is beyond the scope of this paper. But allow me to state that operation of the all-voluntary military is expensive. In part this is due to the fact that in the combat ground forces the rate of attrition is very high. Moreover, fundamental questions have been raised about the calibre — and effectiveness — of recruits with limited educational backgrounds. In any case, the all-volunteer force, with all its limitations and distortions, appears to be acceptable to the nation's political leaders and the bulk of the civilian population. While the system is acceptable, there is considerable uneasiness and a good measure of political debate from the noteworthy faction of the population who feel that the system is not effective enough, as well as being incompatible with democratic values found in the traditional citizen-soldier concept.

As a result, there has been some thinking about a system of

national service, with young people choosing either military or domestic civilian service. Those who hold this perspective are seeking to keep alive the traditional concept of the citizen soldier.

There is no shortage of plans for organising a civilian component of national service. The list of tasks to be performed continues to grow. While national service could be either volunteer or obligatory, it is my view that obligatory national service in the years ahead is an impossibility. (The political support for any extensive obligatory programme does not exist and most likely will not develop in the next decade.) The best that advocates of a comprehensive national service can aspire to, in the near future, is to develop a series of experimental efforts.

Even limited experimental programmes of national service with civilian options are difficult to organise. Advocates of voluntary national service are sensitive to the complex administrative problems that must be solved. Common elements in various proposals for national service include viewing the programme as a national programme. This reflects, in part, the ideology of energetic leaders concerned with the social integration of society. They wish to demonstrate that the nation still has powerful potentials for national integration.

I would have thought that organisation on a state-by-state basis or even by metropolitan centres would make administrative problems simpler. Many plans called for national service to be run by public, non-profit national agencies. The effect is to separate the agency from the existing governmental structure. In fact, plans generally call for a national agency to direct the operation and a series of operating sub-agencies to oversee specific programmes.

Most plans involve extensive decentralisation, but I am impressed with the potential difficulties of such efforts. Finally, planning would be oriented to help contribute to co-ordination among existing agencies in health, welfare, education and resource conservation fields. I am more inclined toward a 'loose' plan rather than one spelled out in great detail. To be effective, national service would have to be more of a youth movement than a youth organisation. The youth movement would seek to fill institutional gaps, and be fluid in its approach and organisational structure. The cadres for operating such programmes would have to be young and sympathetic to the idea of national service.

National service is not only a system for rendering needed community and national service. It is also an educational procedure to teach 'in the field' the balance of civic rights and obligations. One central and pressing issue of voluntary national service is to develop a widely-based strategy of recruitment. There has been considerable debate on this point. We are looking for a strong element of diversity in the youth groups recruited. The operational cadres would be drawn from the rank and file. They would have longer terms of duty but they would, in the main, hardly be 'careerist' but subject to regularised turnover.

At stake is the very central question, why are the work features of national service likely to produce more effective citizens? First, national service is committed to a diverse and heterogeneous population. The mixing and social interaction is designed to enhance the self-awareness of those who participate. Second, the work programme of national service should increase awareness of socio-economic realities. Third, and central, is the conviction that such group endeavours serve as forms of education which produce positive responses needed for a democratic society building a welfare state.

National service is in the first instance designed to assist young people make the transition from school to the adult world. I believe this transition can best be achieved effectively by some system of national service or the equivalent. Political support for a system of national service does not exist despite the verbal appeal of the idea in general and especially of particular programmes. Of course, private groups can organise equivalent programmes, but they have failed to do so on any noteworthy basis. Although I emphasise the experience associated with the proposed national service, one can hardly overlook the importance of prior class-room instruction. National service without prior class-room study in civic education is likely to be 'half-baked'.

My research leads me to the conclusion that national service can be defined as working at subsistence level after high school or later on one of the broad range of tasks such as conservation, health, old age problems, in order to participate in learning about the civic institutions of society. It is a device for teaching the student to balance civic rights and obligations. Learning includes especially coming to understand the balance of benefits as opposed to civic obligations. Because of routinised patterns of education one can afford to give a very broad content to national service. The goal is not the reinforcement of traditional patriotism but rather the development of an understanding of the tasks which must be performed in a democratic society.

We are a statistically minded nation; therefore, the suggestion has been made that we should tabulate annually the young people engaged in some form of national service. I have not the slightest idea of the numbers involved; yet I am convinced that, even with the absence of governmental support, participation in some type of private national service is certain to grow year by year. Such an observation, however, fails to confront the central issue of developing a national service programme — governmental or private sector — which will not be dominated by graduates of elite and 'better' colleges, but will include a broad range of participants. No national service system fills its objectives unless it offers the 'rank and file' a national service opportunity.

In plans developed or implemented in the United States, most recent national service programmes involve adding one year to the current curriculum. I prefer, and am prepared to see, that the 16 years required for a college degree be gradually and selectively reduced to 15 years. The 'freedom' year would be devoted to some form of national service. Advanced placement of high school students into college courses is already an essential movement in this direction. The advantages of such a pattern would be immense, especially the financial saving in expenditures for education. Also, given the increasing shortage of young people entering the labour market, the additional labour supply would in the decade ahead be of vital importance to the US economy. Such an analysis rests on my expectation that, gradually, there will be a long-term expansion in the productivity of the US economy. Past performance is not a good indicator of future trends. The short-term surplus of youthful labour will give way to increased shortage, especially of trained young workers.

Despite the increased number of patriotic speeches made by senators and congressmen supporting national service, plus the large amount of favourable publicity in the mass media, the political basis for launching an enlarged national service programme remains weak, in part because of restraints on the US federal budget. However, there is support for national service among both liberal and conservative political leaders. Various bills have been introduced, but the drive for either extensive programmes or even small experimental ones does not command wide political support.

Over the past fifty years, a variety of service programmes open to young people have been created and abandoned, a process which reflects an unstable national commitment to service opportunities. During the Great Depression, young people participated in the Civilian Conservation Corps (CCC) (1933-42) and the National Youth Administration (NYA) (1935-43). The CCC averaged 300,000 participants per year; NYA averaged 500,000. No federal programmes existed from the Second World War through the 1950s. There were, during this period, only small CCC-like programmes at the state level. In the modern era of youth service programmes, the Peace Corps began in 1961 and VISTA in 1964. The 1970s brought the revival of the conservation corps idea in the Youth Conservation Corps (1970-83) and the Young Adult Conservation Corps (1978-82). In addition, major demonstrations of national service in urban areas occurred in Seattle (1973-74) and in Syracuse (1978-80).

However, as of 1982, the nation witnessed the decline of several youth service programmes and abolition of several others. Among those eliminated as part of budgetary restrictions and retrenchment were the National Teacher Corps, the Youth Conservation Corps, and the University Year of Action. Estimates for total numbers of participants in the remaining programmes for 1983 are as follows.

At the federal level, the Peace Corps numbers approximately 6,000. VISTA numbers about 3,000, and the National Health Service Corps roughly 3,000. Of Peace Corps volunteers, about one-half are aged 18-24, the other half being older adults. The size of VISTA remains uncertain. In fact, in 1982, VISTA entered a phase-out schedule, although Congress has been resisting VISTA's elimination. Altogether, one could say that federally-sponsored service opportunities for teenagers and young adults in 1983 are estimated at approximately 10,000 (estimates from National Service Secretariat, Washington, DC).

Several states have taken up the conservation corps idea. The most notable is California, with about 1,900 year-round participants in the California Conservation Corps in 1982. Much smaller programmes in Ohio and Minnesota add 300 more 'slots'. Part-year and part-time programmes in Illinois, Iowa, Kansas, Maine, and other states might add an additional 1,000 positions to make a total of about 3,200 (estimates from Human Environment Center, Washington, DC). Other service programmes may exist at the local government level, but these are few and far between and there is no systematic tracking of these programmes.

In addition, there are a large number of purely voluntary efforts in which young people participate in health, education, recreation, social welfare, religious, political and other volunteer work. In a nationwide survey of volunteer service in 1974, 22 per cent of 14-17-year-olds and 18 per cent of 18-24-year-olds were engaged in part-time volunteer work of one kind or another.[3]

Nevertheless, it is striking that the bulk of US parents on national surveys support the idea that young people should give one year of national service. To some extent such a reply is fashionable; to some extent the replies represent patriotic feelings and the belief that national service will make their children more aware of their obligations as citizens. However, such attitudes expressed in surveys have not led to significant political results.

A fundamental barrier to national service (including local programmes of community service) is the attitude of US youth. Again, public opinion surveys need to be read with great care. In the abstract, there is considerable support for the idea of national service among young people. Almost one-half of young people in the early 1980s expressed favourable attitudes and interest in serving; this is noteworthy. But many responses represented conventional expressions of what were considered appropriate attitudes. I do not doubt that there is considerable genuine feeling among college students and selected young workers 'on the job' about demonstrating that they are 'good citizens'. I cannot make an effective estimate of the real support. Young people are caught in a bind generated by parents and the school system. They are attracted to the adventure and moral value of national service, but also feel obliged to get on with their careers. The US economy is stressed — incorrectly in my view — as likely to get worse. Therefore, there is considerable pressure to get on with education and the world of work. In addition, for some students, national service is considered to be no more than a desirable alternative to service in the infantry and ground combat arms.

But these observations are of secondary importance. There is clearly enough interest in and enough need for national service to launch a range of limited programmes. Of highest priority would be work on conservation programmes, and there is considerable interest in meeting the needs of neglected senior citizens. Programmes for the elderly would be locally managed and organised, while resource conservation should be linked to national and state governmental agencies.

It is appropriate that the United States is not about to launch a large-scale national service programme including both military and civilian options. Existing restraints mean that when programmes are developed, and there will be new programmes in the years ahead, they will be small and more likely to develop adequately. The US pattern of shifting from restraint to excessive rapid expansion appears to be a national pattern which needs to be avoided. Therefore, as the nation gradually moves to new forms of national service, the programmes could be organisationally sound. They will be, and must be seen, not merely as welfare programmes, but as expressions of civic duty by those who actively participate. They must be structured as part of citizen obligation.

While Congress and public affairs leaders consider various approaches to national service — military and civilian — the main outlines of an alternative programme have emerged. Most government loan and scholarship programmes have worked to assist young people to avoid military service. Government loans made it possible for large numbers of students to attend college rather than to enter military service. It is probably not feasible to require military service as a prerequisite for a government loan or scholarship. But it could be politically feasible to require community service for particular government loans and forms of assistance to attend college. The format does not encompass many elements of what I believe are worthy aspects of national service, but makes much sense in the contemporary period. It seeks to link government guaranteed loans for higher education to service by the student in the student's local community, a modified and pragmatic version of the long-standing forms of work/study. It involves national political incentives as well as economic ones. There are various patterns of such an arrangement, but the underlying principle is common. Young men and women who want a loan for college education will receive the loan contingent on a term of meaningful service in the local community.

It does appear that the nation is more and more prepared to accept such a work/study programme. Currently, more than six billion dollars is spent annually for loans and grants to students to attend schools of higher education. Development and enactment of such a work/study programme adds very little to annual governmental expenditures. On the contrary, by making a loan dependent on community service, federal expenditures would be reduced by the value of the work completed by the students.

We return to our point of departure. The vitality of the democratic processes cannot be maintained by the existing range of political forms, such as voting and political participation. In our examination of youth under the welfare state, we are dealing with citizenship in its broadest sense. We are also dealing with the content and consequences of patriotism and the informal system of civic education. Historically, citizenship and patriotism include various forms of local self-help currently associated with the idea of national service. Participation in these practices helped give concrete and fuller meaning to obligations, political and otherwise. The need to make use of this tradition in the United States has grown, strangely enough, with the growth of the welfare state.

Notes

1. Lloyd A. Fallers, *Inequality: Social Stratification Reconsidered* (Chicago: University of Chicago Press, 1973), pp. 3-29.

2. Meyer Fotes and E. Evans Pritchard (eds.), *African Political Systems* (Milford: Oxford University Press, 1940), pp. 1-23, for a related discussion of 'ordered segmentation'.

3. Donald J. Eberly, 'Patterns of Volunteer Service by Young People: 1965 and 1974 ', *Volunteer Administration* 4 (Winter 1976): 20-7, cites data from surveys by the Census Bureau.

9 THE SOCIAL WELFARE LABOUR MARKET

Martin Rein

The central argument in this paper is that the growth of the welfare state directly and indirectly generated a demand for jobs, and that the availability of social welfare employment was an important factor in the integration of women into the paid labour force. Thus a significant part of the increase in the employed female labour force is accounted for by an increase in jobs in the social welfare labour market. A reduction in the role of the state as provider could therefore have a perverse effect on the employment opportunities available for women. This general argument needs to be both modified and extended because, in the real world, these relationships are more subtle and complex. This is a preliminary essay designed to explore this relatively uncharted terrain. I present previously unpublished data focusing on the cases of Israel and the United States.

Welfare State Spending and Welfare State Employment

We cannot infer from the above argument that it is merely the level of public spending or more specifically, the level of welfare state spending that shapes the extent of public employment in welfare, and that the leading welfare state countries are also the leaders of general public employment (see Table 9.1). It is difficult to provide a clear understanding of what is the relationship between the state's roles in welfare services as providers *and* employer. Public employment fulfills at least two roles, which Musgrave describes as 'a by-product of public production' and 'a way of providing employment'.[1] One of the factors that affects the production of services is unionisation in the public sector; 'education and health tend to be among the most intensively unionized occupations in most countries'.[2] The state's motives for the provision of employment are quite varied. There are, for example, political reasons (the pursuit of regional, racial and gender equity) as well as economic reasons (the response to unemployment). Moreover, there

109

is no well-developed theory of social good which can provide a consensual rationale for government's role as employer. And there is no theory which tells us about whether the government itself should undertake the production of such goods and services or whether it should purchase them from para-public institutions or private firms. Musgrave asserts that 'there is no unique feature around which such a theory could be constructed'.[3] As a result of these and other considerations the dynamics of the production of social welfare employment in the economy are not well understood. The variations in practice among countries are especially puzzling.

Of course, research and theory continue to search for explanations of the determinants of public employment. The most widely held explanation for the difference between the level of welfare state spending and the level of welfare state employment is that the driving force for the expansion of public jobs depends on the level and growth of government final consumption for goods and services.[4] We need therefore to distinguish between 'service welfare states' and 'transfer welfare states'; the former are more likely to generate employment than the latter.

This argument seems intuitively convincing, but when we turn to the actual experience of countries we find what an OECD report describes as 'remarkable divergence' among countries. The study tried to decompose public expenditures in order to measure separately government final consumption for goods and services and transfers of households — and then to relate these measures to general public employment. The report concludes that 'there is no fixed linkage across countries between public spending and public employment'.[5]

For our purposes we need an even more refined measure, one which links welfare state spending not to general public employment, but more specifically to welfare state employment. Unfortunately, information on the functional distribution of public employment is available for only a few countries. In Table 9.2 we do find a linear relationship between spending and employment. Within the Scandinavian countries, welfare state employment in the late 1970s was 11 per cent for Finland, 14 per cent for Norway, 20 per cent for Denmark and 25 per cent for Sweden; but in these countries government final consumption for social services was also spread over a much narrower range (from 13 to 20 per cent of GDP) than the spread of social welfare employment (11 to

Table 9.1: General Government Expenditure and Employment as Percentage of GNP (1978-9)

	Total public expenditure	Services[a] as per cent of GNP	Merit goods[b] as per cent of GNP	Cash[c]	Cash plus merit goods as per cent of GNP	Cash-service ratio	General public employment
Denmark	48.1	15.0	16.5	19.7	36.2	1.19	29.6
France	45.2	7.8	14.6	17.9	32.5	1.22	15.8
Germany	46.3	12.3	13.2	18.2	31.4	1.37	15.2
Netherlands	57.7	14.8	20.3	19.4	39.7	0.95	15.4
United Kingdom	41.7	12.7	13.9	11.7	25.6	0.84	22.0
United States	32.7	7.6	8.9	9.8	18.7	1.10	16.5

a. Government final consumption for: education, health, housing and other.
b. Government final consumption, transfers, subsidies and capital investment for: education, health, housing and others.
c. Transfers for: pensions, sickness, family allowances, unemployment, compensation, other benefits.

Source: OECD National Accounts.

25 per cent of total employment). The range of employment is wider than the range of service spending.

In examining the expenditure of other countries, we find that in Denmark, Sweden and the United States employment exceeds spending; in the United Kingdom it is about the same; and in Finland it is lower. Obviously such a comparison can not be done mechanically since it is not appropriate to compare the physical quantities of employment with financial expenditures expressed in current monetary value. These findings do however highlight the variations in employment practice at the same level of spending.

But there are other difficulties in the effort to measure the size of the 'welfare state as a labour market' by estimating the level and type of welfare state spending. As we have seen, there are no decisive practical grounds for determining whether a service should be produced directly by the government sector or sub-contracted to another sector. In a number of countries a substantial portion of welfare state expenditures are funnelled through the private non-profit sector. These organisations form a quasi-public sector because they provide a close substitute for governmental activities. Christopher Hood aptly calls them 'the hidden public sector'. He explains that 'organisations beginning as modest and independent charities may come to assume properties associated with "government" institutions. Independent organizations (such as churches and welfare associations) may become closely involved with governments "CORE" in the delivery of social policy'.[6] When there is a split between government financing and government administration, we find a group of organisations that are difficult to classify as either public or private. These institutional arrangements 'are far too common in the modern world to be dismissed as occasional aberrations'.[7] The failure to take institutional forms into account can lead to a gross underestimate of public employment. For example, the figures cited by the OECD to describe the level of general public employment in the Netherlands is 14 per cent. However, when we include what the Dutch call 'The civil-servant-like employees' the size of the public sector grows by half as much. Thus by redefinition, the Netherlands becomes a state with a rather large public sector employment sector of at least 23 per cent.

Government plays an important direct and indirect role in stimulating demand for employment in the non-state social welfare sector of the economy. We need to have some understanding of the size of this indirect ripple effect. Consider the situation in the

Table 9.2: Government Final Consumption and Government Employment for Welfare

Country	Welfare state public employment	Government final consumption for welfare as per cent of GNP
Sweden	24.9	19.5
Denmark	19.6	16.7
United Kingdom	12.8	12.7
Finland	10.9	12.5
United States	8.8	7.6
Norway	13.6	—

Source: OECD, 'Employment in the Public Sector', 1982; and OECD, 'The Role of the Public Sector', October 1982.

United States. The creation during the 1970s of a large private nursing home industry primarily came about because of the federal government's role in financing Medicare and Medicaid. In this sector alone, social welfare employment (primarily in health) increased from 700,000 to 2.5 million between 1964 and 1980.

How might we more precisely estimate the federal government's direct and indirect share of employment? Lester Thurow has used input-output analysis to estimate the private sector employment indirectly generated by federal service expenditures. In 1976, 13 per cent of private sector professional services employment (mostly in health, education and welfare) was indirectly generated by federal outlays.[8] However, most of the growth in federal social spending since the 1950s has occurred in transfer payments and not in services. Whereas in 1952, federal transfer payments were 32 per cent larger than service outlays, by 1979 they were 50 per cent greater. The one input-output analysis of the effects of federal transfer payments on industry outputs is suggestive. For 1972 the study estimated that nearly 20 per cent of all direct federal transfer payments were spent in non-governmental 'medical, educational services, and non-profit organizations'.[9]

In 1979 federal transfer payments amounted to $206 billion. We can thus surmise that if the industry input-output relationship remained stable between 1972 and 1980, approximately $40 billion in transfer payments flowed into the private human services sector in 1980, generating perhaps an additional 1.5 to 2 million jobs.

In addition to the conceptual and methodological problems inherent in separating public from private, and direct from indirect effects, there is a serious practical problem. From published data it is difficult to distinguish between undirected cash transfers which leave the individual free to spend income as he or she chooses, and services which are provided directly by government or the quasi-governmental sector. In some countries medical care is treated as government final consumption and in other countries as a reimbursement payment and hence defined as a cash transfer. 'In France, for example, a sizable portion of governmental expenditures on health is recorded as a transfer payment for households, whereas in Germany medical bills of insured households are paid by the National Health scheme and are treated as public consumption.'[10] This blurring of the service transfer dichotomy in published statistics makes it difficult to use the concept analytically.

Redefining the Problem

If we are to understand the social welfare economy as the interplay between the production of social welfare goods, services and transfers and the employment of personnel in this productive system, then we need a broader framework than welfare state spending and welfare state employment. We need to take account of all the institutions in society that provide social welfare and employ personnel, not merely the direct role of the state. I want to propose the idea of a *social welfare labour market*. The labour market includes all jobs in the industries of health, education and welfare. In an industry perspective we take account both of social welfare occupations and all other occupations required to assist these occupations in producing the product we call medical care, education and welfare.

While an industry-based measure of social welfare services employment thus has advantages over an occupation-based measure, it does not include workers performing social welfare tasks in other industries, e.g. child-care workers employed in private households or nurses and social workers employed at an automobile plant or doctors in a factory. Thus an industry-based measure results in an underestimate of total social welfare employment. The extent of this underestimate is an empirical question.

The social welfare labour market includes employment defined in terms of *both* industry and occupation, i.e. all jobs in the social welfare sector.

Mapping the Social Welfare Labour Market: The United States and Israel

In this section I first present data on the structure of the social welfare labour market at a point in time: Israel in 1972 and the United States in 1970. In the next section I examine trends over time. The data on the employed labour force in the 1970s come from the national census in each country. The analysis is based on published tables in which two-digit industry and occupations are cross-classified separately for men and women.

The specific social welfare *occupations* selected are: physicians, nurses, health technicians, nurses' aides, social recreation workers, teachers, vocational education counsellors, health and school administrators, social workers, child-care workers, teachers' aides, etc. The lists are not directly comparable in the two countries, although the categories in both are similar. The social welfare *industry* includes only health, education and welfare. That part of culture, recreation, sport and public administration which can be considered social welfare is excluded. Our estimates are therefore conservative. When the data is re-analysed, attention will be given to the problem of comparability. Hence the present findings must be treated as preliminary.

The data in Table 3 are organised in terms of a simple dichotomy. All industries and occupations are classified as included or not included in the category 'social welfare'. From the cross-classification of industry and occupation, we can add all social welfare occupations regardless of their industry, together with all the occupations that fall within the social welfare industry. This provides us with a measure of the *social welfare sector*, i.e. all social welfare jobs in the public, private and non-profit sectors of the economy.

The most striking conclusion from this data for the 1970s is the broad similarity in the size and structure of the social welfare *sector* in both countries. Overall 14-15 per cent of the total civilian labour force is employed in the social welfare sector. The proportion of men working in the social welfare *sector* is about 8 per cent in both countries. About one-fifth of all employed women in the United States and 30 per cent in Israel work in the social welfare *labour market.*

In the 1970s more than two-thirds of all social welfare employment in the United States and Israel were held by women. The social welfare labour market is not only heavily female in both countries, but has become even more so over time (to be discussed later).

Next, we decompose employment within the social welfare sector into three groupings: (1) *Primary social welfare employment,* in which the social welfare occupation also represents the primary purpose of the industry, for example teachers in schools, doctors and nurses in hospitals, and social workers in welfare departments. These social welfare occupations include both professional and non-professional personnel like kindergarten aides, nurses' aides and other para-professional workers. (2) *Secondary social welfare employment* constituted of welfare occupations located outside of social welfare industry. The social welfare task is secondary to that of the industry in which the person works. These workers are of two types: (a) social welfare personnel, who work in a variety of economic branches such as manufacturing, finance, etc. — doctors and social workers employed in factories, banks and other non-welfare settings. (With the growth of fringe benefits, many business firms employ social welfare personnel.); (b) social welfare workers employed by private households as child-care workers. Finally, we turn to (3) *non-social welfare occupations in the social welfare industry.* These can be thought of as *support jobs* — maintenance, clerical and managerial.

These relationships can be displayed in a two-by-two table, where employment is cross-classified by industry.

We first highlight the main findings for women in the two countries (see Table 9.3). In 1970 we find that about two-thirds of Americans and Israelis employed in the social welfare sector work in social welfare occupations in the social welfare industry.

In the United States, 'support jobs' comprise almost one-third of all social welfare jobs for women, as compared to only 22 per cent in Israel.

The structure of the social welfare sector in both countries is broadly similar for men. Two-thirds are employed in primary jobs (somewhat less in the US), and about one-quarter in support jobs (somewhat higher in the US). Between 5 and 11 per cent are in

Figure 9.1: The Structure of the Social Welfare Industry

Occupation	Industry		
	Social welfare		Non-social welfare
Social welfare	Primary	1	2 Secondary
Non-social welfare	Support	3	4 Non-social welfare sector

occupations outside the social welfare industry.

It is tempting to think that the level and pattern found in Israel and the US can be generalised to other countries. However, some preliminary German data suggest that in 1970 only 12 per cent of women are employed in the social welfare sector as compared to 30 per cent in Israel and 21 per cent in the United States.

We need to further differentiate this portrait of the social welfare labour market and examine trends over time. Here, we do not have data to permit a symmetrical analysis of the two countries. But even a less systematic comparison raises a number of important questions that have significant implications for public policy.

I would like to consider three issues briefly: (1) professional employment; (2) part-time employment; and (3) the growth of secondary employment in the social welfare labour market. Originally, I had expected to find that all three of these issues would be linked in the following way. The female labour force has not only grown in size, but changed in composition. The most important change was the entry of mothers into paid employment, a phenomenon different from that at the turn of the century when, in the US, only daughters living at home and mothers heading families, worked in the post-war period. The labour market entry of mothers in intact families (secondary workers) produced a pressure for part-time employment. This new job market was largely to consist of professional social welfare employment within the social welfare sector where work-sharing as well as part-time and part-year work was possible.

As mothers entered part-time professional social welfare employment, they stimulated the further expansion of this market,

Table 9.3: Percentage Distribution of the Civilian Labour Force by Industry, Occupation and Sex

A: Israel 1972, Civilian Employment

Occupation	Female Industry		Male Industry		Male and female Industry	
	Social welfare %	Not social welfare %	Social welfare %	Not social welfare %	Social welfare %	Not social welfare %
Social welfare	19.9	3.5	4.3	0.8	9.2	1.6
Non-social welfare	6.0	70.0	7.0	91.7	3.9	84.4
	100% = 355,485		100% = 750,700		100% = 1,106,185	

Women 32.2% of the employed labour force.

B: United States 1970, Employment (in thousands)

Occupation	Females Industry		Males Industry		Male and female Industry	
	Social welfare %	Not social welfare %	Social welfare %	Not social welfare %	Social welfare %	Not social welfare %
Social welfare	16.4	1.8	4.5	0.9	8.9	1.2
Non-social welfare	8.2	73.7	2.7	91.9	4.8	85.1
	100% = 29,967		100% = 48,960		100% = 78,627	

Women equal 37.7% of the employed labour force.

Source: Israel, The Date Archives; The Faculty of Social Science; The Hebrew University. US, The United States census.

as they were in need of care-takers for their own children. If these child-care workers were to be employed by the state in government day-care centres, then welfare state or primary social welfare employment would grow. But if working mothers hired private child-care workers, then secondary social welfare employment would expand accordingly.

What is the empirical evidence for such a scenario? First, how dependent are women in the professions on social welfare occupations? In 1970 in the US, nearly 80 per cent of 4.6 million female professionals worked in social welfare occupations, as compared to 35 per cent of the 6.9 million male professionals. In Israel, although the figures are lower, they are equally impressive. If one takes all professional jewish women in 1980, we find that 70 per cent (142,000) of them are employed in social welfare occupations.[11] Thus, the first part of our argument — that professional women overwhelmingly work in the social welfare sector — is confirmed.

There is considerable evidence from the 1980 EEC labour force survey that women in Western Europe are employed as part-time workers. Two broad patterns emerge. In the Netherlands, Denmark and the United Kingdom two-fifths of the employed women work part-time, i.e. less then 34 hours per week. Between 20 to 30 per cent of these part-time workers work less than 20 hours per week. By contrast, in France and Germany only 25 and 31 per cent of women work part-time and only 10-15 per cent work 20 hours or less.[12]

But these data do not directly address our argument because they do not permit us to describe the role of part-time employment in social welfare. In addition, the European statistics are based on hours worked during a designated survey week. We cannot assume that this information is a proxy for customary or normal work patterns throughout the year. The labour force survey in Israel permits us to overcome both of these difficulties. Using self-reported status and information on weeks worked during the year, we can construct a more refined measure of part-time and part-year employment. The data presented in Table 9.4 show that in 1981 in Israel, only 60 per cent of all employed women worked full-time and full-year as compared to 85 per cent of men. Women comprise only 28 per cent of the full-time, full-year labour force compared with 60 per cent of the part-time, part-year labour force. About one-quarter of all women hold regular part-time jobs throughout the year; and 14 per cent work only part of the year on either a full- or part-time basis.

While a large minority of women in Israel clearly work part-time and part-year, there does not seem to be much evidence to show that such jobs are especially concentrated in the social welfare labour market. About 39 per cent of full-time, full-year workers are employed in social welfare as compared with 44 per cent of part-time, full-year workers (Table 9.4). These differences are very small. Thus it does not appear that in Israel it is social welfare employment that is creating the supply of part-time work.

The next part of the argument concerns the self-generating nature of womens' employment, when working women generate the demand for the employment of other women. The distribution of employment in cells 1 and 2 shed some light on this issue (see Figure 9.1).

In Israel, the continuing growth of the social welfare sector was not concentrated in primary social welfare employment (social welfare occupations in the social welfare industry). Instead, the relative importance of primary social welfare jobs decreased sharply. In 1972 they accounted for 66 per cent of employment in the social welfare sector but only 42 per cent in 1981. What appears to be driving the continuous growth of the social welfare

Table 9.4: Part-time and Part-year Employment by Sex and Social Welfare Employment in Israel, 1981

	Female		Male	
		Social welfare as percentage of total		Social welfare as percentage of total
Employment status	Percentage distribution	employment status	Percentage distribution	employment status
Full-time — full-year	60.0	38.5	85.0	7.8
Full-time — part-year	8.3	25.4	7.2	4.7
Part-time — full-year	25.7	43.7	6.0	16.7
Part-time — part-year	6.0	45.1	1.8	20.6
	100.0%		100.0%	
	428,374		777,560	

labour market is an increase in secondary social welfare employment (social welfare jobs outside of the social welfare industry).

There are two different types of secondary or related social welfare occupations: professionals working in industry, and child-care workers employed by households. Further analysis is needed to clarify the relative growth of each type of secondary employment, but the data do seem to suggest a substantial growth in child-care workers. While secondary social welfare employment was initially stimulated by primary social welfare employment, largely because that was a major condition for female employment, secondary employment has now almost overtaken conventional jobs. Over the decade, the balance of professional and non-professional work has shifted, creating a marked change in the overall structure of the social welfare labour market.

This discussion of the size, structure and change in social welfare female employment suggests that the scenarios I have sketched is plausible. I want now to turn to my main thesis, that the social welfare labour market is crucial in integrating women into paid employment.

How Women have Fared in Social Welfare Employment in the United States

We examined employment patterns in all sectors of the social welfare economy — public, private, non-profit and for-profit. Overall employment trends in the social welfare sector can be briefly characterised as follows: between 1940 and 1980, the social welfare labour market grew from 7 to 9 per cent of the total labour force, thus accounting for one-quarter of the nation's net job increase. During these years, the internal composition of the industry changed. Jobs in education no longer dominated as employment growth has shifted to health. With these shifts, the industry is becoming increasingly 'privatised'. In 1979, 45 per cent of all social welfare jobs were in the private sector compared with 38 per cent in 1952.

The expanding social welfare economy has been an important and under-recognised source of job opportunities for women. In 1980 nearly one-third of the 37 million women in the employed labour force worked in the social welfare industry compared with only 10 per cent of men in the work force. Social welfare employment was especially important for black women. About 37 per cent of all non-white women in the labour force in 1980 were employed in the social welfare sector. In terms of job growth between 1940 and 1980, 41 per cent of all new employment for non-white women occurred in the social welfare industry.

'Great Society' programmes in the 1960s heightened the importance of social welfare employment for all groups, particularly for women. Between 1960 and 1980 social welfare accounted for 41 per cent of the job gains for women compared with 21 per cent for men. The job gain for black women was an even more dramatic 58 per cent.

While the sector's labour force historically has been heavily female, it has become even *more* feminised during the period 1940-80, thus raising the question of whether this stimulation of demand for female work has also resulted in channelling women ever more intensively into traditional female occupations. In 1940 women comprised 59 per cent of the social welfare industry and 70 per cent by 1980.

Is Sex Segration the Price of Employment Integration?

In the 1968 to 1980 period, we can detect the industry's distinct counter-cyclical role for women (see Table 9.5). Welfare has been a sheltered sector of the economy, less affected than many others by major business cycles (though clearly affected by political electoral cycles). The National Bureau of Economic Research estimates six economic turning points (peaks and troughs) in the period 1968 to 1980. Social welfare employment was more important for women as economic troughs approached and less important during peaks, when private sector job growth absorbed greater numbers of women seeking work. In the late 1960s, when the economy was robust, social welfare contributed 35 per cent of the job increase for women. In the early- to mid-1970s, when the economy experienced a severe recession and women lost a disproportionate number of private sector jobs, social welfare accounted for 42 per cent of the employment increase for women. In the late 1970s, however, when the economy partially recovered and fiscal strains slowed public sector employment growth, the contribution of social welfare employment gains declined to 28 per cent for women and 8 per cent for men.

Table 9.5: Share of Annual Increase of Employment in the Social Welfare Economy by Sex

	Female employment increase per year				Male employment increase per year			
	1964-80	1964-70	1970-6	1976-80	1964-80	1964-70	1970-6	1976-80
Share of total increase	33.13	35.06	42.16	28.82	18.51	17.14	42.66	7.56
Private social welfare	21.48	19.48	24.72	17.03	7.89	4.41	10.96	5.05
Non-profit	12.48	13.08	10.15	10.67	4.25	3.04	4.31	3.13
Profit	8.70	6.30	14.57	6.41	3.64	1.27	6.65	2.00
Government social welfare	11.95	15.58	17.44	10.79	10.62	12.73	31.70	2.52

Table 9.6: Social Welfare Employment Gain by Sex

	Israel				United States (in thousands)			
	Females		Males		Females		Males	
	%	(N)	%	(N)	%	(N)	%	(N)
1972					**1960**			
Social welfare	29.9	(106,450)	7.7	(57,430)	20.8	(4,037)	5.8	(2,051)
Other	70.1	(249,035)	92.3	(688,249)	79.2	(15,412)	94.2	(33,028)
Total	100.0	(355,485)	100.0	(745,670)	100.0	(19,450)	100.0	(35,129)
1981					**1980**			
Social welfare	39.2	(174,598)	8.5	(68,528)	30.6	(11,372)	10.0	(4,844)
Other	60.8	(271,074)	91.5	(740,867)	69.4	(25,817)	90.0	(43,390)
Total	100.0	(445,672)	100.0	(809,395)	100.0	(37,198)	100.0	(48,234)
Increase 1972-81					**Increase 1960-80**			
Social welfare	75.6	(68,148)	17.4	(11,098)	41.3	(7,335)	21.3	(2,793)
Other	24.4	(22,039)	82.6	(52,627)	58.7	(10,404)	28.7	(10,312)
Total	100.0	(90,181)	100.0	(63,725)	100.0	(17,739)	100.0	(13,105)

Source: Data for Israel is from the Data Archives; The Faculty of Social Sciences; The Hebrew University.
Data for the UN Survey is from publication data in the Current Population Survey.

The Growth in Female Employment: Comparing Israel and The United States

Table 6 compares the role of the social welfare industry in generating jobs for men and women in Israel between 1972 and 1981 and in the United States between 1960 and 1980. Although the years are not comparable, the figures are nevertheless interesting.

Between 1972 and 1981 Israel experienced a net growth in the civilian labour force of 13 per cent. Almost two-thirds (61 per cent) of this increase in the labour market is attributable to the entry of women into paid employment. These figures include non-paid household members, but not Arabs from the occupied territories. In turn, the growth of the social welfare sector absorbed three-quarters of the increase in the female labour force of women.[13] A similar, but less dramatic story occurred in the United States. Between 1960 and 1980 there was a rather impressive increase of about one-third in the size of the total employed labour force and women accounted for almost 60 per cent of the expansion. In turn, the social welfare sector was responsible for about half (47 per cent) of the net increase in the employment of women.

In Israel the social welfare sector accounts for 30 per cent of all jobs held by women in 1972 and 39 per cent in 1981. In the United States, over the much longer time period of 1960-80, the share of jobs in social welfare increased from 21 to 31 per cent. This suggests a trend towards divergent patterns. In both countries the share of males working in the social welfare sector increased more modestly, from 7.7 to about 8.5 per cent in Israel and from 6 to 10 per cent in the United States.

When we examine the gender distribution of employment within the social welfare sector we find that in 1980-1, about 70 per cent of all social welfare jobs were held by women in both Israel and the United States. In 1972 for Israel the figure was 64 per cent; and in 1960 in the United States, 59 per cent. In both countries it appears that over time, employment in the social welfare sector has become more feminised.

Explaining Women's Employment Gains in the Social Welfare Economy

Several different (though complementary) explanations can be advanced to account for the heavy representation of women in social welfare employment. These can be summarised as welfare state expansion, gender socialisation, technical improvements and political factors.

The welfare state interpretation is a demand-side model. In both countries women were drawn into the labour force in large numbers because of the 'take-off' in governmental social welfare expenditures. Expanding welfare state responsibilities took such varied forms as social security, welfare, housing and employment programmes. Together these programmes sharply expanded state and local health, education and welfare services. In the United States this interpretation appears to be rejected by analysts such as Emma Rothschild,[14] who seeks to explain job gains for women in the 1970s primarily in terms of the private sector shift from manufacturing to services. In her analysis, three service industries in particular loom large: eating and drinking establishments, health and business services. These industries have grown in response to the twin 'crises' of the family and the corporation. According to Rothschild, the family as an institution reproducing the labour force has declined and industries such as food and health care have correspondingly grown to fill the vacuum. With the decline of the extended family and the ageing of the population, the nursing-home industry has grown. Corporations are ill-equipped to meet the needs of women employees for social services or for part-time work. They prefer instead to sub-contract such business services as data processing to smaller firms that can employ a part-time and largely female labour force. Yet aspects of a demand model to account for human service employment gains for women are troubling. Even when controlling for differences between the sexes in the numbers entering the labour force since 1960, the question still remains — why were women still more likely than men to be employed in social welfare? This led to a labour supply model in which the attributes of the labour force creates its own demand. One type of explanation for the crowding of women into the expanding social welfare economy may be found in broader cultural patterns and even in power relationships between the sexes. A gender model of role socialisation addresses the question of why women would disproportionately enter the 'helping' professions. A power interpretation addresses the question of how and why men have kept women out of traditionally male occupations.

The socialisation hypothesis stresses the similarity in character of the work performed in the social welfare economy to women's traditional roles in the family. In the family, women have been socialised into supportive and nurturing roles. Thus their non-market activities involved the social reproduction of labour. As women moved into the paid labour market, many continued to perform these traditional women's roles in service industries such as social welfare.

The power interpretation recognises that while men need the earnings of women in order to improve the family's economic position, men also have an even larger stake in not altering their position of power both in the work-place and in the family (as the primary breadwinner). Hence the segregation of women into lower-paid and less desirable jobs in the service sector (including social welfare) and away from better-paid and more desirable unionised jobs, provides the material foundation enabling men to enjoy a more privileged position in work and family life.

A different political argument is found in the work of Michael Shalev. He believes that it is in the state-building function that we can find a clue which might account for the growth of social welfare employment among women. He argues that in order to make Israel attractive to newcomers and to prevent those already living in Israel from emigrating in periods when the economy is stagnant:

> The state has been active ... in building up (mostly public) employment openings for surplus qualified (white collar and professional) labor. The expansion of the public education and health sectors in the early 1970's for instance cannot be fully understood without reference to the looming possibility of structural unemployment among these groups.[15]

There are other explanations: (1) economic and social motives encourage women to want to work; and/or, the educational system prepares them for professional jobs in human services. A supply-side push is thus created. (2) Men control entry into service sector jobs and have successfully expanded the demand for lower-level female work in the service sector.

Finally yet another type of political explanation can be advanced, one which has its roots in the technical problem or occupational re-classification. In all societies the re-categorisation of the labour force is subject to continued political pressure. Organised groups have a very large stake in redefining their job titles to that of a higher status. Many are successful in their efforts. For example, in France some shoemakers classified as manual workers were able to get their jobs reclassified as mechanical orthopaedists employed in the health industry.[16] When an occupation is placed in the health sector it can better regulate and control working conditions and salaries.

Workers in institutions for the elderly and children were classified as working in the hotel and restaurant industry. A technical re-classification occurred in 1972 in the United States when these workers were regrouped into a new occupational category 'social service worker'. This new category made visible over 2 million social service workers that were hidden in an industry category that did not fully capture what they did. According to this explanation, it was not necessarily the expansion of the industry, but the redefinition of the industrial categories that explains part of the growth of the social welfare sector. The above list is, of course, not exhaustive. We should not feel compelled to choose among these different interpretations. Each sheds some light on a different aspect of the dynamics of welfare employment growth.

Conclusion

We conclude this paper with our initial observation that the growth of employment in the social welfare sector of the economy is not simply a reflection of the size and growth of the production of public welfare services. The link between government, final consumption for welfare and the welfare state as a labour market is not strong. Similar commitments of resources for health, education and social services can have different welfare employment effects, and dissimilar spending can yield similar results. To deal with this problem we proposed a broader concept of the social welfare labour market, which included all social welfare employment in the public, private and non-profit sectors. The advantage of this perspective is that it encompasses, at least in principle, all the relevant employment in social welfare. There is no reason to expect that variations in practice will be easier to explain within this framework. Data from Germany show that despite a high level of welfare state spending the size of the social welfare labour market is very small.

All this suggests that we do not have a very good understanding of the social process at play. We also have a very incomplete map of employment in the social welfare sector. We do know that the sector has become more feminised over time and more privatised (at least in the United States); that it has been responsible for absorbing a large portion of the increase in the female labour force; and that it is the major outlet for the employment of professional women. The hunch that the phenomenon of part-time employment among women may be concentrated in the social welfare sector turned out to be incorrect, at least for Israel.

Even as we begin to learn more about the structure of the social welfare industry and the processes that generate it, the economic environment in which policy evolves has changed. Some governments, especially in the United States and Britain, are committed not only to slowing down the rate of growth of welfare state employment, but also to reversing it. And these objections occur in a period of large and growing unemployment. The explanation for wanting to cut public jobs when unemployment is rising, is that there are too few producers supporting an increasingly dependent population. The evidence for dependency or non-productivity is based on an estimate of the number of persons dependent on the public sector for income from transfers and from public employment in proportion to the number of persons employed in the market sector. The figures are then converted to thousands of man-years and the following conclusion is reached for the Netherlands: 'The ratio of the number of persons receiving an income from the public sector to the number employed in the market sector — thus rose from 55 per cent in 1963 to 80 per cent in 1973 to 110 per cent in 1980.'[17] Richard Rose will try to show that this argument can be generalised for other countries.[18]

This analysis requires the implicit assumption that all workers in the market sector are productive while those receiving income from the public sector are unproductive. But as Rudolph Klein sensibly points out:

> If the 'employment generating aspects of the welfare system is to be seen as a positive advantage — rather than as a sign of original sin — then it follows that we should be concerned about the policy implications of promoting this objective. ... if the welfare jobs — teaching, nursing, etc., did not exist, neither would work for many of the women now in paid employment. And, certainly, in the case of Britain, if there were no such jobs

for women, the whole pattern of income distribution would be radically altered since the most important prediction of whether any given family will be in the upper half of the distribution and above the poverty line — is the presence within it of a working wife.[19]

If the state cuts back on its role as producer and employer, the effects on women and the families in which they live could be reversed. But we need to distinguish intent from performance. Here the British experience, although it cannot be generalised, is instructive. Reducing public sector manpower is a major objective of the Thatcher government. Yet a review of experience shows that between 1977 and 1982 the civilian labour force declined by five per cent, and the public sector declined by about one per cent. However, the public social welfare sector of health, education and social services increased by three per cent. Moreover its share of all the jobs within a declining public sector increased from 52 to 59 per cent. Finally, the share of welfare state employment as a percentage of total civilian employment grew from 12.4 to 13.5 per cent.[20]

It appears from this experience that even when a country sets out to reduce the size of the welfare state as a labour market, it may not succeed. Of course, this does not mean that the past can be interpreted as a prelude to the future.

Notes

1. Richard A. Musgrave, 'Why Public Employment?', *Public Finance and Public Employment*, Proceedings of the 36th Congress of the International Institute of Public Finance, Jerusalem, 1980, pp. 9-10.

2. Rudolph Klein, 'Social Welfare: Options for Change', unpublished paper prepared for OECD, January, 1983.

3. Musgrave, p. 8.

4. There is a political struggle over the scope of the state, which has focused not only on the level of social spending, but also the size of the state. This politically constituted debate about scope has focused on two issues: the relationship between on and off budget items; and the use of transfers and services as a mechanism to expand public employment.

5. *Employment in the Public Sector*, OECD, Paris, 1982, p. 53.

6. Christopher Hood, 'The Hidden Public Sector: The Quangocratization of the World?' University of Glasgow, mimeo, 1983, p. 18.

7. Ibid. p. 2.

8. Lester Thurow, the *Zero Sum Society*, New York Penguin Books, 1981, pp. 165-6.

9. Irving Stern, 'Industry Effects of Government Expenditures: An Input-Output Analysis', *Survey of Current Business*, Vol. 55, No. 5, May 1975, pp. 9-23.

10. OECD, 'The Role of the Public Sector', OECD Secretarial, October 6, 1982, p. 5.

11. *Labor Force Survey, 1980*, Special Series, No. 690, Central Bureau of Statistics, Jerusalem, 1982.

12. EEC Labor Force Survey for 1980, unpublished statistics.

13. This figure appears high. Note that in 1972 a 2 digit industry and occupation code was used and for 1981 a 3 digit code. However, some people suggest that the figures might be higher if an earlier base year was used, because much of the expansion in social welfare expenditure took place in the early 1970s.

14. Emma Rothschild, 'Reagan and the Real America', *The New York Review of Books*, 5 February, 1981.

15. Michael Shalev, 'Social Protection, the Labor Movement and the State: Outline of a Case Study', mimeo, 1983, p. 17.

16. For an interesting analysis of the process with statistical evidence, see Laurent Thevenot, 'Evolution du Personnel de Sante 1968-1971', National Institute of Statistics and Economic Studies, Paris, mimeo, May 1979.

17. H. van der Wielen, 'The Growth of the Public Sector and Its Interaction with the Market Sector in the Netherlands', a paper presented at the Berlin Conference on Measuring the Size and Growth of the Public Sector, June 1981, mimeo, p. 16.

18. Richard Rose (ed.), *Public Employment in Western Nations*, Cambridge University Press, forthcoming.

19. Rudolph Klein, 'Social Welfare: Options for Change', mimeo, 1983, p. 13.

20. 'Employment in the Public and Private Sector 1976 to 1982', *Economic Trends*, February 1983, Table B, p. 83.

10 THE WELFARE STATE AND THE VOLUNTARY SECTOR: THE CASE OF THE PERSONAL SOCIAL SERVICES

Ralph M. Kramer

Despite the enormous expansion of governmental social services during the last 20 years, voluntary non-profit social agencies have grown in number and importance. In many countries where they are used as public social service providers, voluntary agencies have become highly dependent on government funds. This process is part of a pervasive mingling of public and private funds and functions, which has resulted in a mixed economy of welfare. The similarity of service delivery problems confronted by welfare states with varying degrees of reliance on the voluntary sector also suggests that the auspices of the provider agency may be less significant than other organisational variables.

As the welfare state has contracted, however, both the political left and right have rediscovered the special advantages of the voluntary sector. Analysis of their arguments reveals some unrealistic expectations and unfounded assumptions. A less doctrinaire and more experimental approach is proposed which would shift the focus from government or voluntary sponsorship to the design of social policies which would optimise the values of access, adequacy, accountability, efficiency and effectiveness in the delivery of personal social services.

It is fitting to begin a discussion of the voluntary sector of the welfare state with the observation of one of its intellectual founders, Lord Beveridge, who described the historical source of the democratic welfare state as 'voluntary action crystallized and made universal'. Yet Lord Beveridge saw a continuing place for various forms of voluntarism, particularly in 'doing those things which the State should not do'. Unfortunately, this simple guideline has not proved to be very useful because the boundaries of governmental action have been stretched enormously and the differences between institutional sectors are no longer clear.

There is still no theory for the role of voluntary organisations in complex industrial societies with comprehensive systems of state social services. Because there is also no generally accepted taxonomy of voluntary organisations, there is a frequent failure to distinguish between voluntarism, volunteerism, voluntary associations and voluntary agencies. Voluntarism consists of both a set of values (volunteerism) and a set of structures (voluntary organisations). The values can be expressed in such behaviour as citizen participation in policy making, planning, advocacy, administration and fund-raising, and in freely giving oneself to directly helping another person or group. Voluntary organisations fall into two classes according to the primacy of their social welfare functions. First, *voluntary associations* are membership organisations which usually have a social purpose — a 'cause' — and usually seek to benefit their constituency. They include service and fraternal organisations, religious and charitable societies, political parties, and unions. Second, *voluntary agencies* are also of many different types, depending, for example, on the degree of participations of consumers in their governance. We are concerned with those that are essentially bureaucratic in structure, governed by an elected, volunteer board of directors, employing professional or volunteer staff to provide a continuing personal social service to a clientele in the community. At various times voluntary agencies have also been known as 'private agencies', 'non-profit organisations', and even as 'public agencies'. Closely related to voluntary agencies are various forms of self-help or mutual aid groups which may provide some services for their members.

During the growth of the welfare state during the last 20 years, voluntary agencies did not, as some expected, diminish in number or decline in importance. The number of voluntary agencies increased substantially, and new types emerged such as 'alternative agencies', many of which were even started and supported with governmental funds. The expansion of the welfare state was accompanied by a pervasive mingling of public and private funds and functions, based upon a separation of financing from service delivery. Governmental funds were transferred by means of subsidies, grants and payments for service, often in the form of contracts, to voluntary non-profit organisations to provide an ever-growing number of personal social services to a clientele for whom there was a public responsibility.

Welfare states varied considerably in the extent to which they relied on voluntary agencies. The Netherlands, where voluntary agencies constitute the primary social service delivery system, stands at one end of the continuum; Sweden, where practically no voluntary agencies are used although some are subsidised for purposes of advocacy, stands at the other. Not only is it possible to do without a voluntary sector for social service delivery, as Sweden has demonstrated, but much of the voluntary sector can be nationalised and incorporated as part of the government, as in Quebec in 1974. Closer to the Netherlands is West Germany, where about half of the social services are subsidised by government but are provided by voluntary agencies. Other countries with similar pattrns are Belgium, Switzerland, Austria and Italy. The United States is about in the middle, preferring the voluntary agency as an agent and sometime partner to complement a dominant governmental system that uses a variety of service providers. The United Kingdom stands closer to Sweden because of the dominance of its statutory agencies, while France, Israel and Canada stand somewhere between it and the United States.

A summary of governmental-voluntary service patterns and public fiscal policies in the United States, the United Kingdom, the Netherlands and Israel is as shown in Table 10.1.

In each country, the particular division of responsibility between governmental and voluntary agencies is not formalised, but it reflects a distinctive history and socio-political context. While the welfare states differ in the extent of their reliance on non-governmental organisations for the provision of social services, they all share a basic perception of voluntary agencies: these agencies are expected to be innovative and flexible, to protest particularlistic interests, to promote volunteer citizen participation and to meet needs not met by government. Through provision of opportunities for citizen participation, sponsorship of social agencies, dispersal of social power, and an increased sense of civic efficacy, voluntary social agencies are believed to strengthen the pluralist and democratic forces of a society. Together with government and profit-making organisations, voluntary agencies may relieve, replace, or reinforce the primary social systems of family, neighbours and friends. In relation to the public sector, voluntary agencies may substitute for, influence, extend and improve the work of government, or they may supplement, offer complementary services different in kind, or function as a public agent.

Voluntary agencies were used by governmental agencies because, as in the United Kingdom, the local authority social

Table 10.1: Governmental-voluntary Service Patterns and Public Fiscal Policies

	Service Patterns	Fiscal Policy
United States	Mild preference for voluntary agency as an agent and sometimes as a partner, *complementing* a dominant, governmental system that uses a variety of service providers.	A decentralised, grants economy with over one-third of the governmentally financed personal social services provided by non-profit organisations through purchase of service on a contractual or third-party payment basis.
England	Voluntary agency as a partner (junior or silent), *supplementing*, via gap-filling and substitution, for resource deficiencies in a system of primary statutory responsibility for direct administration of comprehensive, universal, personal social services.	Priority for statutory funding and provision. Very limited grant-aids for voluntary agency administration, with local authority payments for service mainly on a deficit-financing basis.
The Netherlands	Voluntary agencies are the primary service delivery system, based on the principle of *subsidiarity*, with government almost exclusively as financier, having only a residual role in service delivery.	Governmental subsidies for administration and social insurance payments provide at least 90 per cent of the income of voluntary agencies.
Israel	High degree of inter-penetration of institutional sectors, dominated by central government, with voluntary agencies as *complementary* but not necessarily as the preferred provider.	Limited governmental subsidies and deficit financing for a wide range of services.

Source: *Voluntary Agencies in the Welfare State* by Ralph M. Kramer (Berkeley, California: University of California Press, 1981), p. 146.

service departments did not have appropriate, specialised or sufficient resources; or because, as in Holland, they were, for historical, religio-political reasons, the providers of first choice; or for more pragmatic reasons in the United States and Israel, where they could provide an economical, flexible service which was often a means of avoiding bureaucratic or budgetary constraints. These public fiscal policies enabled voluntary agencies to greatly enlarge the scope of their services and more than compensated them for any decline in contributions. As they became increasingly dependent on governmental funds, voluntary agencies became, in effect, public agents, raising worrisome questions about their autonomy and their public accountability. The future fate of voluntary agencies became inexorably linked to that of the welfare state and they have become highly vulnerable to reductions in public spending.

In addition, the organisational differences between them and other providers of personal social services — in government and in the market — have diminished somewhat as they all draw their funds from the same governmental sources, are subject to the same regulations, and utilise the same type of professionals and other staff members. Over the years, voluntary agencies have become more bureaucratic and professionalised, and in the United States, more entrepreneurial and political.

In general, the welfare state has encouraged an inter-organisational environment in which the traditional dichotomy between public and private has become artificial and obsolete. The blurring of sectoral differences is reflected in labels such as the 'new political economy', 'the contract state', the 'mixed economy of welfare', or 'welfare pluralism'. They all refer to the inter-penetration of five institutional systems through which the personal social services are provided: government, voluntary agencies, the market, corporate employers and the informal social systems, including the family. Governmental funds are the most important element and account for the existence of the same types of personal social services under different auspices, although not necessarily for the same population. What is evident is that we have not yet developed the appropriate concepts, models, paradigms and theories to reflect this new reality of the mixed economy of welfare.

On the international level, there is great similarity in the types and patterns of personal social services in the welfare states, despite the differences in their reliance on voluntary agencies. Welfare states have also encountered similar problems in the operation of their greatly expanded delivery systems for the personal social services including over- and under-utilisation and other problems of access, spiralling costs, and lack of accountability. Personal social services in most welfare states are usually described as fragmented, lacking coherence and co-ordination and riddled with 'bureau-pathologies'.

This experience suggests that auspices *per se*, or whether the governmental or voluntary sector is used for service delivery, may be less significant than is generally believed. For example, organisational sponsorship may be less influential than other variables such as size, extent of bureaucratisation, professionalisation, complexity, type of service technology, etc. In fact, very little is known about the effects of auspices, i.e. what difference it makes if personal social services are provided by a governmental agency, a voluntary agency, a profit-making organisation, an employer, or a neighbourhood association.

Most consumers believe that whether sponsorship is governmental or voluntary is not nearly as important as the manner in which the service is delivered — that is *how* is more important than *who*. It has been asserted that there are as many differences among voluntary agencies as between them and governmental organisations. Yet many claim that non-governmental organisations are intrinsically preferable to those under public sponsorship because of their greater discretion, responsiveness and innovative capacity. Others are concerned that by substituting for, instead of supplementing the governmental services or by providing an alternative, the voluntary agency may perpetuate second-rate services and mask basic weaknesses in governmental services. Another point of view is that competition should be encouraged between governmental, non-profit and profit-making organisations operating as parallel systems, while recognising that only government can provide universal services as a matter of right.

A concern with the significance of voluntary or governmental sponsorship is particularly relevant now in considering the future of the welfare state in a period of austerity. In the face of retrenchment and other efforts to halt the expansion of the welfare state, there has been a revival of interest and renewed political pressure to rely more extensively on the voluntary sector, particularly in the United States and United Kingdom. Both countries have experienced, in varying degree, a backlash against public spending and considerable distrust and disillusionment with government administration, as well as growing support for re-privatisation and the empowerment of voluntary organisations to carry out public purposes. Ideological backing for the voluntary sector comes both from the left and the right, and stems from its perception as a bulwark against further governmental intervention, or at least as an alternative if not a substitute for it, while some even see voluntarism as a way of recovering a lost sense of community. However, in this attempt to reverse the process of *gemeinschaft* to *gesellschaft*, it may be unwise to assume too soon that we have reached the limits of state welfare. A facile acceptance of the end of the welfare state can become a premature, self-fulfilling prophecy, too easily tolerating governmental failure to continue providing benefits that only the state can ensure. Voluntarism is no substitute for services that can best be delivered by government, particularly if coverage, equity and entitlements are valued. Nor does the voluntary sector have the capacity to compensate for drastic cuts in governmental allocations for the personal social services.

Enthusiastic supporters of empowerment tend to lump together indiscriminately all forms of volunteerism and mediating structures and to regard them as equally desirable and effective in combatting excessive governmental size. There are, however, considerable differences between the use of volunteers as unpaid staff and peer self-help, between mutual aid, neighbourhood, and community-based service organisations, and between the multiple forms of citizen participation, as well as in the institutional structures of family and religion. It is quite understandable in a shrinking economy that, for example, there would be a revival of interest in the use of volunteers as a substitute for paid staff. In California, supporters of reduced taxation fantasised about a wave of good-neighbourliness that would sweep the state in a collective volunteer effort to restore services lost as a result of budget cuts. But experience has shown that, as a cheap form of labour, volunteers can exacerbate tensions among staff and between non-governmental organisations and trade unions. They are no substitute for necessary services best delivered by professionals and other types of paid staff.

Sufficient attention has not been given to the great diversity in the effectiveness of voluntary organisations as service providers and in nurturing citizen participation. Proponents of the voluntary sector often fail to appreciate that its strengths are at the same time the source of its limitations. Whether based on locality, ethnicity, religion, or another sectarian interest, voluntary organisations as service providers are inherently narrow and exclusionary in their scope. Because the individual is dependent for social services on the initiative, resources and capabilities of a particular group with which he is administratively identified, the substitution of voluntary for governmental agencies can result in even more, uneven, inconsistent, and inequitable services. Although evidence of their service delivery capability is rather sparse, experience with various forms of neighbourhood organisation suggest that they can become just as institutionalised, rigid, inaccessible, unresponsive, and undemocratic as professionalised bureaucracies.

There is also a romantic myth of a Golden Age of voluntarism in local communities in which neighbours helped each other. This popular belief underlies proposals such as those embodied in the 1982 Barclay Report in the United Kingdom advocating the provision of resources to informal networks of social relations to deal with the community care of the mentally ill, the infirm aged, physically and mentally handicapped persons, etc. Scorned by Professor Robert Pinker in his dissent from the majority report as 'a romantic illusion that we can miraculously revive the sleeping giants of populist altruism', such substitutions of voluntary for governmental effort are subject to three sets of constraints: (1) the social networks may be non-existent, or unacceptable to the person in need of care, or vice versa; (2) the available resources may be inadequate, or the informal relationships cannot be sustained with the required intensity, duration and competence; (3) accountability for public funds and the performance of a public function are especially difficult for such social systems. It is often forgotten that the present, more formalised modes of care and support developed because of the failure of the local community, the informal and more voluntaristic institutional systems to perform these functions.

In conclusion, I suggest that thinking, in terms of the traditional sectors, of voluntary provision substituting for governmental provision may not be productive. Apart from resting on a set of invidious organisational stereotypes and ignoring the blurring of sectoral boundaries, a focus on governmental versus voluntary deflects attention from major policy questions of equity, i.e. who is getting what services? Instead of asking which sector should be responsible, it may be more important to determine *what* should be done and, thus, de-emphasise 'ownership of the means of production'.

Since we have very little information about what difference governmental or voluntary sponsorship has on the quality, quantity and client impact of a service, a less doctrinaire, more experimental and pluralistic approach would be appropriate. The task then becomes one of designing policies which will assure a desired level of personal social services, using different funding devices and a variety of service providers — with the objective of optimising such values as access, adequacy, accountability, cost-efficiency and effectiveness. In experimenting with different organisational mixes, we can begin to learn what might be expected from various types of service providers, and to discover in an empirical manner, as Beveridge put it, what those things are 'that the State should not do'.

PART FOUR

THE EXPERIENCE OF THE WELFARE STATE IN
DIFFERENT COUNTRIES

11 WELFARE STATE REGRESSION IN SCANDINAVIA? THE DEVELOPMENT OF THE SCANDINAVIAN WELFARE STATES FROM 1970 TO 1980

Lars Nørby Johansen and Jon Eivind Kolberg

Introduction

It seems a commonplace observation that the Scandinavian countries consitute a distinct group within the larger family of modern welfare states. The literature abounds with labels such as 'Scandinavia as a paragon of welfare virtues', 'the Scandinavian model' or 'Scandinavia as a laboratory of welfare policies'.

The Scandinavian countries' much vaunted reputation as welfare leaders is bolstered by a variety of indicators. Some commentators point to the high levels of welfare spending prevailing there, or to comparatively high post-war growth rates. Others focus on the composition of public expenditure in general and of social security expenditure in particular and, accordingly, attach importance to the high share of resources channelled into final government consumption or social benefits in kind (see, for example, Kohl, 1981). Still others spell out the significance of quantitative spending indicators and point instead to a specific institutional profile. Thus, Korpi and Esping-Andersen (1982: 6-7) assert that the Scandinavian welfare states may be distinguished by three features: (1) comprehensiveness of state intervention to provide welfare: (2) institutionalised social entitlements: and (3) a social security system based on universalistic coverage and solidarity. In short, the Scandinavian welfare states are unique in that they can boast an almost perfect fit with the 'institutional redistributive model' of social policy (Titmuss, 1974; Mishra, 1977).

Yet the widespread belief that Scandinavian welfare states are something special extends a mere descriptive portrait — be that in terms of spending indicators of institutional profile. It also includes the notion that the Scandinavian model is a product of the post-war era, and that the strength of Social Democratic parties and unions is the pivotal factor to account for this development.

143

If we accept the contention about a distinct Scandinavian model, it follows that this model also is a product of an unprecedented and sustained period of economic growth — especially during the late 1950s and 1960s. It therefore makes sense to ask whether the Scandinavian welfare state model has been able to withstand the economic stagnation of the 1970s. This will be the main topic of this paper. Focusing on the performance of the Scandinavian welfare states under conditions of economic stagnation is also justified by the fact that Social Democratic governments have been less stable during the 1970s than hitherto. Bourgeois governments or weak Social Democratic minority cabinets have more often than not appeared in the course of the 1970s. Moreover, the economic recession after the oil crisis in 1973-4 was accompanied by widespread anti-tax and anti-welfare sentiments — most notably in Denmark where in 1973 Glistrup's Progressive Party dramatically changed the political landscape (Heidenheimer *et al.*, 1975; Wilensky, 1975 and 1976; Hibbs and Madsen, 1981).

Thus, if we depart from the assumption that there is in fact such a thing as a Scandinavian welfare state model, that this model is a product of post-war economic growth and inextricably related to Social Democratic strength, one would expect this model to have been under severe strain during the last decade. On the other hand, if the changed economic and political conditions turn out not to have altered the essentials of the Scandinavian welfare states, the line of thought alluded to above should be questioned.

Structure of the Paper

This paper will pursue a descriptive and inductive approach. Descriptive because it is necessary to provide a fairly thorough mapping of the development of social security expenditure and of institutional changes from 1970 to 1980. This is the only way to cut through prevailing myths about welfare state roll-back or myths about continuing welfare state excesses. Inductive because we cannot start out with fixed theories or hypotheses when the subject matter is so badly illuminated and of such a recent nature.

The paper will begin with a brief description of the economic malaise in the Scandinavian countries. In particular, it will be shown how the economic recession has hit the Scandinavian countries differently. The next section will attempt to trace how strategies of crisis management are reflected in the development and composition of public expenditure in general and of social security expenditure in particular. As far as social security expenditure is concerned, the analysis will be carried out at both an aggregate level and at a level of individual social benefit. In this way, it should be possible in principle to control for automatic growth components such as demographic changes and increases in the number of beneficiaries.

The third section is concerned with possible institutional changes. This is crucial to the argument. The point is, that even though no significant changes (or cuts) have occurred with respect to aggregate social security spending or individual benefit levels, institutional changes may very well have undermined the tenets of the so-called Scandinavian welfare state model.

The final part will provide a sketchy discussion of possible explanations of the development of the Scandinavian model during economic stagnation.

Economic Stagnation in Scandinavia

As shown in Table 11.1, real economic growth has been markedly slower after the oil crisis in 1974 compared to the preceding period. This gloomy picture of reduced economic growth is of course shared by most OECD-countries, but in this context of inter-Scandinavian comparison it is striking that Norway has been able to maintain her pre-1973 economic growth rate. In fact, Norway's economic growth has increased in the years following 1973, whereas Denmark and Sweden both experienced a staggering drop in economic activity.

The major reason for this difference is obviously that sky-rocketing energy prices have been a severe blow to Denmark and Sweden, whereas Norway has profited greatly from the very same

Table 11.1: Average Annual Real Economic Growth (GDP) in the Scandinavian Countries, 1960-82

	1960-7	1967-73	1973-80	1980-2
Denmark	4.7	4.0	1.6	0.7
Norway	4.7	3.8	4.7	1.3
Sweden	4.5	3.6	1.8	0.7

Source: OECD, *Economic Outlook. Historical Statistics 1960-1980* plus national sources.

factor. Put differently, the traditional vulnerability of open, dependent and small countries and the concomitant ineffectiveness of traditional macro-economic strategies of crisis management have been severely felt in Denmark and Sweden, but not in Norway — at least not to the same extent. Thus, the combination of increased burdens of import caused by exploding energy prices and stagnant export markets has exposed Denmark and Sweden to mounting deficits on the trade balance. Moreover, the demand for foreign capital and the ensuing burdens of payments on loans and interest on debts aggravated by unprecedentedly high interest rate have made problems of large deficits on the balance of payments even more astounding. In contrast, Norway could tolerate huge deficits on the trade balance and balance of payments reflecting enormous imports of capital, goods and services to build up an infrastructure to the oil adventure and in expectation of oil receipts to come.

The difference between Denmark and Sweden on the one hand and Norway on the other is reflected in another area of economic imbalance — deficit on the public household. If we take the deficit on the total public budget (including both current and capital transactions) this deficit has been exponentially increasing in Denmark and Sweden — especially over the last few years. In contrast, Norway has maintained a surplus throughout the decade — even strongly increasing towards the end of the period thanks to revenues from oil taxes. In order not to reduce domestic demand further in the already deflated economies by raising taxes or cutting social security benefits, Denmark and Sweden have increasingly resorted to deficit financing. However, deficit financing is not costless. As we shall see now, the burdens of deficit financing in terms of interest on public debt do not only produce repercussions on the profile of public expenditure but also on redistributive processes.

Public Expenditure

It was the rapid speed of the expansion of the public economies during the 1960s that led some commentators to single out the Scandinavian countries as a distinct group characterised by markedly high growth rates. If we measure the scope of the public economy by total public expenditure as a percentage of GDP it is apparent from Figure 11.1 that the growth has not come to a halt during the 1970s. On the contrary, in all three countries the expansion of the public economy has continued at the rate similar to that of the previous decade.

Yet there are some noticeable differences among the Scandinavian countries in terms of level, rate of change and timing. Throughout the period Sweden has had the highest level of public expenditure relative to GDP — not only among the Scandinavian

Figure 11.1: Total Public Expenditure as a Percentage of GDP: the Scandinavian Countries

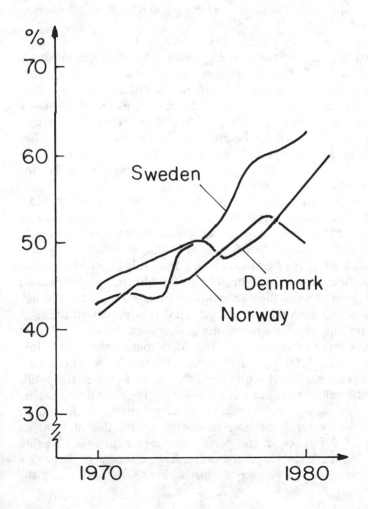

countries but also among OECD countries. On average, Denmark had the second highest level and Norway the lowest level. Sweden also strikes the record when it comes to the rate of growth with a stunning 18 per cent increase from 1970 to 1980. The corresponding figures for Denmark and Norway are 13.8 per cent and 8.2 per cent. As to timing, it is striking that (1) Norway experienced a marked growth of public expenditure in the early 1970s (in contrast to Denmark and Sweden); (2) the global economic recession in 1973/4 almost immediately manifested itself in Denmark and Sweden in terms of 'bumps' in the public expenditure-ratio; and (3) the late 1970s witnessed an accelerating growth of public expenditure in Denmark and Sweden but deceleration in Norway.

These intra-Scandinavian variations reflect to a certain extent national differences in economic growth. The development of the denominator (GDP) of this somewhat elusive measure of the 'size' of the public economy has been markedly different for the Scandinavian countries. Be that as it may, the development of public expenditure relative to GDP testifies to a growing *divergence* among the Scandinavian countries in the course of the 1970s. Where, at the beginning of the decade, the 'size' of public economy was pretty much the same in Scandinavia, the following years brought about a widening gap.

However, one cannot preclude that this divergence hides important similarities in the way in which total public expenditure is allocated to various economic activities. In order to see if that is the case, the relative distribution of public expenditure by economic categories is reproduced in Figures 11.2, 11.3 and 11.4.

If we first look at the distribution of public means absorbed by *final consumption* on the one hand and *transfers* mediated through the public sector on the other hand, a rather clear pattern emerges: Denmark and Sweden are distinct in that these countries allocate relatively more resources to public final consumption than does Norway. This difference is important because government final consumption is a better indicator of the extent to which the public economy really absorbs resources in society in contrast to transfers which just signify redistribution mediated through the public sector. As we shall see later in further detail, this hints at an important difference in the profile of the Scandinavian welfare states. Denmark and Sweden are to a large extent 'service welfare states' compared to Norway's 'cash welfare state'. Although the

Figure 11.2: Total Public Expenditure by Economic Categories: Denmark

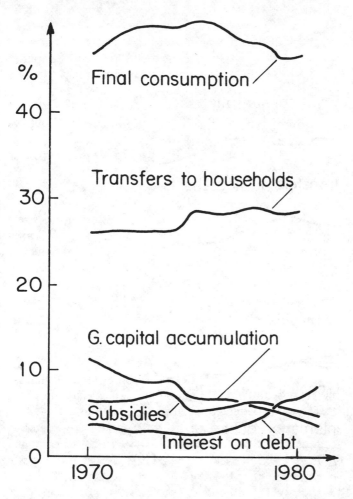

difference in this respect apparently is only marginal between Denmark and Sweden it is nonetheless interesting that Denmark, on average, allocates relatively more resources into public final consumption than Sweden. If we also take into account the fact that Sweden spends considerably more on defence than Denmark, it appears that the latter is more service-oriented than the country of Gunnar Myrdal's much vaunted service state.

Finally, it goes to say that the Scandinavian countries have not

Figure 11.3: Total Public Expenditure by Economic Categories:
Norway

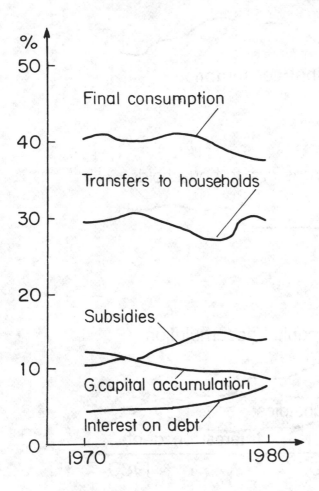

been converging on this score during the 1970s. In all three countries there is a slight tendency towards a relative decline of final
consumption expenditure — especially towards the end of the
period, and more so in Norway than in Denmark and Sweden.

Now, it should not be overlooked that transfers include more
than direct transfers to households. Norway has indeed spent relatively more on transfers to households, but only slightly more.
What really makes the difference appears to be *subsidies*.

Figure 11.4: Total Public Expenditure by Economic Categories: Sweden

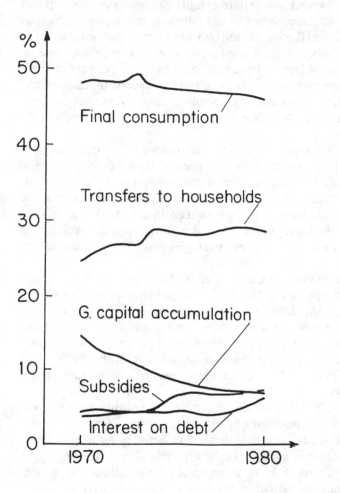

Throughout the period, Norway has devoted twice as much, relatively speaking, to subsidies compared with Denmark and Sweden. However, it is striking that from 1975 Sweden significantly increased the proportion of subsidies. In contrast, the level of subsidies in Denmark has not only been rather low but also stable.

Though these figures may seem crude, they nonetheless signal fundamental differences in responses to the economic crisis. Denmark has reacted to the international economic slow-down of the late 1970s by a typical liberalistic strategy relying on the 'cleaning' effects of the market mechanism. In contrast, Norway (and, from 1975, Sweden to a certain extent) has been pursuing a policy of limiting domestic impact of the international economic crisis by fuelling substantial subsidies into private firms or public enterprises. This is probably one of the reasons why the jobless rate in Denmark soared from 1.1 per cent in 1973 to 9.7 per cent in 1983, whereas unemployment in Sweden did not exceed the 'acceptable' 2 per cent limit of structural unemployment until the very last few years (from 1981). Needless to say, unemployment has been negligible in Norway.

The 1970s witnessed a steady decline in public *capital accumulation* and investments. This is a general tendency observable in most OECD countries, but in a Scandinavian context it is interesting to note that the decline of public capital accumulation and investments has been most pronounced in Denmark and least in Norway. This underscores the intra-Scandinavian variation in macro-economic and political strategies also found in the differential use of public subsidies.

The accelerating scope of deficit financing in Sweden and Denmark is reflected in the form of rapidly increasing burdens of *interest on public debts* towards the end of the period; a tendency that is more pronounced in 1980-3. In Denmark, public expenditure for interest on debts now exceeds 10 per cent of total public expenditure. To give an example of what that means: in 1983 interest on public debt is estimated to exceed expenditure to old-age pensions.

The varying distributions of public expenditure by real economic categories among the Scandinavian countries may serve as a memento of the fact that the borderline between industrial policy, regional policy and social policy is blurred. This should be kept in mind when interpreting the development of social security expenditure to which we now turn.

Social Security Expenditure

It may be useful to separate the survey of social security expenditure from some widely used aggregate measure of the scope of publicity provided benefits and services. This is done in Figure

11.5 which shows social security expenditure as a percentage of GDP and as a percentage of total current public expenditure. In all three countries the share of social security expenditure of GDP has risen rather steeply from 1970 to 1980, most notably in Sweden (14.8 per cent) and least in Norway (6.4 per cent) with Denmark in between (10.8 per cent).

Again, it should be recalled that this difference first and foremost reflects the underlying developments of the denominator, GDP. As we shall see soon, the real growth of social security expenditure follows a different track. It is more interesting that the share of public expenditure devoted to social benefits and services has been going down in all three countries towards the end of the decade. In Denmark and Sweden, this new trend may probably be 'explained' by the accumulated impact of deficit financing in terms of rapidly increasing interest on public debt. The economic crisis has put mounting pressure on the social security system. But due to the fact that an increase of taxes in order to finance the gap between public expenditure and revenues would produce unacceptable contractions in the economy the governments have instead resorted to deficit financing. In turn, deficit financing, and the ensuing burdens of interest on public debt, absorbs an increasing share of public expenditure with the effect that proper social security expenditure take up a decreasing share of total public expenditure. This is the paradox of deficit financing: the public economy expands partly as a result of the impacts of the economic recession on the social security system, but proper social security expenditure take up a decreasing share of the expanding public economy.

Figure 11.6 showing the distribution of social security expenditure by major programmes, provides a first survey of the *spending-profile* of the Scandinavian welfare states.

Not surprisingly, the lion's share of social security expenditure goes to *pensions* (old age, invalidity and survivors'), and related welfare measures. In Sweden, the steady increase of expenditure to pensions is most likely caused by accumulating impacts of the superannuation scheme (ATP). In Denmark, there is tendency towards decreasing outlays to publicly provided pensions. The fact that this tendency appears to be reversed in 1979 may be explained by the introduction of a special reform on 'severance pay' (*efterløn*), i.e. a special remuneration provided for older workers and employees who voluntarily retire from the labour

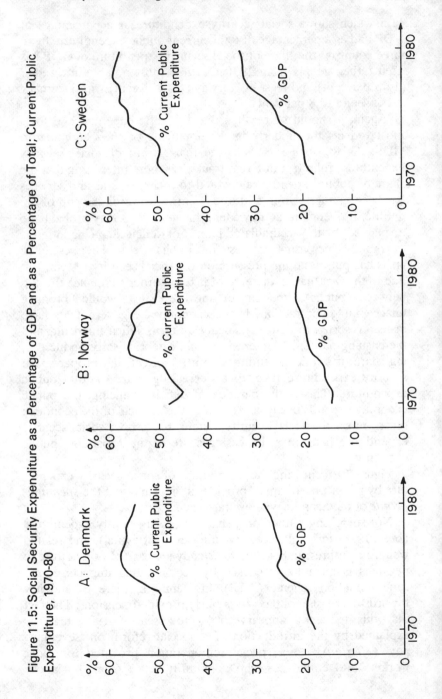

Figure 11.5: Social Security Expenditure as a Percentage of GDP and as a Percentage of Total; Current Public Expenditure, 1970-80

Figure 11.6: Distribution of Social Security Expenditure by Programmes, 1970-80; at Current Prices

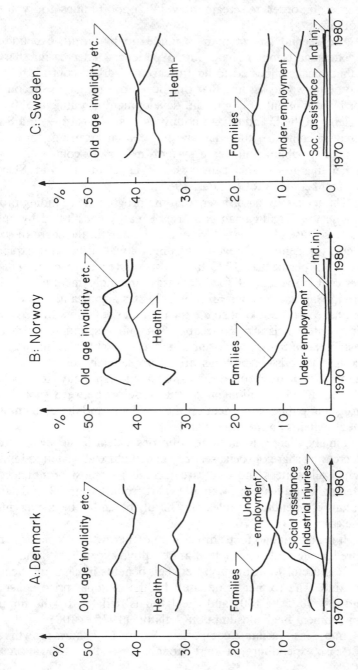

market in order to create new job opportunities for younger workers.[1]

The second largest item is made up by *health* expenditure. Sweden and Denmark have both experienced a decreasing share of public means allocated to health care in marked contrast to Norway. One would assume that this development may be accounted for by a different timing of the development of public health care systems in the Scandinavian countries. As a laggard — in a Scandinavian context — there has simply been more latitude for expansion of a public health care system in Norway compared to the rather mature health care systems in Denmark and Sweden (Heidenheimer and Elvander, 1981).

The most striking difference in the programme spending profile among the Scandinavian countries is easily constituted by public outlays caused by *unemployment*. In Denmark, the share of social security expenditure devoted to unemployment benefits exploded from 3.5 per cent in 1973 to a post-war record of more than 13 per cent in the late 1970s. In contrast, unemployment expenditure in Norway and Sweden are not only at a significantly lower level but have also been kept stable throughout the period. Moreover, in this context it is also noticeable that public spending on means-tested *social assistance* assumes greater weight in Denmark indicating that crisis symptoms are more severely felt there. Yet it should not be overlooked that Sweden and especially Norway have chosen different options as to the trade-off between subsidies to firms and public investment on the one hand and direct unemployment benefits on the other hand.

Finally, there is in all these countries a clear tendency towards a decreasing share of social security expenditure allocated to families (child allowances and day care facilities) — most pronounced in Denmark and least in Sweden. Apart from that, the Scandinavian countries' spending profiles may hardly be said to be converging in the course of the 1970s.

It is now time to focus directly on real growth of social expenditure leaving aside the somewhat deceptive expenditure ratios.

It is useful to distinguish between benefits in cash and benefits in kind. The former is deflated by the national price consumer indices (1975 = 100) and the latter is deflated by the imputed government final consumption deflators (1975 = 100).[2]

In order to facilitate comparison Figure 11.7 shows growth rates for cash expenditure, in-kind expenditure and total social security

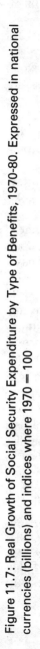

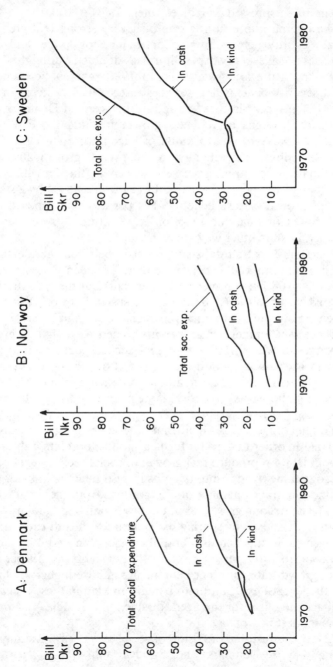

Figure 11.7: Real Growth of Social Security Expenditure by Type of Benefits, 1970-80. Expressed in national currencies (billions) and indices where 1970 = 100

expenditure expressed by indices where 1970 = 100.

The overall impression is one of a very strong real growth of social security expenditure. Controlling for price and wage increases social security expenditure has doubled during the 1970s. To be more precise, from 1970 to 1980 real public outlays to social security benefits and services rose by 124 per cent in Norway, 111 per cent in Sweden and 88 per cent in Denmark. And there are no signs of reduced growth towards the end of the period. However, the two kinds of expenditure (in cash and in kind) contribute differentially to the overall growth among the Scandinavian countries. In case of Sweden, the growth of total social security expenditure is to a large extent caused by a staggering real growth of cash benefits (194 per cent) as opposed to the real growth of final consumption expenditure (40 per cent). In Norway, it is the other way around.

The Danish pattern falls somewhat in between these extremes. The growth of in-kind expenditure there has been more rapid than in Sweden (68 per cent versus 40 per cent) but the growth of cash benefits has been less (210 per cent versus 194 per cent) *in spite* of the enormous outlays to unemployment benefits in Denmark.

These developments may be interpreted as a sign of growing convergence when it comes to real social security expenditure: Norway is catching up with the high level of social security spending in Denmark and Sweden, and is approaching the service orientation of the social security system prevailing in these two countries.

Yet there may still be significant differences programme by programme. In order to dig a bit further into this problem Tables 11.2, 11.3 and 11.4 reproduce real growth of social security expenditure by programme divided into benefits in cash benefits in kind.

One can draw a number of observations from these figures:

(1) The striking growth of outlays to benefits in kind in Norway is primarily caused by soaring expenditure to health care facilities. The growth in this field is markedly higher than in both Denmark and Sweden (109 per cent versus 25 per cent and 19 per cent). Also, growth rates of other benefits in kind are higher in Norway. But the level of expenditure to benefits in kind in these other fields (welfare measures for the aged, disabled and families) is unevenly more modest in Norway.

(2) In contrast, the provision of social services is generally comprehensive in Denmark and Sweden although it varies from

Table 11.2: Social Security Expenditure by Major Programmes and by Type of Benefits, 1970-80: Denmark. At constant prices (million Danish kroner)

	Health		Unemployment		Old-age, invalidity, etc.		Families	
	Cash	Kind	Cash	Kind	Cash	Kind	Cash	Kind
1970	1067	11261	852	360	11353	4064	3461	2501
1971	941	11781	1316	428	12279	4758	3576	2852
1972	1535	12387	1146	434	13243	5325	3857	3168
1973	1661	12560	1081	435	13703	5891	3804	3431
1974	3719	13611	3217	486	16012	6459	3776	3226
1975	4058	13381	5246	525	16962	6502	3842	3181
1976	4794	13759	5728	522	16756	6573	3675	3099
1977	4703	13631	7185	605	17583	6530	3436	3155
1978	4877	13988	7188	952	18308	6777	3223	3555
1979	4866	14339	6480	1626	20090	7573	2908	3973
1980	4765	14028	6402	1843	20706	7845	2807	4535

Table 11.3: Social Security Expenditure by Major Programmes and by Type of Benefits, 1970-80: Norway. At constant prices (millions Norwegian kroner)

	Health		Unemployment		Old-age, invalidity, etc.		Families	
	Cash	Kind	Cash	Kind	Cash	Kind	Cash	Kind
1970	634	5921	197	175	7146	347	2202	430
1971	1078	4932	194	184	8162	377	2120	636
1972	1096	7135	234	152	8484	523	2143	373
1973	1033	7930	222	145	9318	570	2149	382
1974	1812	8640	171	142	12110	772	2067	477
1975	2439	9336	312	142	12570	781	1964	195
1976	2508	10349	445	113	13181	991	2008	562
1977	2502	10999	418	259	14445	1167	1988	575
1978	3756	11428	501	308	14616	983	1985	887
1979								
1980	4872	12345	691	321	15434	964	2706	1399

Table 11.4: Social Security Expenditure by Major Programmes and by Type of Benefits, 1970-80: Sweden. At constant prices (millions Swedish kroner)

	Health		Unemployment		Old-age invalidity, etc.		Families	
	Cash	Kind	Cash	Kind	Cash	Kind	Cash	Kind
1970	3891	16985	674	1947	13220	2533	3207	4040
1971	3948	17636	915	2665	14996	2781	4068	4371
1972	3849	18038	863	2590	15865	2989	4835	3689
1973	3828	19418	769	2574	17245	3048	5500	3611
1974	10970	16677	893	2196	23636	3086	6722	3611
1975	11903	17950	786	2524	25775	3672	6818	4218
1976	13728	18141	846	4227	29406	3809	6634	4817
1977	13743	18556	1024	4784	32869	3948	6756	5181
1978	14240	19458	1382	4676	35403	4211	6910	4741
1979	14118	20085	1421	4054	37769	4170	7225	4728
1980	13697	20176	1301	3674	39370	5194	7455	5048

programme to programme. In the field of unemployment Sweden relies heavily on benefits in kind as opposed to the importance attached to benefits in cash in Denmark. This fits in with the observation that Swedish labour market policies are geared towards the prevention of unemployment or the shaping of the supply of labour force by means of active labour market policies such as job training, employment services, etc., whereas the Danish unemployment policy primarily aims at alleviating the material costs for the individual by means of generous unemployment benefits. In the field of social services for the aged (homes for the aged, home help services, etc.) and for families (day care facilities, nursing homes, etc.) Denmark appears to offer more comprehensive social services than Sweden. Not only does Denmark allocate relatively more resources to social services in these fields, but, per capita, spending is more than twice as high in Denmark as in Sweden. These differences assume great importance when interpreting the adequacy of cash benefits. Put differently, adequacy or generosity of social benefits should not only be judged in terms of (cash) compensation ratios but also with due regard to the public provision of social services for a given group.

(3) Some of the breaks in the reported time-series may be accounted for by the introduction of new reforms. For example, in Denmark the doubling of expenditure devoted to sickness benefit from 1973 to 1974 is caused by a thorough health security reform (enacted in 1972 with effect from 1973) setting the compensation ratio in case of sickness at a rate of 90 per cent of previous earnings. Likewise, the dramatic 1978 increase of public spending on sickness benefit in Norway may be attributed to the introduction of a reform which provided full compensation in case of sickness (100 per cent). At least one break is caused by changed procedure of statistical reporting: the sudden and sharp increase in expenditure on pensions from 1973 to 1974 (in all three countries) is in part the result of the fact that outlays on statutory pensions (for example, for civil servants) were only reported from 1974 onwards!

(4) Finally the real growth of social expenditure varies significantly across countries, programmes and type of benefits (in cash and in kind). In Denmark, the overall growth of social security expenditure is heavily influenced by a 710 per cent increase (*sic*) of unemployment benefits. It is also a distinct Danish feature that consumption expenditure allocated to the provision of social services

for pensioners and families with children runs relatively faster than cash transfers to these groups. The provision of benefits (in cash and in kind) for families and children deserves special attention. From about 1975 outlays paid in the form of child allowances and similar cash benefits decreased steadily with the result that there is a total decrease of some 9 per cent (the *only* example of a real negative growth (or cuts) in all the programmes, for both types of benefits and in all three Scandinavian countries). Yet expenditure on benefits in kind — most notably day care facilities — rose by 81 per cent from 1970 to 1980. This indicates that government attempts to reduce expenditure by cutting child allowances have been more than outweighed by increasing expenditure on social services provided for the same group. In Sweden, increased public spending on (old-age) pensions appears to be one of the most important factors behind the overall growth of social security expenditure observable there. Apart from final consumption expenditure allocated to employment services and services for pensioners, outlays to benefits in kind display comparatively modest growth rates. As mentioned above, it appears that Sweden's profile is gradually changing from a service-oriented welfare state to a cash-oriented welfare state.

The programme-specific growth rates have already been commented upon in the Norwegian case.

Average, Individual Benefits and Compensation Ratios

The survey of the development of social expenditure in the Scandinavian countries during the 1970s may have produced a somewhat bewildering picture of cross-national and programme variations. However, one should not lose sight of the basic conclusion: a spectacular (real) growth of social security spending. One cannot be sure whether overall growth is mainly caused by demographic changes or increasing numbers of beneficiaries produced by changes in the business cycle leaving the individual beneficiary less well off. To be more precise, the growth of social security expenditure is caused by an interplay of demographic factors, criteria of eligibility, changes in numbers of beneficiaries and changes of benefit levels. If we can somehow single out the relative weight of these components we can provide a first clue to the question of whether the individual recipient has been hit by cuts or has lost ground *vis-à-vis* members of the labour force.

We can approach this procedure of decomposition only in the case of pensions. But as will be recalled, pension expenditure takes up about 40-50 per cent of total social security expenditure. Due to the fact that old-age pensions have been universal in Scandinavia throughout the decade we can keep eligibility constant and limit ourselves to changes of total pension expenditure (at constant prices), changes in numbers of pensioners and changes of average per pensioner (at constant prices). In order to facilitate comparison changes are expressed in the form of simple indices (1970 = 100). The results of this simplified method of decomposition are shown in Table 11.5.

In the case of *old-age pensions* it is obvious that real growth of total expenditure on old-age pensions is not only caused by demographic changes. The purchasing power of old-age pensions has increased significantly — on average, more than real wages. The differences between the Scandinavian countries may be attributed to the existence and age of superannuation schemes. Denmark's poor performance reflects the non-existence of an effective superannuation scheme. Sweden's lead over Norway is most likely related to the matured scheme in Sweden (introduced in 1960 in contrast to Norway's 1967 scheme).

As far as *invalidity pensions* are concerned, Sweden is outstanding in terms of both increasing numbers of recipients and improved benefit levels.

In order to give a more accurate picture of the position of recipients of cash benefits *vis-à-vis* those actively employed, Table 11.6 reproduces compensation ratios in typical cases for a variety of social benefits.

The interpretation of Table 11.6 seems straightforward: (1) in general, compensation ratios have considerably increased over the period — even after the breakthrough of the economic recession. (2) Compensation ratios for old-age pensioners in Denmark are comparatively low. But it is precisely in this context that one should pay attention to the more comprehensive supply of social services for the aged. On the other hand, Denmark boasts the most generous unemployment benefits. (3) Norway's full compensation in case of sickness (sickness pay) is unmatched within an intra-Scandinavian perspective. Swedish compensation ratios are generally high.

By now it should be abundantly clear, that the Scandinavian

Table 11.5: Total Expenditure, Numbers of Pensioners and Average Benefits per Pensioner by Type of Pensions, 1970-80. At constant prices

	Denmark			Norway			Sweden		
	Expenditure	Number	Exp/no	Expenditure	Number	Exp/no	Expenditure	Number	Exp/no
Old age pensions									
1970	100	100	100	100	100	100	100	100	100
1975	117	110	107	147	137	101	151	112	134
1980	132	119	111	204	153	130	240	114	167
Invalidity pensions									
1970	100	100	100	100[a]	100[a]	100[a]	100	100	100
1975	138	129	106	105	100	105	225	154	147
1980	139	135	103	132	112	118	228	156	185
Survivors' pensions									
1970	100	100	100	100	100	100	100	100	100
1975	106	103	104	101	91	110	146	105	139
1980	88	94	94	111	91	122	161	83	194

a. Norway 1971.

Table 11.6: Post-tax Social Benefits for a Male Industrial Worker as a Percentage of Post-tax Income by Type of Benefits, 1970-81

		Sickness benefits			Unemployment benefits			Retirement/ invalidity pension			Old-age pension			Survivors' pension		
		(a)	(b)	(c)	(a)	(b)	(c)	(a)	(b)	(c)	(a)	(b)	(c)	(a)	(b)	(c)
Denmark	1970	42	53	55	63	63	65	77		90	42	57		38		66
	1972	54	67	68	67	67	68	80		88	41	59		37		63
	1974	64	64	66	61	61	61	71		82	48	62		39		63
	1978	79	81	82	79	81	82	70		82	42	57				
	1981	80	81	82	80	81	82	76		88	47	65				
Norway	1970	37	40	46	37	40	46	41		48	41	59		38		67
	1972	51	51	62	51	51	62	43		56	43	61		39		66
	1974	51	50	59	51	50	58	39		61	56	66		36		61
	1978	100	100	100	64	64	64	64		81	75	96				
	1981	100	100	100												
Sweden	1970	83	73	74	79	69	69	85		92	85	91		74		98
	1972	80	74	75	80	79	84	80		90	80	92		74		90
	1974	90	90	90	67	63	67	73		75	66	77		68		75
	1978	94	94	94	77	77	77	68		72	68	92				

Source: *Social Security in the Nordic Countries*, various volumes.

(a) — Single man; (b) — married man, childless; (c) married man with 2 minor children, including child allowances.

welfare states have been able to withstand the strain imposed upon them by economic stagnation in the late 1970s. Cuts in social security spending have certainly not been made in order to reduce the mounting pressure on the public budgets. Whatever indicators or measures are applied, the 1970s have not only witnessed real growth of social security expenditure, but also an incessant, if not accelerating, growth.

But, as already said in the introduction, the uniqueness of the Scandinavian welfare state model is not only derived from high spending levels, accelerating growth rates or generous benefits, it is also founded on a distinct institutional profile. And it still remains to be shown to what extent institutional features may have been changed.

Institutional Changes

If we depart from the tenets of the 'institutional redistributive model' of social policy, and we accept the contention that the Scandinavian welfare states are unique in their near-perfect fit with this model, the search of essential institutional changes should focus on the following issues.

(1) *Breaches of the principle of universalism.* A universalistic social legislation is allegedly an important characteristic of the Scandinavian welfare states. It is also an essential ingredient of the 'institutional redistributive model'. Accordingly, we will look for tendencies towards selectivity or changes in social legislation that are targeted towards special problem groups.

(2) *Changes of entitlements to social benefits.* For Titmuss, the basic distinction between his three models of social policy was the way in which individual needs are satisfied. The 'residual model' relies on the private market and the family as the basic channels through which needs are met. Welfare institutions only come in if these channels fail. The 'industrial achievement-performance model' prescribes a type of social policy where social needs are met 'on the basis of merit, work performance and productivity'. In short, social entitlements are based on labour market participation and, thus, reflect the distributive logic of the market. In contrast, the 'institutional redistributive model' transcends the distributive logic of the market. Entitlements are based on social citizenship and equality and are, thus, divorced from market criteria. We will

look for changes of social entitlements that signal a departure from the institutional model.

(3) *Privatisation.* Tendencies towards increased privatisation in the form of, for example, fee-for-services or private pension schemes will also be conceived of as departures from the institutional model.

(4) *Cuts of benefits.* It is believed that the institutional model not only prescribes social benefits at a subsistence level, but benefits that secure an adequate compensation. Accordingly, we will look for cuts of benefits that leave recipients of social benefits less well off.

Selectivity — Changes in Criteria of Entitlements

Denmark has experienced changes in social legislation that portend a selectivistic departure. Firstly, entitlement to child allowances has been made income related, i.e. benefits are graduated downwards according to family income up to a certain income limit. Above that limit, allowances are not granted. It should be stressed that income relating of this kind is not equivalent to a discretionary means test. The right to child allowances is, in principle, still universal, but benefits are automatically related to income. As alluded to above, these changes have been rather effective in terms of reducing expenditure devoted to this programme.

Secondly, a new concept of 'social income' has been introduced in order to tighten the relationship between income and social benefits. The new concept deviates from normal taxable income in that it includes the value of certain assets (and the value of pensions for civil servants) and excludes the value of certain tax deductions. The 'social income' was justified by a need to establish a 'fair' measure according to which income-related benefits could be distributed. The point is, however, that this new measure has been applied to a number of social benefits that were not previously income related.

Thirdly, the present bourgeois government has re-introduced one waiting day in case of sickness benefits. Yet there are also changes that run counter to this development. In the field of unemployment insurance entitlements and duration periods have become less restrictive. Part-time employees, younger employees and employees with little or no participation record on the labour market have gained access to unemployment benefits. And existing duration periods have been prolonged — in fact suspended.

These extensions were primarily introduced in the mid-1970s at a time where the recession was believed to be short lived.

In sum, the Danish experience testifies to an increasing select-ivity in terms of income-related benefits, but typically in fields out-side the labour market. Benefits that are more directly related to the labour market — e.g. unemployment benefits — have, para-doxically, become divorced from labour market participation and performance. In Norway and Sweden, child allowances are still flat rate and universal. In general, the phenomenon of income related benefits is not as pronounced there as in Denmark. As to sickness benefits, the previous Swedish bourgeois government introduced one waiting day which, however, was repealed by the present Social Democratic government. The issue of waiting days in case of sickness has also been brought to the fore in Norway. The Con-servative government and business associations have launched a proposal to introduce two waiting days and reduce compensations. These attempts have failed so far.

The most important example of the role of labour market par-ticipation for social entitlement is easily the existing super-annuation schemes in Norway and Sweden (see Esping-Andersen and Korpi, 1983). Although Denmark has an ATP scheme it is of negligible importance compared to Norway and Sweden. Den-mark's pension system is still a non-contributory system solely financed through taxation, with universal flat-rate pensions (plus some income-related supplementary allowances). But Denmark has other forms of occupationally defined pensions. Civil servants have their own favourable pension scheme. Most other public employees are protected by statutory pension schemes heavily sup-ported by the employer (the state) and based on members' contri-butions. Moreover, a great number of employers in the private sector offer special pension schemes especially for white-collar workers.

Privatisation — Fiscal Welfare

Since 1980 several important services of the Norwegian welfare state have become more expensive for individuals. Fee-for-services has been introduced/increased concerning medical consultations, laboratory tests, drugs, physiotherapeutic treatment, travel expenses and home help for the aged. Some of the items of this list came about as a result of wage settlements between medical asso-ciations and public employers. Fee-for-services amounts to about two per cent of total social security expenditure. In Denmark, fee-for-services is still nonexistent in the health care sector. Both in-patient and out-patient treatment is free for everybody. However, there have been some minor reductions of public subsidies for medicine and glasses; Sweden also has some symbolic fee-for-service elements concerning hospital care.

Private pension and savings schemes are on the borderline between private welfare and fiscal welfare. The element of fiscal welfare creeps in because contributions to most of these schemes are tax deductible. In a Scandinavian context, Denmark is probably outstanding as to the importance of private pension schemes. The redistributive effects of this kind of 'tax expenditure' are — like most tax deductions — highly regressive. The 1970s witnessed an increasing importance of private pension schemes, not because of any specific government acts, but probably because more people ran into higher marginal taxes.

Cuts in Benefits

This item has already been commented upon (see *supra*). It should be mentioned, however, that de-indexation may be an effective means to curtail public expenditure. In Norway, changed indexation procedures, especially regarding the base amount in the pension system, have apparently reduced public expenditure. Another example of direct cuts may be drawn from the field of social assistance in Denmark, where a benefit ceiling was introduced in the late 1970s (social assistance must not exceed the maximum of daily cash benefit in case of unemployment and sickness).

By way of conclusion it may be said that certain institutional changes have occurred in direct response to a mounting pressure for reducing the growth of public expenditure and social security expenditure. Yet it would be haphazard to interpret these changes as fundamental violations of the Scandinavian welfare states. The essential institutional pillars are still intact. The only systematic departure from the model is found in Denmark in terms of increased selectivity in the provision of social benefits and services and in terms of the importance of private pension schemes. But even there it appears premature to announce an institutional breakdown.

Discussion

It now seems obvious that the problem is not *if* the Scandinavian welfare states have the economic stagnation and political turmoil of the 1970s, but *how*. That this is a real puzzle is also shown by the fact that the 1970s brought about changes in the political setting which would lead one to expect some kind of welfare state regression. At the parliamentary level, Social Democratic parties have generally enjoyed less strength than hitherto. Rather weak Social Democratic minority cabinets or bourgeois cabinets have been the rule in Denmark and Norway, and Sweden has experienced protracted periods of bourgeois government as well. Moreover, the objective of reducing public budget deficits and interest on public debt has increasingly gained political momentum — among Social Democrats as well. And the political-administrative apparatus in all three countries has, in fact, produced an abundance of proposals, budget reforms, administrative reforms, plans, etc., with the explicit purpose of curbing the growth of public expenditure and social security expenditure. Finally, the spread of anti-tax and anti-welfare sentiments in Denmark and Norway during the early 1970s could indicate a lack of popular support for the welfare state. Denmark, in particular, won notoriety as an archetypal example of welfare-state backlash (Wilensky, 1976). If it is a puzzle why a so-called welfare-state backlash occurred in Denmark and not in neighbouring Sweden (Heidenheimer *et al.*, 1975), it appears no less puzzling why this backlash apparently evaporated in the course of the following years *in spite* of the continuing high degree of visibility of taxation (which has even become more visible according to Wilensky's own operationalisation); *in spite* of incessant channelling of state resources into labour-intensive, publicly provided services (Hibbs and Madsen, 1981); *in spite* of new increases of the aggregate tax rate — especially towards the end of the period (Wilensky, 1976); and *in spite* of a growing divergence between pre-tax income and post-tax earnings (Hibbs and Madsen, 1981).

A first tentative clue to the question of how the Scandinavian welfare state model survived both economic stagnation and political attacks may be provided by the following two inter-related hypotheses: (1) the very economic stagnation has engendered an increased political mobilisation of popular support of the welfare state; and (2) the institutional nature of the Scandinavian welfare states produces in and by itself a safeguard against political onslaughts.

That the economic recession and the ensuing insecurity and vulnerability among the citizenry has engendered mobilisation of popular support of the welfare state is indicated by survey analyses. Thus, it has been shown that popular support of the welfare state in Denmark and Norway increased significantly from about the mid-1970s (Kolberg and Pettersen, 1981; Andersen, 1982). In Norway, the percentage of those among the electorate who favoured an expansion of social policy increased from 20 per cent in 1973 to 42 per cent in 1977. In Denmark, the percentage of those who favoured a maintenance *or* a further expansion of social reforms rose from a record low 39 per cent in 1974 to 55 per cent in 1978. Moreover, public employees, i.e. producers of social services, have become increasingly organised and mobilised into support of the welfare state. In this context it is interesting to observe that the single best predictor of popular support for the welfare state is neither traditional class variables nor 'middle mass' notions *à la* Wilensky, but occupational status around the public-private sector nexus. This holds true in both Denmark and Norway (Kolberg and Pettersen, 1981; Andersen, 1982). It should also be recalled that the neo-corporatist setting in the Scandinavian countries gives public employee unions easy access to the centres of public decision making. Finally, client groups have become politically mobilised as well. Old-age pensioners, invalidity pensioners, users of day care homes etc. have their own organisations through which they express grievances against cut proposals. In general, the issue of the welfare state has become thoroughly politicised and polarised in the course of the 1970s. In order to understand why those who have been mobilised in support of the welfare state have been largely successful, it is necessary to turn to the second hypothesis.

Korpi has suggested that an institutional type of social policy — in contrast to a marginal type of social policy — produces pro-welfare-state coalitions among the electorate (Korpi, 1980). Since most programmes are universal and therefore affect large proportions of the population, most households benefit somehow, directly or indirectly from these programmes. If individuals act rationally there will consequently be a strong impetus towards maintenance or expansion of such programmes. Korpi suggests further that an institutional type of social policy tends to encourage coalition formation between the working class and the middle class in support of continued welfare-state policies. The question is what groups constitute the middle class. If it is the petit bourgeois, self-employed craftsmen, or small-holders and farmers, Korpi's line of thought should be questioned. At least in Denmark and Norway it is precisely those groups who express strong anti-welfare sentiments. A potential for coalition formation in support of the welfare state is more likely to occur between the working class and producers of social services, i.e. public employees. As alluded to above, public employees are not only distinct in their pro-welfare-state attitudes; they also constitute the single largest constituency in the electorate.

In all of the three Scandinavian countries the number of public employees increased dramatically throughout the 1970s. In Denmark and Sweden, the number of public employees has now passed one-third of the total labour force. In Denmark, the group of public employees is almost twice as large as the group of blue-collar workers. However, it remains to be shown how the impacts of changes in the social structure on the structure of interests in society have produced new cleavage lines or new bases for coalition formation (see, however, Alber 1982). It appears that traditional class concepts are somewhat inadequate for analyses of the political basis of the (Scandinavian) welfare states.

If we accept the assertion that an institutional type of social policy produces its own safeguard, it still has to be explained why the growth of social security expenditure varied greatly across programmes, types of benefits and countries, and why certain institutional reversals in fact did take place.

In order to account for such variations we can tentatively elaborate the argument: institutionally entrenched resistance or a potential for mobilisation against threats of reversals is not equally distributed across programmes and types of benefits. One would assume that reduced growth, reversals or direct cuts are more likely to occur where the institutional resistance is least. The question is where.

The analysis of the development of social security expenditure provides some clues. Development in Denmark indicates a certain pattern. Apart from unemployment benefits, the growth was most pronounced in case of benefits in kind. This hints that it may be useful to distinguish between cash transfers to households (benefits in cash) and final government consumption (benefits in kind). The point is, that the provision of the two kinds of benefits is subject to two different logics of decision making. The production of benefits in kind is characterised by a rather atomised decision-making process in which producers of social services play a dominant role. There are of course differences in degree as to a potential for coalition-making with clients (read: voters), organisation, professionalisation, etc. But it goes without saying that politicians in general will experience difficulties in counteracting institutionally entrenched interests of this kind. The reported growth of day care facilities and welfare measures for the aged cannot be traced to any overall reform or specific decisions made by government. In contrast, decisions pertaining to cash transfers belong by and large to the realm of politicians and partisan politics. In principle it is easier, *ceteris paribus*, to control expenditure devoted to cash transfers. The provision of child allowances has become more targeted, and benefits have been cut. Also, social assistance benefits and certain benefits provided for the handicapped have been made more selective and reduced. However, attempts to reduce compensation ratios of unemployment benefits have failed. Put differently, it is important whether a constituency of recipients of cash benefits is organisationally rooted in the labour market or not. The strong labour unions in the Scandinavian countries constitute a rather safe bulwark against potential cuts of unemployment benefit, sickness benefit, compensation in case of industrial injuries and labour market related pensions. Groups marginal to the labour market and lacking organisational backing are more susceptible to targeted cuts.

It remains an open question to what extent this kind of reasoning may be extended to the other Scandinavian countries.

If we accept the hypothesis that an institutional type of social policy generates its own safeguard and reduces the likelihood of welfare-state backlash, we must also accept that Social Democratic strength is not a precondition for the maintenance or expansion of this type of policy.

Social Democratic strength may or may not have been conducive to the formation of the Scandinavian welfare state model. But the fact that this model, *grasso modo*, survived economic stagnation and political attacks during the 1970s can not simply be reduced to a question of Social Democratic strength — or partisan politics for that matter.

It also remains an open question whether, if continued, welfare

state expansion in fact benefits Social Democratic core voters–
workers. Deficit financing and increased public outlays produced
by interests on public debt are highly regressive. But that's another
story.

References

Andersen, J.G. (1982), 'Den folkelige tilslutning til social politikken — en krise for
velfærdsstaten?', in Anckar, D., E. Damgaard and H. Valen (eds.), *Partier,
ideologier, väljare.* Åbo: Åbo Akademi, pp. 175-209.
Esping-Andersen, G. and W. Korpi (1983), *From Poor Relief to Institutional
Welfare States: The Development of Scandinavian Social Policy*, paper
prepared for ECPR, Freiburg.
Heidenheimer, A.J. and N. Elvander (eds.) (1980), *The Shaping of the Swedish
Health Care System*, New York: St. Martin's Press.
Heidenheimer, A.J., H. Heclo and C.T. Adams (1975), *Comparative Public
Policy: The Politics of Social Choice in Europe and America*, New York: St.
Martin's Press.
Hibbs, D. and H.J. Madsen (1981), 'Public Reactions to the Growth of Taxation
and Government Expenditure', *World Politics*, vol. XXX111, no. 3, pp.
413-35.
Kolberg, J.E. and P.A. Pettersen (1981), 'Om velferdsstatens politiske basis',
Tidsskrift for Samfunnsforskning, vol. 22, no. 2-3.
Korpi, W. (1980), 'Social Policy and Distributional Conflict in the Capitalist
Democracies. a Preliminary Comparative Framework', *West European Politics*,
vol. 3, no. 3, pp. 296-316.
Mishra, R. (1977), *Society and Social Policy*, London: Macmillan.
Titmuss, R. (1974), *Social Policy*, London: Allen & Unwin.
Wilensky, H. (1975), *The Welfare State and Equality*, Berkeley, California: University
of California Press.
Wilensky, H. (1976), *The 'New Corporatism', Centralization and the Welfare State*,
Beverly Hills and London: SAGE.
Vesterø Jensen, C., 'The Dual Pension System in Denmark', paper, Istituto
Universitario Europeo.

Notes

Notes on statistical sources: the data reported in the paper are taken from different
sources which are rarely consistent. In order to secure a minimum of consistency
and comparability we have generally sought to establish a correspondence between
statistical source and type of information. Thus, data on GDP and public
expenditure are drawn from OECD's *National Accounts Statistics*. Danish data on
public expenditure are, however, reproduced from national sources (*Statistisk
Tiårsoversigt*, Danmarks Statistik, various years). Data on social security
expenditure are drawn from one source, *Yearbook of Nordic Statistics*, various
years. A special committee under the Nordic Council is responsible for establishing
inter-Nordic comparability concerning these data. As far as total social security

expenditure is concerned comparability is generally high. But there are certain problems as to programme-specific expenditure. Specific expenditure items are not always classified under the same programmes in the Nordic countries, and the very definition of programmes has changed over time. Some of the reported changes of programme-specific expenditure simply cover a change-over of expenditure items from one programme to another. Also, one should be aware of the introduction of new items. That is the case for expenditure on 'other statutory pensions' (most notably civil servants' pensions) which were reported only from 1974 onwards. Even after 1974 Swedish data on pension expenditure are based on inconsistent practices as to the inclusion of 'other statutory pensions'. In order to create consistency in the Swedish data and comparability with the data on Denmark and Norway we have extrapolated, for some years, the time-series of 'statutory pensions'. Data on number of recipients, compensation ratios and other types of more detailed information are reproduced from *Social Security in the Nordic Countries*, Statistical Report of the Nordic Countries, various years. Data on compensation ratios in particular should be interpreted with caution. It is not only that these figures are calculated differently in the Nordic countries, but procedures of calculation also change somewhat over time. More importantly, exact criteria of eligibility, duration of benefits, etc. are different from country to country.

1. This 'severance pay' should not be confused with a traditional pre-retirement pension. Eligibility and benefits follow the rules of unemployment benefits and not pre-retirement pensions. There has in fact been a certain substitution effect due to the fact that 'severance pays' are more generous than pre-retirement pensions.
2. The imputed final government consumption deflator is calculated on the basis of final government consumption expenditure at constant (1975) prices according to OECD's *National Accounts Statistics, 1951-1980*. In this way it should be possible in principle to control for different price developments concerning transfers and final consumption. Total social security expenditure at constant prices are, thus, a summation of cash transfers at constant prices (deflated by the price consumer index) and benefits in kind at constant prices (deflated by the imputed final government consumption deflator). No attempts have been made to apply programme-specific final consumption deflators.

12 THE WELFARE STATE — THE CASE OF AUSTRIA

Heinz Kienzl

Full Employment — the Hard Core of the Welfare State

The hard core of the welfare state is full employment; other things are — quoting Hillel of Babylon — only accessories. In the early 1950s the trade unions faced the problem of full employment without inflation. They led the way in the creation of policies to secure full employment while maintaining an internal and external balance in the economy (which means a low inflation rate and a balanced current account). After nearly two years of discussion we established our so-called 'parity commission' (for those interested, the comments on my lecture explain its structure and functioning in more detail). Whenever we have been asked if other countries can take a lesson from our system of economic and social partnership, we have always answered: 'You certainly cannot copy it'. But I must not forget to mention that we learned a lot from the Swedes, the Dutch and the French as far as planification is concerned.

Integration

With the help of welfare state policies, we have had to cope with three important processes of integration since the Second World War. First, we had to re-integrate the war-disabled into the work process, i.e. the soldiers wounded in the war and the returning prisoners of war. The second group of people who had to be integrated were German-speaking people who had been expelled from Eastern countries. They were mainly farmers and had to be re-trained as industrial and self-employed workers. The third group to be integrated were non-German-Speaking refugees from Hungary, Czechoslovakia, Poland and Yugoslavia as guest workers. Those expelled from Poland and Jewish refugees from Russia made up only a small contingent. We experienced sizeable

177

problems in trying to integrate the German-speaking people expelled from Eastern countries into a war-disrupted economy but, nevertheless, we successfully accomplished this task in the 1950s. We experienced financial problems with the integration of refugees of Hungarian, Czech, Polish and Jewish origin but managed to do so in the end. We even successfully absorbed 50,000 Yugoslav guest workers, who obtained Austrian citizenship.

The Costs

As far as the costs of the welfare state are concerned we do admit that they are high and still increasing; and financing them will only be possible in a growing economy. But those costs are relatively low in comparison with those in other European welfare states, as we have managed to keep unemployment low.

The Future

Karl Marx said that capitalism creates the working class which will overthrow it. The welfare state has also created a class which does not attempt to overthrow the system, but considerably challenges it. They manifest themselves in what Willi Brandt called the 'new social movements'. In the beginning these consisted of the members of the new left, and the students who revolted during the late 1960s. This new class supports some romantic dreams; they are anti-American and anti-Israeli; they are for direct democracy and grass root initiatives. The welfare state can only survive as long as they do not exert a dominating influence. At all times social movements have arrived in Austria much later and in an already weakened form. Serious movements which in Germany constitute full dramas appear on the Austrian stage in the form of an operetta. Thus we are hopeful that political changes resulting 'from sociological changes in the welfare state will sink down to the bottom of the pudding — which is the easy-going Austrian way of life.

Table 12.1: Degree of Coverage of the Social Sector

	Expenditure in bn S	Revenue in bn S	Degree of coverage in percentage
1970	25,630	10,412	40.62
1971	28,658	11,989	41.83
1972	32,693	13,946	42.66
1973	36,520	16,303	44.64
1974	44,658	19,180	42.95
1975	53,911	20,991	38.94
1976	58,652	23,634	40.30
1977	63,908	26,270	41.11
1978	69,093	34,549	50.00
1979	73,588	38,048	51.70
1980	71,768	39,065	54.43
1981	79,408	43,651	54.97
1982	93,166	49,012	52.61
1983[a]	101,519	50,395	49.64
1984[a]	114,022	54,481	47.78

a. Provisional.

Table 12.2: Development of Social Quotas (social expenditure in percentage of GDP) in EEC Countries and Austria

	1970	1971	1972	1973	1974	1975	1976	1977	1978	1979	1980	1981
Federal Republic of Germany	21.4 (1)	21.9 (2)	22.7 (2)	23.2 (3)	24.7 (3)	27.9 (1)	—	—	27.4 (2)	26.8 (4)	—	—
France	19.2 (5)	19.1 (6)	19.2 (7)	19.6 (7)	20.0 (3)	22.9 (6)	—	—	25.0 (6)	25.3 (6)	25.8	—
Italy	18.8 (6)	20.2 (5)	21.7 (3)	21.0 (4)	22.6 (7)	22.6 (6)	—	—	23.6 (6)	22.8 (6)	—	—
Netherlands	19.8 (3)	22.0 (1)	23.1 (1)	23.7 (1)	25.6 (4)	26.7 (4)	—	—	28.9 (7)	30.0 (7)	30.7	—
Belgium	18.5 (7)	18.9 (1)	19.9 (1)	20.5 (1)	21.6 (1)	24.5 (2)	—	—	26.4 (1)	27.0 (1)	—	—
Luxembourg	16.4 (8)	18.4 (7)	18.8 (6)	17.5 (6)	17.0 (5)	22.4 (4)	—	—	25.6 (3)	25.3 (3)	26.5	—
Great Britain	15.9 (8)	16.8 (8)	17.4 (8)	17.3 (8)	18.1 (10)	20.0 (8)	—	—	20.4 (5)	20.4 (6)	—	—
Ireland	13.2 (9)	13.6 (9)	13.5 (9)	15.9 (9)	17.8 (8)	19.4 (9)	—	—	17.5 (8)	18.2 (8)	—	—
Denmark	19.6 (10)	21.2 (10)	21.5 (10)	22.3 (10)	25.0 (9)	25.8 (10)	—	—	26.2 (9)	27.1 (9)	28.0	—
Austria	21.1 (4)	21.3 (4)	20.8 (4)	20.8 (2)	21.3 (2)	23.9 (3)	24.4	24.3	26.2 (4)	25.9 (2)	25.9	26.8
	(2)	(3)	(5)	(5)	(6)	(5)			(4)	(5)		

Source: EEC-social accounts; WIFO-calculations

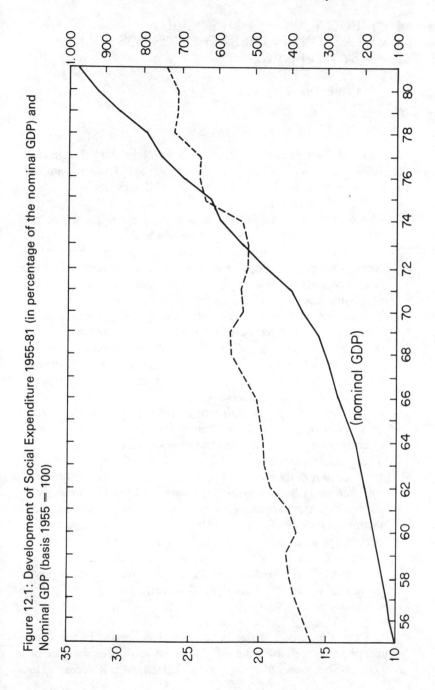

Figure 12.1: Development of Social Expenditure 1955-81 (in percentage of the nominal GDP) and Nominal GDP (basis 1955 = 100)

13 SOCIAL RIGHTS OR SOCIAL RESPONSIBILITIES? THE CASE OF SWITZERLAND

Walter Rüegg

The case of Switzerland confirms in several aspects the general conclusions drawn by scholars of different backgrounds from the development of the welfare state in industrial societies.

(1) The welfare state appears as a necessary consequence of the nation-building processes in industrial societies.

(2) The welfare state succeeded in promoting particular welfare services aimed at improving education and health of the whole population and at protecting people against the risks of illness, accidents, unemployment, disability, old age and misery.

(3) The welfare state failed to reach its underlying general goals, i.e. abolishment of pauperism, redistribution of resources from the wealthier to the poor, social security and equality amongst all its members, political and social integration of its citizens. It favoured, up to now, the middle class and led to a struggle between different middle-class groups for a better share of public funds. *Rebus sic stantibus* it will lead to a redistribution of wealth from the younger to the older generation and, consequently, to a class struggle between generations.

(4) The economical, political and social costs of the welfare state grew more rapidly and to a higher level than its benefits. When the increasing burden could no more be borne without difficulties by an expanding economy, the feeling of a disadvantageous cost-benefit relationship grew everywhere. First, people opposed the growing tax burden; secondly, criticism of the state bureaucracy became a successful political issue, and, last but not least, institutional forms of welfare services began to be supplemented or challenged by different forms of individualised care.

To a certain extent, these features, which appear in the background paper as well as in the contributions to the Jerusalem Conference, can be observed in Switzerland. However, it seems to me that the Swiss case demonstrates the validity of some other basic assumptions which appear as proposals for the aftermath of the welfare state and which, by the particularities of the Swiss social and political system, were experienced before the welfare components of the state turned into a welfare state:

(1) As Karl W. Deutsch noticed in a well-informed and sagacious analysis of the Swiss political system, the Swiss people, by their history, learned that social change and political decision-making not only needs a motor but also a system of brakes.[1] Federalism and direct participation of the citizens in local, regional and, to a certain extent, also in federal votes about welfare issues slowed down the emergence of the welfare state.

(2) The growing expectations for collective security measures did not prevent Swiss voters from opposing the introduction of explicit social rights into the Swiss constitution. The Swiss tradition of the state being fundamentally the direct responsibility of free citizens transposed the soldier-citizen system of compulsory military service to the political sphere in which citizens are supposed to perform public duties without substantial financial compensation. This deep-rooted value of citizen participation in public affairs challenged the professionalisation of political and social expertise which necessarily develops in modern societies and increases the number of university graduates in bureaucratic administrations. The voters still stick to the conviction that citizens not only have rights but also public responsibilities which cannot be reduced to paying taxes. As a consequence, the substantial expansion of welfare components of the state did not fundamentally upset the balance between civil rights and obligations in the value system of the Swiss voters. The notion of 'welfare state', 'social rights', professed by scientists and political leaders, raised the people's suspicions.

(3) The substantial expansion of social security until the 1960s could not destroy the traditional conviction that social responsibilities as fundamental human features were rooted and had to be realised mainly in primary institutions and that secondary institutions had only subsidiary functions. The excessive burden that social security began to put on public funds during the 1970s helped to revive, not only in party programmes[2] but also in official reports of social administrations, even under

socialist leadership, the basic assumptions that social responsibilities of the citizens in their family and community life were
more important than social rights and that the state should be
more concerned in promoting such social networks than to
expand its own welfare services.[3]

Switzerland and Israel have some common features. Both are
small states without any significant natural resources; both have a
democratic constitution from the heads of state down to local and
co-operative authorities; the citizens of both states have a different
cultural background and are liable for compulsory military service.
At a meeting in Jerusalem, it may, therefore, be not unin-
teresting to have a closer look at the Swiss development of a welfare state. The comparison of similarities and differences may
point to some major problems of the welfare state such as cen-
tralism versus federalism, expertise versus civic responsibility, collective security versus private responsibility, professional or reserve
armed forces versus a citizen-soldier military system.

The Citizen-Soldier Military System as a Motor and as a Brake for the Welfare State

The Swiss federal constitution of 1848 states in Article 2 the four
goals of the state: (1) the maintenance of the country's independence; (2) the application of peace and order within; (3) the protection of the freedom and the rights of the Swiss citizens; (4) the
promotion of their common welfare. With this last goal, the
declaration of welfare — undoubtedly influenced by the preamble
of the constitution of the United States — the Swiss people made
no attempt to found a welfare state as some modern promoters
would like to conclude.[4] But the Swiss state of 1848 was not conceived as the 'night-watchman-state' caricatured by Lassalle in
Germany.[5] It was the general conviction of the liberal founding
fathers that, through education, social progress, 'control of the
nature within and outside man by reason' could be promoted and
poverty, misery and other social evils erased. Education as a
national task had to be performed by compulsory military service
for all men and by compulsory elementary school education for all
children.[6]

The Swiss army, which after 1848 integrated the independent

armed forces of the cantons, was conceived not only as an instrument of defence against foreign aggression and of peace and order inside the state, but also as a school of the nation. Participation in the citizen-army was at the same time a duty and a right of the free citizen. Taking the two opposites together, military service was an expression of, and, at the same time, a laboratory of civic responsibilities. The same applies to the elementary education. It was conceived as a civic obligation which could be enforced by the cantons. Modern observers claim that the compulsory school education was not meant as an obligation, 'but as a guarantee for the right to education for the children who had to be protected against unwitting parents and authorities'.[7] Therefore, elementary school education was rather an institution of and for social responsibilities. Contrary to the army, the school was entirely left to the cantons. The division of tasks between the federal state and the cantons was expressed by a slogan which seems to go back to the constitutional revision of 1874: To the federal government the canons, education to the cantons.

Therefore, from the emergence of the first welfare components, the education of all citizens through army and elementary school, reflects the two poles of institutionalised civic responsibilities: elementary education near to primary group experiences, therefore centred on the development of the individual personality, and the citizen-army on the other end in which the individual has to be willing to sacrifice his life for the community.

Thus the Swiss elementary school is, to a large extent, governed by local boards which appoint the teachers, provide for the buildings and defend the interests of the parents and children. The cantons train the teachers, organise the curricula, control its results and subsidise local expenditure for salaries, investments and maintenance. The main responsibilities are located as near as possible to the primary groups of family and neighbourhood. More remote public institutions have subsidiary functions, the federal government only having the institutional right to establish and to subsidise institutions of higher learning.

On the other side, the military system as a national task had to be organised by central government. Therefore it is not surprising that the emergence of the state bureaucracy is connected with the organisation of armed forces in the late Middle Ages. That social security subsidies were first established by the state in the military framework is less well known or explored. But in its historic origins as well as in its extreme realisations, the welfare state is closely connected to military affairs. To a certain extent, this also applies to the citizen-soldier system. The risks of health, accident and disability were first insured on a national basis for persons in military service. The introduction of old-age and survivors' insurance which — beside education — is the most important welfare component of the Swiss state, and which was introduced into the constitution in 1924, could only be implemented by law in 1948 on the model of an income-compensation plan for persons liable for military service which was introduced during the Second World War by the federal government through a special authority which parliament had granted for the duration of the war. Also other welfare components of the Swiss state go back to war experiences with the fundamental constitutional change of 1947 by which the federal government was charged to protect and promote with economic measures the people's welfare and the citizen economic security.

Five structural features of the Swiss citizen-soldier system slowed down development into a welfare state.

(1) The conception of citizen-soldier avoids the formation of standing armies composed by professional soldiers or conscripts fully engaged for a longer period of time and thus separated from civil life. For several decades of his adult life, the citizen-soldier forms part of the army. Outside the military training periods, too, he is responsible for his equipment and training and, as an officer, has to assume commanding functions. He is thus constantly reminded that he cannot only assert his rights from the state but also has to fulfil concrete obligations towards it.

(2) But even more crucial are the institutional effects: officers up to the rank of colonels-in-chief, while working in their civil professions, have to administer the control of their troops, to prepare military exercises and are responsible for their own further training; the army has indeed an educational effect on the development of leadership skills in civil and political life, just as the founding fathers of 1848 intended for the whole male population. On the other hand, this system of civic responsibilities applies to the whole domain of home defence, in which, for example, the organisation of provisions of raw materials and food for war-time and other emergency situations is left as the responsibility of private persons; and private industry eases the burden (and at the same time the bureaucracy) of the state. In 1976 private contributions (taxes not

included) towards defence measures amounted to 25 per cent of the defence budget.[8]

(3) The close connection between military and civil responsibilities strongly effects the composition of the political elites. At the beginning of the Confederation, the taking over of military commands and parliamentary mandates largely went hand in hand.[9] Even now, one is tempted to establish a correlation between the officer's rank and the relative change to be elected into the federal parliament. Results in the 1971 elections for the *Nationalrat* (House of Representatives) were:

	Of the candidates %	Of those elected %
Subaltern officers	7	8.7
Captains	7.5	12.8
Higher ranks	9.5	21.0[10]

The strong interweaving of civil, military and political elites gives an important role to private interests in the decision process of the state legislation, particularly in the field of social policy.[10b]

(4) Of particular importance are also the effects of the citizen-soldier principle on the supplement of parental and neighbourhood social networks through citizens' participation in organisations which include extra-military activities, such as shooting societies, athletic clubs and samaritan associations.

(5) Whereas even in defence, with its extreme conditions, public tasks are delegated to individual and collective private responsibilities, the central state element is also limited by delegating a certain part of the military organisation to cantonal and local authorities. Such a delegation and decentralisation of power make a smooth functioning and an appropriate perception of an integrated state policy more difficult, but it certainly allows greater, more informal and formal, legitimation of the central authority by self-responsible institutions on a cantonal and local level.

These five aspects of civic responsibilities, as they have developed in a federal citizen-soldier system, have the effect of a brake system for the development of a centralised welfare state. One of its most successful promotors, Professor Tschudi, Federal Councillor (Minister of Interior) from 1960 to 1973, describes it as follows:

A characteristic feature of our system is the high degree of decentralization in the social security administration. This solution is not so much the result of the history and growth of the different insurance plans, as it is a political choice. In our federalist nation the cantons must have the possibility to co-operate in the application of the laws. In the social field, the cooperation between government and the associations of employers and employees has been successful. Only the accident insurance and the military insurance are administered by a central authority; all the others — the health, unemployment, old age and survivors' insurance, the disability insurance, the income compensation plan, and the children's allowances — are handled by different public funds or by funds of associations.[11]

The Development of the Social Security System in Switzerland

With a few exceptions, the federal government only plays a subsidiary role in the social security system, compared with the role of cantonal and private institutions. The analysis of these exceptions illustrates the briefly-explained democratic brake system of the individual citizen's social responsibilities.

(1) Following the economic recession in the 1870s and the growing organisation of neglected workers' interest, the federal government, inspired by the pattern of Bismarck's social legislation, tried to introduce a compulsory health and accident insurance plan especially for workers. In the parliamentary debates, where a constitutional change was sought, a formula had to be found which took into account the then established private and cantonal health insurance funds. The constitutional change passed a plebiscite in 1890. But in 1900 a law, agreed upon in parliament after lengthy debates, was rejected by a popular referendum. Farmers and small tradesmen all opposed it, but also in the working class a 'part of the basis mistrusted the social-political interventions by the state and rejected them as much as ever'.[12] In 1911 a more modest federal law on health and accident insurance was accepted because it was limited to those dependently employed in industry, transportation and the building trade, and replaced severe factory legislation which made employers responsible for occupational accidents. In 1918 the Swiss National Accident Insurance Institute was founded as the first and only federal

institute in the field of social security. But the thought of a national health insurance system was given up in favour of a law which was to allow the federal government to support existing or future private and cantonal health insurance institutions.

(2) In 1901 a federal military insurance was established without difficulties which was to protect military persons against accidents and injuries during the military service. There were not any civil interests involved here. That is why the centralistic regulation was readily accepted.

(3) The third and, until now, most powerful form of national welfare security could, as mentioned above, only be established in 1948, i.e. old-age and survivors' insurance. As the quotation from Professor Tschudi shows, even this insurance is not administered by a central authority. Attempts to introduce old-age and survivors' insurance in the 1920s failed, mainly because a second central bureaucratic institution was to be avoided after the creation of the Swiss National Accident Insurance Institute, founded in 1918, which soon came to be criticised as a 'bureaucratic power body' and a 'first class robbery institution'.[13] But a purely federalistic solution was not feasible for economic and organisational reasons. The Second World War proved to be a powerful motor for a state policy in this field. On the one hand, the solidarity experienced in the war and the widespread fear of a post-war recession had dismantled the psychological restraints against a more powerful state welfare policy. On the other hand, the federal government in its full power of authority during the war had created an income compensation plan for persons liable for military service. According to this model a new national insurance plan could technically be realised without establishing a new central institution.

> The basic novelty consisted in financing the plan from contributions by employers and employees, calculated in proportion to the salaries. Special compensation funds, created by the employer associations and the cantons, administered the plan. Switzerland's most important social plan was adopted in 1947 by popular vote with an overwhelming majority: the old-age and survivors' pension plan as a national insurance which covers the total population; employees, self-employed, and also the non-working population.[14]

The consciousness of national threat during the Second World

War thus brought a decisive expansion of the welfare components of the state. This could also be observed in the constitutional change which gave the federal government a series of possibilities to intervene in the freedom of trade and industry. Article 31[bis] placed these measures explicitly under the goal of promoting the people's welfare and of economic protection of the citizen. In comparison with the cited general purpose of Article 2 of the federal constitution, this new constitutional article listed those areas in which state interventions in the constitutional freedom of trade and industry were made possible. These new federal competences opened up the way which the working class had been paving in vain after the failure of the general strike in 1918. The new constitutional regulations were perceived as the 'actual programme of the Swiss welfare state'.[15] Subsequently, not to prevent the recession feared for the post-war years, but in the wake of the economic boom in the 1950s and 1960s, great progress was achieved to expand the welfare state components. In the field of social security, the old-age and survivors' insurance was first supplemented by a disability insurance. After eight revisions the pensions received are almost ten-fold. In 1972 the federal government was entrusted by a constitutional change to provide for an overall old-age security system which is aimed at 'maintaining the previous standard of living to a reasonable extent' and is based on (1) the federal old-age, survivors' and disability insurance, (2) new federal regulations for an occupational pension scheme, and (3) self-provisions.

Parallel to this expansion of welfare components of the state, efforts were made in the 1960s to totally revise the federal constitution. In 1977 they led to a constitutional bill anticipating the welfare state with explicit social rights, granting the corresponding competences to the federal government and limiting the rights of the cantons and individuals.[16] It is characteristic for the political turn that the bill met with vehement criticism when it first appeared and that today hardly anybody believes in its realisation any more.

In the late 1970s the welfare state as a goal became a problem[17] and was violently criticised.[18] Also in popular votes during the last ten years most attempts failed to expand the planning competences and to provide the necessary financial means to the federal government. Instead of discussing the new constitutional move, the parliament will debate this year 'First measures for a redistribution of tasks among the federal government and cantons' which are to pass both the load of responsibilities and the competences from the federal government to the lower levels by changing constitutional and legislative regulations.[19] A similar shift of trend could be observed when the so-called second pillar of old-age insurance, the occupational pension scheme, was established. Constitutionalised in 1972, the *Nationalrat* (House of Representatives) first passed a draft of a bill in 1977 which essentially corresponded to that of the government. The opposition against the centralistic and bureaucratic tendencies contained in it made the *Ständerat* (Senate) work out a simpler solution which took into account the interests of private pension funds. In 1981, the House of Representatives was at one with the Senate, and the bill became a law in 1982.[20]

Compared to other OECD states, with the exception of Japan, Switzerland shows the lowest public expenditure, amounting to less than one-third of the gross national product. The public welfare expenditure and the share of public employees in total number of employed persons give a similar picture compared to other industrial nations.[21] Nevertheless, the thought of a welfare state is politically dead in Switzerland. The authorities try to take into account the political will of the majority of the electorate for 'more freedom and self-responsibility'[22] in a pragmatic way by carefully decentralising welfare measures. Whether these measures determined to gain votes are due to the state of business or whether they point to a structural trend that could be of interest to the development of a welfare state shall be discussed in the final section.

Intermediary Institutions as a 'Work of Art'

In his analysis of democracy in America, Tocqueville pointed out that the democratic thought of equality would necessarily lead to an expansion of the central government. The reasons he assigned for it finally went back to a principle of equality, that is the will of all men to be independent of each other. This basic view of the same isolated independence of all individuals may lead to anarchy as well as to the recognition of a homogeneous central supreme power directing all citizens by itself (*l'idée d'un pouvoir unique et central qui mène tous les citoyens par lui-même*).[23] Tocqueville gives the following reasons why the citizens do not decide to have an anarchy but a central state.

The democratic strivings for simple, homogeneous, common

ideas, constitutions, forms of government, the democratic anti-
pathy to inequalities, privileges and differences lead to an abso-
lutism of the thought of equality in the collectivism, the society and
its representatives, the state. If every citizen is equal to the other, is
judged according to the same principles, the community through
the state gets the right and duty to take every citizen by his hand
and guide him. On the other hand, the direct social consequences
of the thought of equality, individualism and privatism, make it
more difficult for the citizen to participate. He is inclined to hand
over public affairs to the state as the obvious representative of collective interests. This tendency is even increased by the growing
striving for welfare which makes material disorder unbearable for
democratic societies. Material security and, therefore, welfare can
only be guaranteed by the state because the principle of equality
excludes the granting and accepting of personal aid. Envy and
even hate towards those on a higher level, which is embedded in
the thought of equality, favours the central power of the state
before which all citizens are equally powerful or powerless respectively.

The welfare state with its central power seems to be a necessary
consequence of the democratic thought of equality for Tocqueville. That Tocqueville also named most factors which modern
political economy attributes to the expansion of public expenditure
was recently shown by the economist Peter Bernholz[24] in Basel. In
spite of his pessimistic analysis, Tocqueville did not regard this
development as unchangeable. The main purpose of his book was
to fight against the tendencies leading towards natural power of
centralisation. '*Je pense que dans les siècles démocratiques qui vont
s'ouvrir l'indépendance individuelle et les libértés locales seront tou-
jours un produit de l'art*'.[25] As Tocqueville admiringly observes in the
American democracy, this 'work of art' is the result of voluntary associations of citizens. '*Les sentiments et les idées ne se renouvellent, le
coeur ne s'agrandit, et l'esprit humain ne se développe que par l'action
réciproque des hommes les uns sur les autres*'.[26]

As far as I can see, Karl Mannheim was the first sociologist who
analysed the 'natural' tendency of democracy towards the centralisation of power,[27] as it was predicted by Tocqueville. His point
of departure is that, under the conditions of industrial ways of life,
'a society in which the habit of rational thinking is unevenly distributed cannot exist anymore'. The necessary process to the fundamental democratisation, as he called it, which was at the same time

a process of rationalising and making our conditions of life even more scientific, calls for counteracting powers. It increasingly hands over: (1) the insights and decisions which elite groups used to make on a common life orientation, accessible also to further groups, to a 'limited number of politicians, economists, administrative technicians and lawyers for purely objective reasons'. 'Hand in hand with the monopolisation of knowledge goes (2) the concentration of administrative action of a bureaucracy which more and more distinguishes itself from other social groups'. Furthermore (3) the technocratic state elite receives the decisive concentration of military power. General democracy in the nineteenth century was not only guaranteed by industrialisation but by compulsory military service, 'by the plain fact that one man meant one gun and a thousand men a thousand guns', whereas today the power is determined by 'how many men can be killed or terrified by a single bomb'.

Therefore, the continuation of a fundamental democratisation depends on the extent to which future war technology has to rely on the entire population as well as a relatively small professional army. On the other hand, the continuous differentiation of modern society increases the importance of 'small local units and associations'. Without their consent, the complicated instrument of a society as a whole cannot be handled by the political and economical bureaucracy.[28]

What consequences can be drawn from Mannheim's insights for our topic?

(1) Mannheim departs from a centralistic trend of modern democracy towards professionalised, possibly academic leadership. This has developed in an unprecedented explosion of student numbers during the past decades. For good reasons the political and economical elites have argued that the economic prosperity of industrial nations depended on the application of scientific knowledge. Since researchers and technicians are mostly trained at universities, publically guaranteed egalitarianism for entry into universities became the nucleus of a reform of the elite and thus common among progressivistic parties, the *communis opinio* and the social scientific theories in the mass media. Professors and students have tended generally to favour this expansion. Not only did many of them espouse progressivistic political and moral standpoints, which led them to affirm the right of larger proportions of

the young generation to higher education and the material benefits following from it, but also they have a vested interest in the expansion. It would supply more resources for their own research and more appointments for their most promising students. What Tocqueville finds characteristic for the relationship between the citizen and the state in democracies, applies also to professors and students: they often do not agree with the particular form of government of their country, but seldom oppose public regulations and aids from which they profit.

In most countries the expansion of central government has played a major role in the realisation of the welfare state and has thus confirmed the trend of democracy, exemplified before by Tocqueville and Mannheim, towards centralisation of all its tasks related to the promotion, transfer and application of scientific thinking.

In Switzerland, too, this trend could be observed. But the advantages of a welfare state did not make up for the obstacle of a higher percentage of academics trained with the help of the central government. During the boom years a small majority of cantons rejected a bill which was to guarantee the right to education to be anchored in federal competence. But a few years later, a law on the promotion of cantonal universities, which would have embedded federal competence even further, was clearly rejected by the electorate.[29] The percentage of student beginners could never take the 10 per cent hurdle. According to American and German calculations which demand 20-30 per cent of an academic elite for a modern industrial state, Switzerland would be doomed for industrial and economic failure. Fortunately nothing points in this direction yet.

The resistance of the Swiss people against the publicly promoted expansion of academic elites can not only negatively be led back to scepticism towards scientific expertise and bureaucracy of the welfare state. It positively means the equality of social positions, held by a manifold group of elites and relatively open to all, who only distinguish themselves gradually and potentially from the non-elite group through particular performance and their efficiency potential. As far as education is concerned, this is expressed in a strong promotion of vocational training as well as in the improvement of higher technical, commercial, artistic, social and medical schools and other intermediary institutions between elementary schools and university.

These intermediary institutions play a major role for the mixing of social classes, make way for social rise, allow an open educational system and do not isolate their elites in an artificial surrounding from the rest of the population as the catholic priest schools, the French *grandes écoles* or the Anglo-Saxon boarding schools tend to do.

The social identity as it develops in primary and secondary groups by different forms of work and life, value conceptions and behavioural expectations, can rarely be integrated without difficulties into a new framework of action. Social rise generally takes several generations and needs intermediary structures to materialise unless it is gained by fighting and high social costs. When it leads step by step from one social class to the other, the values, norms, attitudes and role patterns only differ slightly, professional and cultural images, personal models, language, habits and behavioural patterns cause minor problems of integration and make it easier to assume social responsibilities.

(2) For Tocqueville intermediary institutions are a 'work of art'. For Mannheim they are the necessary basis of legitimation for democratic societies. In social policy matters they are linked with the principle of the individual's social responsibility, the so-called principle of subsidiarity which consists in asking for social security only in addition to self-help, and which is considered as one of the main obstacles against the tendency of democracies to develop into totalitarian welfare states with bureaucratic leadership. It departs from the primary responsibility of the family and the social surrounding to provide education and develop the personality of an individual. The state may only interfere if self-help proves to be insufficient.

Because this proof is always a question of economic, political and cultural definition, also in societies which are based on this principle, the conversion of scientific experience into public health, economic, social and educational policy has mutilated traditional self-help mechanisms of the individual and his reference groups.

However deeply-rooted the principle of social responsibility is in our societies, is reflected in the emergence of social and economic self-help activities and groups. Only recently scientists began to pay particular attention to this new phenomenon and pointed to the aspects which transcend the purely economic side and let the actor experience these forms of work as 'part of increased inde-

pendence, autonomy, competence, opportunities'.[30] This movement should not be qualified as a trend back to pre-industrial
forms of society and life, but should be seen as the realisation of a
society in which the individual, free from economic pressure, pur-
sues the activities chosen by himself. This is not a levelling of the
elites in a classless society, as Karl Marx postulated it, but is due to
continuous differentiation of all modern societies.[31]

Surveys conducted by our institute on the economic and social
situation of Swiss citizens above the age of 60 show that the elderly
practise and receive social responsibility to a very high extent.
Almost 89 per cent were visited by their children during the month
of interrogation, 83 per cent by grandchildren, 86 per cent by
friends and acquaintances, 62 per cent by other relatives. About
half of them are members of one or more associations. Only 4 per
cent felt lonely or bored; 5 per cent claimed close and 10 per cent
open institutional or private aid. The payment of old-age insurance
is insufficient for 7.5 per cent. Most recipients increase their savings. Average wealth of the elderly citizens amounts to more than
double that of those still working.[32]

Apparently the intermediate structures between the individual
and the state work well as far as old-age aid is concerned. The
same holds true for other fields of social responsibility. In spite of
the development of the welfare state, the net of voluntary associations in Switzerland is very tight. For example, the Swiss
Women's Association of Voluntary Social Work, with its 62
branches and more than 60,000 members, supplements public welfare measures by flexible and often innovative private initiatives.

The recent self-help groups were formed as protest movements
against the centralistic elite structures of a welfare state. They try
to replace or supplement the weakened intermediary structures
between state and individual through spontaneous groupings. It
can be hoped that they will finally strengthen the respective institutions or revive intermediary groupings, local or regional associations, which have developed historically but become stunted in
the welfare state.

(3) Karl Mannheim subjected the future of our democracy to a
probably shocking but, in view of the present world situation, very
realistic condition, i.e. the question of how much war technology
has to rely on the whole population beside a relatively small
professional army. Behind this argument hides a fundamental value
axiom of democracy: It can only survive if all citizens are ready to

invest part or, in case of necessity, the whole of their existence for the common cause. This fundamental value axiom of democracy on which the citizen-soldier system is based also applies to the civil sphere: public affairs are expected fundamentally to be the responsibility of all citizens so that no special class of 'politicians', alien to the people, can emerge. Professional and life experiences are to be used for political activities on different levels of public welfare. Even more important is the network of personal, traditional, cultural and economic ties of the individual citizens who affirm and give vitality to this network in a multifarious form, but at the same time maintain a certain distance from the authority of the state.

The mandates awarded by the people are not only to be subjected to regular confirmation by the electorate, as Schumpeter demands for the democratic elite. They have to be carried out basically as a social responsibility with such a modest reward that there is no incentive for professional execution of such mandates. This ideal can hardly be realised in full, of course. But with its main feature of a citizenship feeling responsible for public welfare, it is the only counterweight to the execution of power by a professional state bureaucracy in a welfare state.

Notes

1. Karl W. Deutsch, *Die Schweiz als ein paradigmatischer Fall politischer Integration*, Bern: Haupt, 1976, p. 41.

2. Programmatische Schriften der Schweizerischen Volkspartei (SVP). Aktionsprogramm '83. Bern, April 1983, p. II, 19. — Zielsetzungen 83/87 der Freisinnig-Demokratischen Partei der Schweiz, verabschiedet am 6.5.1983.

3. Verwaltungsbericht 1983 der Fürsorgedirektion der Stadt Bern. März 1983, p. 4: 'Wenn wir die Nächstenhilfe im Verwandten-, Bekanntenkreis oder sogar im Quartier nicht intensivieren, so können wir den künftigen Bedürfnissen nicht genügen. Der Aufbau sozialer Netze, in denen nicht nur die jüngeren, sondern auch die älteren Menschen einander helfen und im Krankheitsfall oder bei Verlust der eigenen Selbständigkeit beistehen, muss vermehrt von Staates wegen gefördert werden'.

4. Hans Peter Tschudi, 'Der schweizerische Sozialstaat. Realität und Verpflichtung', in *Schweizerische Wirtschaftspolitik zwischen gestern und heute*, Festgabe zum 65. Geburtstag von Hugo Sieber. Hrg. von Egon Tuchtfeldt. Bern: Haupt, 1976, pp. 131-48.

5. See the informative essay on 'Welfare State' by Lord Asa Briggs in Philip P. Wiener (ed.), *Dictionary of the History of Ideas*, vol. IV, pp. 509-15, New York: Scribner's Son, 1973.

6. See Walter Rüegg, *Anstösse, Aufsätze und Vorträge zur dialogischen Lebensform*, Frankfurt: Alfred Metzner, 1973, p. 187.

7. *Die Schweiz. Vom Bau der Alpen bis zur Frage nach det Zukunft. Ein Nachschlagewerk*, Zürich: Ex Libris, 1975, p. 135.

8. Ueli Augsburger, 'Die Leistungen der Wirtschaft zugunsten der Landesverteidigung', *SAMS-Informationen*. *Bulletin des Schweizerischen Arbeitskreises Militär + Sozialwissenschaften*, 2 (1978) no. 2, p. 23.

9. This is illustrated by a famous nineteenth century story of an old, half-blind member of the parliament who, stumbling against colleagues, used to offer automatically the same excuse: 'Pardon, mon colonel'.

10. Erich Gruner, Martin Daetwyler and Oscar Zosso, 'Aufstellung und Auswahl, der Kandidaten der Nationalratswahlen in der Schweiz, Dissertation Universität Bern, 1975, p. 406. See Hanspeter Kriesi, *Entscheidungsstrukturen und Entscheidungsprozesse in der Schweizer Politik*, Frankfurt: Campus, 1980, p. 533.

11. Hans Peter Tschudi, *Social Security*. *Modern Switzerland*, The Society for the Promotion of Science and Scholarship, 1978, 209f.

12. Jürg H. Sommer, *Das Ringen um die soziale Sicherheit in der Schweiz*, Diessenhofen: Rüegger, 1978, p. 97.

13. Jurg H. Sommer, ibid., p. 130.

14. Hans Peter Tschudi, *Social Security*. *Modern Switzerland*, p. 201f.

15. *Die Schweiz*, pp. 112, 302.

16. Expertenkommission für die Vorbereitung einer Totalrevision der Bundesverfassung, *Verfassungsentwurf und Bericht*, Bern: Eidg. Drucksachen- und Materialzentrale, 1977, 2 vols.

17. Peter Bernholz, 'Freiheit, Staat und Wirtschaft. Auf der Suche nach einer neuen Ordnung', *Zeitschrift für die gesamte Staatswissenschaft*, 133 (1977), pp. 575-90. *Wohlfahrtsstaat, Anspruch und Wirklichkeit*, Zum 60, Geburtstag von Bundesrat Dr. Hans Hürlimann. Hrg. von H.P. Fagagnini und Hans Witz. Olten: Walter, 1978.

18. Guy Kirsch, 'Der Wohlfahrtsstaat', *Die Orientierung*, no. 75, Bern: Schweiz, Volksbank, 1980.

19. Botschaft über erste Massnahmen zur Neuordnung der Aufgaben zwischen Bund und Kantonen vom 28 September 1981.

20. Paul Gygi, 'Das Bundesgesetz über die berufliche Vorsorge', *Wirtschaftspolitische Mitteilungen*, 39 (1983), no. 4, Zürich: Wirtschaftsförderung.

21. Bruno Frey, 'Wie gross ist der öffentliche Sektor?', *Neue Zürcher Zeitung* (*NZZ*) (1981), no. 25, p. 37. Peter Bernholz, 'Expanding Welfare State, Democracy and Free Market Economy: Are they Compatible?', *Zeitschrift für die gesamte Staatswissenschaft*, 138 (1982), p. 586f; 'Der Wohlfahrtsstaat auf dem falschen Weg? Steigende Staatsausgaben als negativer Beschäftigungsfaktor', *NZZ* (1982), no. 277, p. 17.

22. Slogan of the biggest Swiss political party, the Freisinnig-Demokratische Partei. See Guy Firsch, 'Die Flucht aus der Eigenverantwortung. Warum glauben wir noch an den Wohlfahrtsstaat?', *NZZ*, (1982), no. 233, p. 17.

23. Alexis de Tocqueville, *De la démocratie en Amérique*, vol. II, Quatrième partie, Chapitre II: Que les idées des peuples démocratiques en matière de gouvernement sont naturellement favorables à la concentration des pouvoirs. Oeuvres complètes. Paris: Gallimard, Tome I, vol. 2, 1951, p. 297ff.

24. Peter Bernholz, *Zeitschrift für die gesamte Staatswissenschaft*, p. 589ff.

25. Tocqueville, *De la démocratie en Amérique*, vol. II., 2me p., ch. III: Que les sentiments des peuples démocratiques sont d'accord avec leurs idées pour les porter à concentrer le pouvoir, p. 203.

26. Tocqueville, ibid., vol. II, 2me p., ch. V, p. 113ff: De l'usage que les Américains font de l'association dans la vie civile.

27. Karl Mannheim, *Mensch und Gesellschaft im Zeitalter des Umbaus*, Darmstadt: Gentner, 1958 (englisch, 1940), p. 54ff.

28. Karl Mannheim, ibid., p. 57.

29. See Walter Rüegg, 'Switzerland: The Re-affirmation of Autonomy', in

Hans Daalder/Edward Shils (eds.), *Universities, Politicians and Bureaucrats. Europe and the United States,* Cambridge University Press, 1982, pp. 393-435.

30. Walter Rüegg, 'Eliten in der Demokratie. Reform und Repräsentation', in *Elite, Zukunftsorientierung in der Demokratie. Veröffentlichungen der Walter-Raymond-Stiftung Band 20,* Köln-Bachem, 1982, pp. 9-28; quotation p. 21.

31. For self-help groups see: Ernst Wieltschnig *et al.,* 'Die Rolle von Selbsthilfegruppen von Chronischkranken im Gesundheitswesen der deutschen Schweiz', Arbeitsberichte aus dem Institut für Soziologie der Universität Bern, no. 6, Bern, 1983.

32. Willy Schweizer, *Die wirtschaftliche Lage der Schweiz,* Bern: Haupt, 1980. Ernst Wieltschnig, *Altern in der Schweiz. Ein theoretisch-empirisches Konzept,* Bern: Haupt, 1982. Viggo G. Blücher, *Altern in der Schweiz. Arten und Grade der Unabhängigkeit,* in print, p. 56.

14 THE EXPERIENCE OF THE WELFARE STATE IN JAPAN AND ITS PROBLEMS

Rei Shiratori

I

After recovering from the damages which Japan suffered during the Second World War, the conservative government, which had constantly ruled Japan except for a period of eight months under a centre-left coalition government in 1947-8 quickly adopted the so-called 'rapid GNP growth policy' as one of its fundamental policies. For example, Prime Minister Ikeda proudly announced the 'double income policy' in January 1961. This rapid growth of GNP policy was successful as you can see in Tables 14.1, 14.2 and 14.3, partly because of the Korean War and the eruption of the Vietnam War. The problems occurred, however, because the rapid growth of GNP policy since 1960 was too successful and the growth rate was too high. First, large scale mobilisation of population from rural areas to big cities facing the Pacific Ocean, as shown in Table 14.4, simultaneously caused the problem of over-density of population in Pacific-facing megalopolis areas as well as over-scarcity of population in the northern (Tohoku) and south western (Shikoku island) parts in Japan. This over-density of population then caused such urban problems as the increase in juvenile delinquencies, traffic noise and accidents, poor living conditions, etc. At the same time, the over-scarcity of population in rural areas destroyed the traditional stable agricultural communities and autonomous agricultural economy of the villages leaving only old people, housewives and children in the villages as labour forces. The destruction of big families in rural areas and atomisation of families in big cities that occurred during this period of rapid growth of the GNP substantially changed Japanese social structures.

Secondly, this too rapid industrialisation in Pacific-facing cities caused pollution problems of all kinds. Because administrative response to the new social environments could not catch up with the changing of social situations, pollution victims in those rapidly

Table 14.1: Relative Positions of Gross National Products of Selected Countries (1951-81)

	Japan		USA		Germany, FR		France		UK	
	Amount (US$ billion)	Index (U.S.A. = 100)	Amount (US$ billion)	Index (U.S.A. = 100)	Amount (US$ billion)	Index (U.S.A. = 100)	Amount (US$ billion)	Index (U.S.A. = 100)	Amount (US$ billion)	Index (U.S.A. = 100)
1951	14.2	4.3	328.4	100.0	28.5	8.7	35.1	10.7	41.4	12.6
1955	22.7	5.7	398.0	100.0	43.0	10.8	49.2	12.4	53.9	13.5
1960	39.1	7.8	503.8	100.0	70.7	14.0	60.0	11.9	71.9	14.3
1965	88.8	12.9	688.1	100.0	115.1	16.7	99.2	14.4	100.2	14.6
1968	146.4	16.8	873.4	100.0	133.8	15.3	127.6	14.6	105.2	12.0
1970	203.1	20.5	992.7	100.0	185.5	18.7	145.5	14.7	124.0	12.5
1975	498.2	32.2	1,549.2	100.0	420.6	27.1	339.7	21.9	234.8	15.2
1978	963.3	44.7	2,156.1	100.0	642.6	29.8	476.5	22.1	317.6	14.7
1979	998.9	41.4	2,413.9	100.0	762.8	31.6	576.1	23.9	409.9	17.0
1980	1,035.8	39.4	2,626.1	100.0	820.8	31.3	656.0	25.0	523.6	19.9
1981	1,127.0	38.5	2,925.5	100.0	686.7	23.5	—	—	—	—

Note: Current US dollar figures are calculated according to the annual average exchange rates of the IMF, *International Financial Statistics* (refer to table 6-7). USA = 100 for all years.

Source: Bank of Japan, *Comparative International Statistics*, 1966, 1977, 1982.

Table 14.2: GNP and GNP per Capita (1980) and Growth Rate of GNP (1971-80)

	GNP (nominal)[a]		Annual growth rate (real)	
	US$ billion	Per capita (US$)	1971-5 %	1976-80 %
USA	2,626.1	11,535	2.6	3.7
Japan	1,035.8	8,870	4.7	5.0
Germany, FR	820.8	13,333	2.1	3.6
France	656.0	12,214	4.0	3.3
UK	523.6	9,359	2.0	1.4
Italy	396.5	6,951	4.1	3.8
Canada	253.3	10,582	5.0	3.0
Brazil	237.4	1,929	10.8	6.5[c]
Netherlands	167.6	11,855	3.2	2.5
Australia	148.2	10,135	3.4	2.5
India	133.6[b]	205[a]	2.9	2.9[c]
Sweden	122.6	14,771	2.7	1.2

	GNP (nominal)[a]		Annual growth rate (real)	
	US$ billion	Per capita (US$)	1971-5 %	1976-80 %
Mexico	121.3[b]	1,749[b]	5.6	5.1
Belgium	116.5	11,813	3.5	2.9
Saudi Arabia	116.2	12,965	12.8	9.5[c]
Switzerland	101.5	15,929	0.8	1.6
South Africa	80.0	2,730	4.1	3.4
Indonesia	69.8	460	8.0	7.5
Denmark	66.4	12,964	2.0	2.6
Korea, Republic of	59.2	1,553	9.5	7.6
Philippines	35.5	733	6.0	6.3
Thailand	32.9	698	6.3	7.7
Malaysia	23.5	1,749	10.4	8.6
New Zealand	23.3	7,510	4.0	0.7

a. U.S. dollar figures are calculated according to the annual exchange rates of the IMF, *International Financial Statistics* (refer to table 6.5).

b. 1979.

c. 1976-1979.

Source: Bank of Japan, *Comparative International Statistics*, 1982.

Table 14.3: Nominal GDP and Real Growth Rate by Country (1969-81)[a]

	Japan			USA			Germany, F.R.		
	Nominal GDP (¥ billion)	Nominal Growth Rate (%)	Real Growth Rate (%)	Nominal GDP (US$ billion)	Nominal Growth Rate (%)	Real Growth Rate (%)	Nominal GDP (DM, billion)	Nominal Growth Rate (%)	Real Growth Rate (%)
1969	62.181	17.7	12.3	937.1	8.1	2.8	597.0	11.6	7.8
1970	73.285	17.9	9.8	985.5	5.2	-0.2	678.8	13.7	6.0
1971	80.632	10.0	4.6	1,068.5	8.4	3.3	754.9	11.2	3.2
1972	92.306	14.5	8.8	1,175.0	10.0	5.6	826.0	9.4	3.7
1973	112.420	21.8	8.8	1,310.4	11.5	5.5	918.6	11.2	4.9
1974	134.169	19.3	-1.0	1,414.4	7.9	-0.7	987.1	7.5	0.6
1975	148.031	10.3	2.3	1,531.9	8.3	-0.9	1,034.0	4.8	-1.9
1976	165.851	12.0	5.3	1,697.5	10.8	5.3	1,122.8	8.6	5.2
1977	184.460	11.2	5.3	1,894.6	11.6	5.4	1,200.5	6.9	3.0
1978	202.638	9.9	5.0	2,126.2	12.2	4.6	1,286.4	7.2	3.2
1979	218.616	7.9	5.1	2,370.1	11.5	2.8	1,393.9	8.4	4.5
1980	234.949	7.5	4.4	2,576.5	8.7	-0.2	1,488.9	6.8	1.9
1981	248.534[b]	5.8[b]	2.9[b]	2,871.1	11.4	2.0	1,552.9	4.3	-0.0

Table 14.3: continued

	France			UK			Italy		
	Nominal GDP (F. billion)	Nominal Growth Rate (%)	Real Growth Rate (%)	Nominal GDP (£ million)	Nominal Growth Rate (%)	Real Growth Rate (%)	Nominal GDP (Lira billion)	Nominal Growth Rate (%)	Real Growth Rate (%)
1969	700.7	14.0	7.0	46,607	7.1	1.4	51,691	10.1	5.7
1970	782.6	11.7	5.7	51,107	9.7	2.2	57,937	12.1	5.0
1971	872.4	11.5	5.4	57,339	12.2	2.7	68,510	8.9	1.6
1972	981.1	12.5	5.9	63,461	10.7	2.3	75,124	9.7	3.2
1973	1,114.2	13.6	5.4	73,025	15.1	7.5	89,746	19.5	7.0
1974	1,278.3	14.7	3.2	83,114	13.8	−1.0	110,719	23.4	4.1
1975	1,452.3	13.6	0.2	104,907	26.2	−0.5	125,378	13.2	−3.6
1976	1,678.0	15.5	5.2	124,656	18.8	3.6	156,657	24.9	5.9
1977	1,884.6	12.3	3.1	143,911	15.4	1.3	190,083	21.3	1.9
1978	2,141.1	13.6	3.8	164,901	14.6	3.3	222,254	16.9	2.7
1979	2,439.6	13.9	3.3	192,329	16.6	1.4	270,198	21.6	4.9
1980	2,758.7	13.1	1.1	225,560	17.3	−1.4	339,068	25.5	3.9
1981	3,094.4	12.2	0.2	—	—	—	398,125	17.4	−0.2

a. Based on individual country data.
b. Based on GNP.

Source: Bank of Japan, *Comparative International Statistics*, 1982.

industrialised cities increased sharply during the 1960s. The administrative staffs of both central and local governments, on the contrary, were more keen to pursue the rapid growth of GNP by investing in production related capital projects such as building factory sites and industrial roads, and neglected investment in citizen's life related social capital projects such as building parks and schools.

In a sense those bureaucrats held the very optimistic view that 'economic development *automatically* induces improvement in the quality of life and fulfillment of social welfare systems'. Former Prime Minister Tanaka clearly expressed this opinion, stressing the importance of industrialisation and the expansion of production. He said in 1972 in his book *Reconstruction of Japan Archipelago* that 'we should first increase our national incomes, in the second stage we should supplement the lack of our social investments, and in the third stage we should proceed in the enlargement of social welfare'.

In this phrase, we can see his confidence in the process of development; that 'there will be no social welfare without economic growth beforehand'. We can also find his optimistic view that economic development (i.e. growth of GNP per capita) will automatically produce a welfare society without any special efforts in government policies being made.

The tragedy was, however, that there was no causal relation between economic growth and the fulfillment of the social welfare system in the real world. What the real world told us, contrary to Prime Minister Tanaka's optimistic view, was that economic development did not necessarily lead the nation to a welfare state.

Figure 14.3 is the result of the quantitative analysis of cross-national data carried out at the end of 1972, by myself, in order to examine the relationship between GNP per capita and the quality of a citizen's life. The vertical scale shows the amount of GNP per capita in 1970, while the horizontal scale indicates the quality of a citizen's life (life quality indicator).

In order to analyse the relationship between GNP per capita and the quality of life, I first gathered 68 indicators for 42 countries. Secondly, in order to calculate the quality of a citizen's life, I drew the conceptual framework of 'citizen', as shown in Figure 14.2. The conceptual model of a citizen could be traced back in history to the image of the members of autonomous renaissance Italian cities in the fifteenth century. The conceptual model of a citizen could be found in the area where the following four factors overlap: (1) autonomy, (2) freedom, (3) affluence and (4) fraternity. According to this conceptual framework, I classified the 68 indicators into four categories and, by using principle component analysis, I tried to find the common factor, which would indicate the overall concept of citizenship or a civilised life and scaled this quality of citizen's life by country on a horizontal axis. The result is shown in Figure 14.3. The interesting fact is that Japan was situated at a juncture in 1970 where both production-orientated development and welfare-orientated development of society started their different directions.

Figure 14.1: Increase and Decrease of Population by Areas

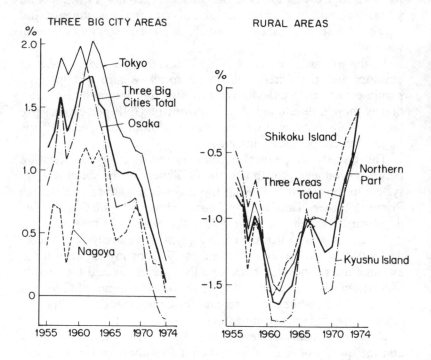

Figure 14.2: The Concept of Citizen

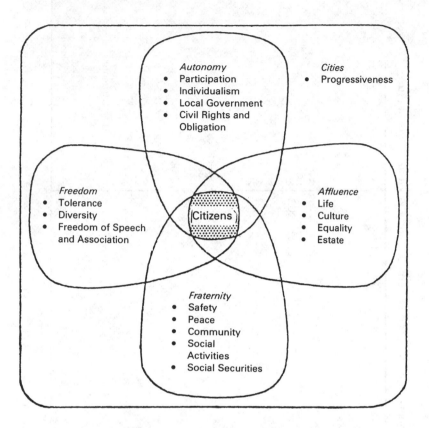

II

Fortunately, in spite of the fact that the then Prime Minister Tanaka stressed the importance of the expansion of GNP and his optimistic view of a natural transition from rapid growth of GNP era into a welfare state era in 1972, *politically* Japan stepped on to the path toward a welfare state in 1972.

We might point out two things that affected the change of policy. First, the influence of news of damage by the destruction of a pipe line in Santa Barbara in 1970 and the discovery of air pollution caused by automobile's exhaust gases in Tokyo in June 1970 upon the people's attitude caused a sudden eruption of citizen's

Figure 14.3: Two Types of Developments: the Production-orientated and the Welfare-orientated

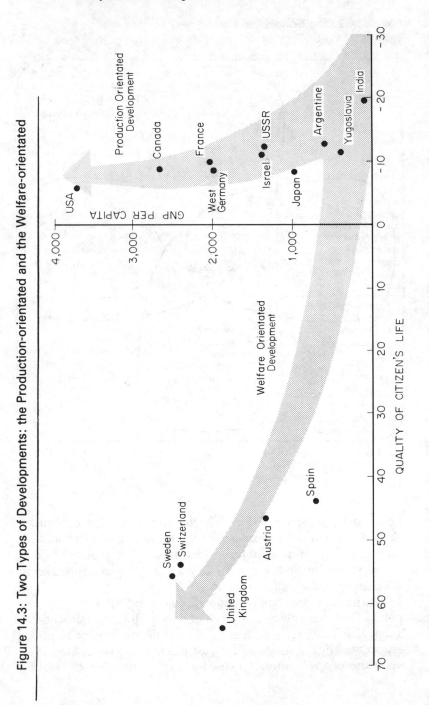

movements against pollution. Secondly, the government could not ignore any longer the increase of the old-age population as a political issue as can be seen in Figure 14.4.

Table 14.4: Average Lifetime by Sex

| | Year[a] | Life expectancy at birth | |
		Male	Female
Japan	1921-5	42.06	43.20
	1965	67.74	72.92
	1981	73.79	79.13
Iceland	1979-80	73.7	79.7
Norway	1979-80	72.25	79.00
Sweden	1980	72.76	78.81
Netherlands	1979	72.4	78.9
USA[b]	1980	70.5	78.1
Switzerland	1968-73	70.29	76.22
France	1977	69.73	77.85
Canada	1975-7	70.19	77.48
UK[c]	1976-8	70.0	76.2
Germany, FR	1978-80	69.60	76.36

a. Latest available year.
b. White only.
c. Only England and Wales.

Source: Ministry of Health and Welfare, Japan. UN, *Demographic Yearbook*, 1979.

Figure 14.4: Persons 65 Years Old and Over: Percentage of Total Population (1850-2000)

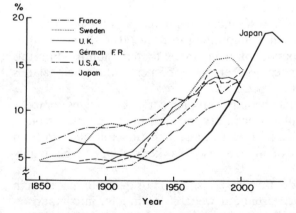

a. For Japan, figures represent the estimates based on the National Census and Foundation Institute on Population Problems.

Source: UN *Population by Sex and Age for Regions and Countries 1850-2000, as Assessed in 1973: Medium Variant*, February 1976.

The year 1972 was generally called 'the first year of the welfare era' in Japan. Free medicare for those over 70 started in January 1973. The national budget for public assistance toward old-age people was increased 53.7 per cent in 1972 fiscal year. The budget for old-age pension was increased 43.5 per cent in the same year. Although the social security budget increased only 13.9 per cent in 1972 (the total budget increased 24.7 per cent), it increased 33.4 per cent in 1973 (total budget, 23.8 per cent).

At present (in 1983), if we consider an average employee in the business world, the social insurance programme is as follows. First, health insurance programmes provide medical treatment, pay medical expenses and provide allowances in the case of illness and injuries. In most cases, health insurance will cover expenses in full for the insured worker, and 30 per cent of the expenses must be paid by the worker in case of illness or injury of dependent family members. The worker's share of the insurance premium amounts to 4.25 per cent of his salary, and his company also pays an equivalent 4.25 per cent.

Employee's pension insurance is designed to provide security for the aged by paying them annuities over a long period of time. If a person has paid premiums for more than 20 years, he is entitled to receive an annuity after reaching the age of 60. In the case of the average worker, the amount will be 145,000 yen ($700) per month. Both worker and company must pay each as premium 5.3 per cent of salary.

The unemployment insurance programme pays the unemployed worker monthly benefits amounting to from 60 to 80 per cent of his salary for a period of from three to ten months. For this employment insurance, workers pay 0.55 per cent of their salaries and the company 0.85 per cent.

Workman's accident compensation insurance provides compensation for death, illness or injury incurred in the course of one's work. In case of death, it pays annual benefits equivalent to from 35 to 67 per cent of the deceased worker's salary to his family members.

When we consider this present situation of the welfare system in Japan, although we started our welfare system later in comparison with industrialised Western countries, we might say that we have already achieved a comparable level of welfare provision.

There are, however, two main problems. First, one year after the first year of the welfare era, i.e. in 1973, Japan ended her rapid

Table 14.5: Japan's General Account Budget (FY 1982)[a]

	Amount (¥ billion)	Change in Amount over Previous year %	Change in Amount over 1975[b]
Aid for Local Government	9,636.5	9.9	2.2
Social Welfare	9,084.9	2.8	2.3
Cost for Public Bond			
Debt Service	7,829.9	17.7	7.5
Public Works	6,655.4	0.0	2.3
Education and R&D	4,863.7	2.6	1.9
Defence	2,586.1	7.8	1.9
Pensions	1,891.8	4.9	2.5
Food Management	990.3	−0.5	1.1
Energy Measures	563.2	13.2	6.4
Aid for LDC's	471.2	10.8	2.4
Small Enterprise Assistance	249.8	−0.0	2.0
Other Items	4,508.0	2.2	1.7
Reserves	350.0	0.0	1.2
General Account, total	49,680.8	6.2	2.3

a. Initial budget only.
b. 1975 — 1.0

Source: Ministry of Finance, Japan.

Figure 14.5: Social Welfare Budget by Countries (1978-80)

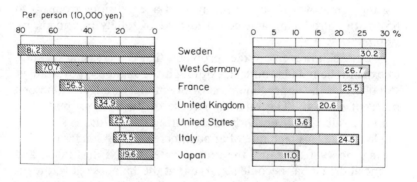

growth of GNP because of the rise in oil prices. Secondly, Japan's old-age population is growing more quickly than that of any other country in the world. Life expectancy at birth is the longest in the world, as shown in Table 14.4, and the birth rate is almost the lowest in the world. The proportion of population aged 65 and over will reach 19 per cent in 2010, as shown in Figure 14.4.

Consequently, with reference to Table 14.6, it is clear that the nominal amount of government pension budget will reach 48.9 times more in comparison with the amount in 1977. Although the average premium of the national pension system was 2,300 yen in 1977, we have to increase the premium up to 8,650 yen (3.9 times) in 2010. If we consider the inflation rate, the premium will reach 78,200 yen (36 times more) in 2010.

The end of the rapid growth of GNP era in 1973 increased the government's budgetary deficit, as shown in Table 14.10. The cost for public bond debt service will reach 10 trillion yen in fiscal year 1984 which is almost equivalent to the social welfare budget and twice as much as educational expenditures.

III

Perhaps, we can solve these financial problems by retaining slow but steady growth of GNP even in the future, as well as by changing the age at which people receive old-age pensions from 60 to 65, or by introducing a selective instead of totally free medicare system.

We have, however, another problem, that is increasing pressure to expand the military budget. Although the Japanese government still observes the upper limitation of the military budget within one per cent of GNP. The rate of increase of the military budget in nominal value has been fairly great during the 1970s, as shown in Table 14.17. This high rate of annual increase is no longer possible during the 1980s because the growth rate of GNP has fallen and financial deficit has become so large that the Japanese government can not continue to issue national bonds in the future. In 1982, for the first time since the end of the Second World War, growth rate of the military budget became higher than that of social security expenditure. Since the so-called 'grant economy' is limited to around 20 per cent of GNP, if we increase the military budget, we

Table 14.6: Prospect of Financial Burden of Government Pension Systems

	No. of persons in the system (A)	No. of old-age pension receivers (B)	A/B(%)	(B/A)	Amount of Pensions Value at 1977 Money value (billion yen)	Nominal value (trillion yen)	Total amount/GNP (%)
1977	5,599	553	9.9	(10.1 persons)	4,536	4.5	3.1
1980	5,758	720	12.5	(8.0)	5,562	8	3.7
1990	6,172	1,137	18.4	(5.4)	9,982	30	6.2
2000	6,388	1,513	23.7	(4.2)	16,557	89	9.7
2010	6,381	1,793	28.1	(3.6)	23,307	220	13.2
(Times)	1.1	3.2	2.8		5.1	48.9	4.3

Table 14.7: Unemployed — Number and Percentage (1978-82)[a]

			Japan	USA	EC	Germany, FR	France	UK
	1978		1,240	6,202	5,973	993	1,167	1,475
	1979		1,170	6,137	6,060	876	1,350	1,391
Number	1980		1,140	7,637	6,805	889	1,451	1,795
(1,000)	1981		1,260	8,273	9,009[b]	1,272	1,773	2,734
	1982	Jan.	1,310	9,298	10,859[b]	1,950	2,034	3,071
		June	1,370	10,790[c]	10,368[b]	1,650	1,867	3,061
	1978		2.2	6.1	5.4	3.9	5.2	5.7
	1979		2.1	5.8	5.4	3.4	6.0	5.3
	1980		2.0	7.1	6.0	3.4	6.4	6.9
(%)	1981		2.2	7.6				
					7.9[d]	4.9	7.8	10.5
	1982	Jan.	2.23[c]					
				8.5[d]				
					9.4[b]	7.5	9.0	11.8
		June	2.48[d]	9.8[c, d]	9.1[b]	6.2	8.2	11.9

a. See footnote (c) under 9.9.
b. Ten countries
c. July 1982.
d. Seasonally adjusted.

Source: Ministry of Labour, Japan. *Monthly Labour Statistics and Research Bulletin*, May 1982; EC, *Employment and Unemployment Statistical Bulletin.*

Table 14.8: Unemployed by Age Group (1980)[c] (Male only, unemployed total = 100)

Age group	Japan[a] %	USA %	EC[b] %
—24	21.6	46.4	36.7
25-44	37.8	37.7	—
45-	40.5	15.9	—
Total	100.0	100.0	100.0

a. March 1980.
b. October 1980. Based on *Employment and Unemployment Statistical Bulletin.*
c. The definition of unemployed persons and the method of surveying unemployment differ by country, making exact international comparisons difficult. For example, only US figures include persons laid off among unemployed. New graduates waiting to be employed and others working for the first time are included among unemployed in the US but not in Japan. In addition, persons working for compensation for one hour or more during the survey period and those engaged in individual proprietorships and farms, even those not receiving compensation, for one hour or more are not included among the unemployed in Japan.

Source: Japan Productivity Center, *Labor Statistics*, 1982.

Table 14.9: Wage Differentials According to Age (1980)

| Age Groups | Manufacturing Industry Production Labourer[a] | | Administrative Clerical |
	Japan	Germany,[b] FR	Japan
-17	61.5	58.8	66.2
18-20	82.5[c]	88.1	79.1[c]
21-24	100.0[d]	100.0	100.0[d]
25-29	122.9	105.5	127.0
30-34	143.1	108.0	158.4
35-39	158.5	108.2	185.9
40-44	163.0	106.9	203.4
45-49	159.8	105.4	216.0
50-54	157.2	103.0	221.0
55-59	133.8	99.8	193.2
60-	99.9	95.9	145.1
Total	139.7	103.5	171.6

a. Male only.
b. 1972.
c. 18-19 years
d. 20-24 years

Source: Japan Productivity Center, *Labor Statistics*, 1982.

Table 14.10: GNP Estimates and Budget Surpluses/Deficits in Japan (FY 1972-82)

| | Annual Growth Rate of GNP[a] | | Budget Surplus/Deficit[b] | |
	Estimated %	Actual %	Amount (¥ billion)	Budget Ratio[c] %
1972	12.9	16.6	639.6	7-0
1973	16.4	21.0	778.9	6.2
1974	12.9	18.4	−338.1	−2.2
1975	15.9	10.0	291.7	2.2
1976	13.0	12.2	138.8	0.9
1977	13.7	10.9	198.9	1.2
1978	12.0	9.5	770.5	3.6
1979	9.5	7.4	333.5	1.4
1980	9.4	7.7	−276.3	−1.0
1981	9.1	5.2	−2,881.8	−9.1
1982	8.4	?	−5,500.0[d]	−15.0[d]

a. Nominal.
b. Of General Account.
c. Of supplementary budget revenues.
d. Estimated by Japanese Government for initial budget in range of 5-6,000.

Source: Ministry of Finance, Japan, *Nihon Keizai Shinbun*.

have to cut either social welfare expenditures or educational expenditures.

My personal view is that Japan can contribute more to world security and peace by increasing official economic development assistance than by increasing the military budget (see Table 14.18).

IV

In January 1979 the late Prime Minister Ohira made a speech in the Japanese parliament proposing a 'Welfare society, Japanese style'. He explained his idea by saying: 'I would like to build up a Welfare Society in the following way while retaining a traditional Japanese spirit of self-respect and self-reliance, human relations which are based upon the spirit of tolerance and the traditional social system of mutual assistance. I should like to add the public welfare system to a fair degree to them'.

When people talk of the welfare society, Japanese style, it always contains three elements: (1) public assistance programmes and public services, (2) self-reliance carried out by families, and (3) welfare facilities and services carried out by the local community and private organisations such as business enterprises.

Table 14.11: Earnings and Tax Ratios in Three Countries (1981)[a]

Annual Earnings[b]	Marital Status[c]	Japan %	Tax ratios USA (New York) %	UK %
¥3,000,000	S	9.5	18.5	22.9
(US$ 13,825)	M	7.4	13.4	18.9
(£5,814)	2C	3.9	10.0	18.9
¥5,000,000	S	14.5	27.0	25.7
(US$23,041)	M	12.9	20.7	23.4
(£9,690)	2C	9.8	17.9	23.4
¥7,000,000	S	18.9	33.4	27.7
(US$32,258)	M	17.5	26.5	25.4
(£13,566)	2C	14.7	24.0	25.4
¥10,000,000	S	24.8	39.4	32.9
(US$46,083)	M	23.5	33.6	30.9
(£19,380)	2C	21.0	31.5	30.9

a. Tax includes income and local tax.
b. US$1.00 — ¥217. £1.00 — ¥516.
c. S — single, M — married, and 2C — married with two children.
Source: Ministry of Finance, Japan.

Table 14.12: Annual Earnings and the Tax/Benefit Position of a Typical Worker in Major Countries (1980)c (in US$)

	Annual Gross Earnings^b (A)	Total (B=C+D+E)	Payments to government			Cash Transfers from the government (F)	Disposable income (G=A−B+F)	Disposable income Ratio (G/A) %	Rate of income tax paid [(C+D)/A] %	Rate of social security paid (E/A) %
			Income tax (C)	Additional income tax (D)	Social security (E)					
Switzerland	22,210	4,105	196	1,582	2,327	1,003	19,108	86.03	8.01	10.48
Germany, FR	18,489	4,756	1,851	—	2,905	990	14,723	79.63	10.01	15.71
Netherlands	18,057	5,956	2,288	—	3,668	1,374	13,475	74.63	12.67	20.31
Japan^c	16,960	1,735	650	393	692	—	15,225	89.77	6.15	4.08
Belgium	16,022	3,478	1,670	100	1,708	1,944	14,488	90.42	11.05	10.66
Australia	15,689	2,636	2,636	—	—	505	13,558	86.42	16.80	—
Canada	15,210	2,105	1,039	710	356	447	13,552	89.10	11.50	2.34
USA	14,949	2,782	1,233	633	916	—	12,167	81.39	12.48	6.13
UK	14,866	3,966	2,963	—	1,003	1,003	11,933	80.27	19.93	6.74
France	12,106	1,549	—	—	1,549	1,062	11,619	95.98	—	12.80
Italy	10,284	1,859	1,057	—	802	818	9,243	89.88	10.28	7.80

a. Male, manufacturing sector worker with a two-child family where the wife is not working.
b. US dollar figures are calculated according to the annual average exchange rates of the IMF. *International Finance Statistics.*
c. US$1.00 = ¥226.75.

Source: OECD. *The 1980 Tax/Benefit Position of a Typical Worker in OECD Member Countries.*

Table 14.13: Marriage and Divorce Rates[a]

	Marriages[b]	Divorces[c]		Marriages[b]	Divorces[c]
USA	10.6	5.3[e]	France	5.8	1.39
UK	7.4[d]	2.93	Germany, FR	5.8	0.53
Japan	6.6	1.32[e]	Italy	5.7[d]	0.18

a. Annual rate per 1,000 population.
b. 1981
c. 1978
d. 1980
e. 1979

Source: UN, *Monthly Bulletin of Statistics, Demographic Yearbook.* 1979, Ministry of Health and Welfare, Japan.

Table 14.14: Crime and Arrest Rate (1980)[a]

Crime rate per 100,000 inhabitants:

	Homicide	Forcible rape	Robbery	Property crime
USA	10.2	36.4	243.5	5,319.1
Germany, FR	4.4	11.2	39.3	3,960.0
France	4.2	3.5	65.8	2,942.5
UK[b]	2.6	9.3	30.5	4,157.4
Japan	1.4	2.2	1.9	995.8

Total arrests per 100 offenses:

USA	72.3	48.8	23.8	15.5
Germany, FR	95.6	72.3	53.0	28.9
France	79.4	76.6	26.4	17.4
UK[b]	88.1	87.0	28.8	35.4
Japan	97.2	89.0	75.5	55.0

a. Due to differences in crime definitions stated by each country, the comparisons between countries may not be perfect.
b. Only England and Wales.

Source: National Police Agency, Japan.

Table 14.15: Level of Higher Education[a]

| | | Percentage of relevant age group[b] | | |
		Total	Male	Female
USA	1975	45.2	46.3	44.2
Japan	1980	37.9	42.4	33.3
France	1979	25.7	21.3	30.3
Germany, FR	1978	23.2	25.2	21.2
UK	1977	22.1	25.3	18.9
(ref.) Rate of junior high school graduates continuing on to senior high school (%)				
Japan	1981	94.3	93.2	95.4

a. Higher school education means: USA — figures of new entrants at university level: France, Germany, FR — figures of those qualified for higher school education (university level): Japan — total figures of new entrants at university level, junior college level, national training institute for nursing teachers and senior level of technical colleges.

b. Per cent of equivalent age population.

Source: Ministry of Education, Japan, *Statistical Abstract of Education, Science & Culture*, 1981, *Asahi Shinbun*.

Table 14.16: Defence Expenditure and Numbers in Armed Forces in Twelve Leading Countries (1981)[a]

	Defence expenditure (P) (US$ million)	Defence expenditure per capita (P) (US$)	Ratio of defence expenditure to government spending (%)	Defence expenditure to GNP ratio (%)	Numbers in armed forces (1,000)
USSR	185,000[b]	—	—	12-14[b]	3,673.0
USA	171,023	759	23.7	5.5[b]	2,049.1
China	56,941[b]	56[b]	—	—	4,750.0
UK	28,660	512	12.3	5.1[b]	343.6
Saudi Arabia	27,695	2,664	31.0	—	51.7
France	26,008	483	20.5	3.9[b]	504.6
Germany, FR	25,000	405	22.6	3.2[b]	495.0
Japan	11,497	98	5.1[c]	0.9[b]	243.0
Italy	8,887	155	5.1	2.4[b]	366.0
Israel	7,340	1,835	30.6	23.2[b]	172.0
German DR	6,960	415	8.5	6.1[b]	167.0
India	5,119	7	16.9	3.8[b]	1,104.0

a. These data were|originally prepared to show long-term trends by country. Because of differences in method of preparation, precise international comparisons are difficult.

b. 1980.

c. Based on Ministry of Finance, Japan.

Source: The International Institute for Strategic Studies, *The Military Balance 1981-2*

Figure 14.6: Class Perceptions of Japanese Households (1981)

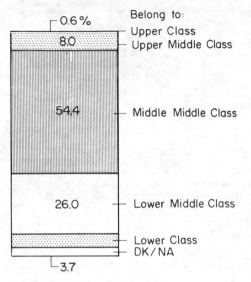

N = 10,000 adults.

Source: Prime Minister's Office, Japan.

Table 14.17: Trends in Level and Share of Japan's Defense
Expenditure (FY 1955-82)

	Defence Expenditure (¥billion)	Change in amount over previous year (%)	Ratio to GNP[a] (%)	Ratio to General Account (%)
1955	134.9	−3.3	1.78	13.61
1960	156.9	0.6	1.23	9.99
1965	301.4	9.6	1.07	8.24
1970	569.5	17.7	0.79	7.16
1975	1,327.3	21.4	0.84	6.23
1976	1,512.4	13.9	0.90	6.22
1977	1,690.6	11.8	0.88	5.93
1978	1,901.0	12.4	0.90	5.54
1979	2,094.5	10.2	0.90	5.43
1980	2,230.2	6.5	0.90	5.24
1981	2,400.0	7.6	0.91	5.13
1982	2,586.1	7.8	0.93	5.21

a. GNP figures are government estimates made for budget compilation purposes.

Source: Defense Agency, Japan.

Table 14.18: Net Official Development Assistance from DAC Countries[a] to Developing Countries and Multilateral Agencies: Net Disbursements (1970-81) (US$million, except as indicated)

	1970-2 Average	1977	1978	1979	1980	1981(P)[b]	% of GNP			Share of Total (%)		
							1970-2	1980	1981	1970-2	1980	1981
USA	3,408	4,682	5,664	4,684	7,138	5,760	0.32	0.27	0.20	43.1	26.7	22.6
France	1,122	2,267	2,705	3,370	4,053	4,022	0.67	0.62	0.71	14.1	15.1	15.8
Germany, FR	714	1,717	2,347	3,350	3,517	2,182	0.32	0.43	0.46	9.0	13.1	12.5
Japan	527	1,424	2,215	2,637	3,304	e3,170	0.21	0.32	0.28	6.7	12.3	12.5
UK	595	1,103	1,460	2,104	1,781	2,194	0.42	0.34	0.43	7.5	6.7	8.6
Netherlands	240	908	1,073	1,404	1,577	1,510	0.63	0.99	1.08	3.0	5.9	5.9
Canada	398	991	1,060	1,026	1,036	1,187	0.42	0.42	0.43	5.0	3.9	4.7
Sweden	158	779	783	956	923	916	0.44	0.76	0.83	2.0	3.4	3.6
Italy	144	198	376	273	672	670	0.14	0.17	0.19	1.8	2.5	2.6
Australia	236	400	588	620	657	649	0.60	0.48	0.41	3.0	2.5	2.5
DAC, total	7,903	15,722	19,986	22,413	26,776	25,461	0.35	0.37	0.35	100.0	100.0	100.0

a. The Development Assistance Committee (DAC) is one of the specialized committees of the OECD. DAC members include Austria, Belgium, Denmark, Finland, New Zealand, Norway, Switzerland and the Commission of EEC, as well as countries shown above.
b. Including previously unrecorded administrative costs.

Source: OECD, *Development Co-operation*, 1981, and *Press Release*, 23 June 1982.

Figure 14.7: Rate of Taxation and Social Security Disbursements to National Income (1979)

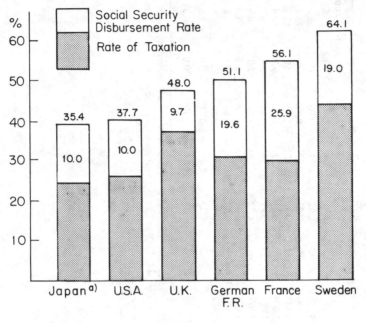

a) FY 1982.
Source: Ministry of Finance, Japan.

It is true that the Japanese rate of taxation and governmental social security disbursements to national income is comparatively low, as shown in Figure 14.7, in spite of the fact we are enjoying an almost equal standard of living to European countries. It is also true that the Japanese family system, which has a more solid bond than other industrialised countries (as shown in the low divorce rate, Table 14.13), and the Japanese community system, which has more stabilised spiritual interdependent relations of fraternity (as shown in the low crime rate, Table 14.14), contribute to this low rate of taxation and small government social security disbursements.

Besides those two factors, perhaps what we can rely on the most in solving the problems of the financial burdens of a welfare state, I should say, is the high standard of Japanese education (as shown in

Table 14.14) and the quick response of the people which this high standard of education causes.

Note

Much of the statistical data I quote here appeared in *Japan 1983, An International Comparison*, published by Keizai Koho Centre (Japan Institute for Social and Economic Affairs), and I partly owe the descriptions of the welfare system in business corporation to *Nippon, the Land and Its People, 1982*, edited by Nippon Steel Corporation and published by Gakusei Sha Publishing Co. Ltd.

15 ANGLO–AMERICAN EXCEPTIONALISM OR IS THE WELFARE STATE IN DANGER?

S.M. Miller

Some argue that the strains in and pressures on the welfare state in the United States and Britain are exceptional, that other nations have difficulties with their social programmes but no major onslaught is underway, and that other nations do not have politicians like Reagan and Thatcher in power who campaign on their opposition to vast social expenditures.

Indeed, some would go further and contend that Prime Minister Thatcher has had to ease her welfare-state attacks and dampen her more militant intellectual supporters' intentions of radically reducing the scope of the National Health Service. In the United States, polls are cited to show that the welfare state in principle is widely supported and that the Reagan cuts in means-tested programmes have led to revulsion as media reports of hunger and homelessness centre attention on the impact of programme contractions. A few think in terms of a liberal backlash against the earlier Reaganite backlash against welfare programmes. The general argument, then, is that other nations have not experienced pronounced assaults against social programmes and that even in the US and Britain politicians have learned their political costs in contracting welfare-state programmes.

It would be comfortable to accept these assessments that the welfare state experiences only some discomfort, not a major threat. But, to take the United States, there continue to be strong objections to the purported conduct of means-tested programmes from centre, right and left despite the public opinion polls which show a general support of helping those in need. The growing opposition to the cuts in programmes is partly due to the unfairness issue — the Reaganite tax cuts for the very wealthy have propelled a right-wing as well as a left-wing populism which objects to stroking and feeding the fat cats in society. The media attention to the horrors of the casualties of the reduced welfare state has not challenged notions that there are major things wrong with welfare-state programmes. People do want social programme cuts that do not hurt people, a position which they think tenable because of their perceptions of major abuses in many means-tested programmes. Indeed, there is an interesting, disturbing effort to portray more universal programmes like social security pensions and unemployment insurance benefits as aid to the un-needy and greedy middle classes; these programmes should be means-tested, thereby drastically reduced, and private savings be made major props for families not receiving wage income.

True, the Reagan cuts have shifted attention to the impact of the cuts from the once-highlighted welfare abuses, although Reaganite officials continue to try to shift the spotlight back to criticism of programmes. And the Reaganite plans are, perhaps, exceptional in their scope and openness. The aim is to reduce wages in order to improve American competitiveness in the greatly expanded international marketplace, to expand savings, investment and productivity by reducing business taxes, to reduce social expenditure and greatly increasing (in an apparently mindless way) military expenditures, and to pursue (in a stumbling way) the restoration of American power in a very changed world scene.

But economic difficulties may lead other countries to some of these objectives: the expansion of physical investment or capital; the contraction of the public sector relative to the private, capitalist sector. We have called this development 'the recapitalising of capitalism'.[1] Norway and Denmark, perhaps less dramatically than the United States, are seeking the reduction of social expenditures. Other nations may veer towards major changes in their welfare state programmes because of three major failures.

One failure is that to which Shmuel Eisenstadt has referred: the failure of the *vision* of the welfare state. It has not politically healed society; it has not made people happy although it has alleviated pain; it has not resulted in much satisfaction with the programmes themselves; and it has not transformed society.

The second failure has received surprisingly less notice — *the failure of the promise of post-war capitalism*. In Britain and the United States expectations about the growth, stability, and equity of capitalism have collapsed. In the 1950s when the American economy had obviously escaped from the fear of a post-war depression and growth was steady and apparently secure, Arthur F. Burns, Eisenhower's chief economic advisor, could express his confidence that the American economy was producing an 'income revolution' in which not only were standards of living improving for all but the slices of the economic pie were being more evenly distributed. *Fortune Magazine*, an important magazine for business executives, proclaimed that capitalism was producing the 'Permanent American Revolution' of growth and happy change. In the 1960s the Kennedy-Johnson economists felt that they could 'fine-tune' the economy into stable growth; indeed, for a short period the fear was of 'fiscal drag' — the steadily growing economy would generate so much tax revenue that government would have to speed up expenditures if it did not want to slow growth by taking in more funds than it spent.

In Britain, Anthony Crosland, a leading figure of the Labour Party, argued in 1957 in his influential *The Future of Socialism* that Keynesian-managed growth, a rising public sector yielding a welfare state, and a more accessible educational system would produce a socialism of rising standards of living and greater equality without taking over the commanding heights of the economy. A managed capitalist economy could yield the fruits of full employment and greater equality once thought to be only available in a socialist society.

These images of *the perfectability of capitalism and the welfare state have been badly damaged.* The economy and society have not been easily conquered.

Some of these issues have been apparent for some time. About a dozen years ago two articles appeared at the same time and grappled with them. Both, by chance, were called 'The Limits of the Welfare State' and were written without the awareness of each other. One was published in the American journal *The Public Interest* and was written by Nathan Glazer, now the co-editor of that publication. It argued that the penalties and complications involved in trying to change society through expanded governmental intervention were too great and disturbing. Interventions should be curbed and equality goals contracted.

The other 'Limits' argued that the welfare-state approach to greater equality was too limited, that basic economic policies had to be effected if improvements in the distribution of income and wealth were to be accomplished. It argued that 'passive intervention'[2] of the welfare state was inherently limited in transforming society and that deeper intervention in the economy than merely stimulating growth in Gross National Product was needed: social aims would have to influence economic policies. I was the author of that second article which was published in *Social Policy*, the British social science weekly. The welfare state could not make up the inroads on equality of capitalist functioning. 'Whose economic growth' was the issue and the character of macro-benefits was important.

Clearly, the mood of the first article has captured the day. The movement is toward contracting efforts to produce greater equality, not to expand them. But the broader issue is that the hope for both capitalism and the welfare state has withered, at least temporarily.

The third failure is that of *practice*, the experience of the welfare state. I find myself surprisingly and awkwardly in agreement with Arthur Seldon if his over-statements are disregarded. There *are* problems in the conduct of the welfare state. Many of the left and centre as well as the right recognise difficulties in social programmes, difficulties of bureaucracy, dependency, authoritarianism, inappropriate professionalism. That is why the need is to *defend and change* the welfare state. Unfortunately, in the United States at least, there are few positive changes toward autonomy and participation. Rather, the slashing of programmes is not changing them to improve the situation of those who use them. Nor can one have confidence that privatising the public sector, contracting out services, and the like, are positive. One of the worst scandals of the American public sector is the support given to nursing homes by the Medicare and Medicaid programmes; the quality of performance in these private services has often been criminal. The market principle has not led to improved services.

But, as Eisenstadt has pointed out, the welfare state has brought in its train new relationships.[3] The organisation of the families of those labelled mentally retarded and their effective lobbying have led to increased and more diversified public resources to aid them and a decline in their segregation (what is now termed 'mainstreaming') rather than isolating them in schools and other institutions. The requirement in many public programmes that local citizens participate in programmes has often been abrogated and downgraded but it has often led, nonetheless, to modifications in the conduct of programmes.

Despite such advances, the need is for more than a patch-up of existing policies and programmes to compensate for the Reaganite–Thatcher inroads. A philosophical and political basis is lacking if the welfare state is to be substantial and stable. An important yet rare recognition is that growth (and even affluence) induces poverty and inequalities. As Peter Townsend has argued, new poverties emerge as societies grow, standards of living change, and new barriers to full participation in that society emerge.[4]

In the advanced capitalist countries now trying to emerge from economic strains, the essential question is who shall bear the burden of change in a capitalism in difficulty?

The moral support for the next welfare state must be rebuilt. The themes of fairness and caring seem to be the essential basis for a welfare state. The issue seems to be whether morality, economics and political effectiveness can be joined.

I reject Crosland, Seldon and neo-Marxists like O'Connor. Like Eisenstadt, I believe that we have to think freshly about the welfare state: old problems exist; new problems emerge, especially about financing; new risks appear (e.g., in the blocked mobility of particular groups); new segregations and stratifications result from the restructuring of societies in a period of economic pressure and international transformations.

I hope that the United States is exceptional. But I doubt it. At the least, it shows *coming attractions* for some nations, (which may appear in their political theatres soon), and the *pressure points* for nations which may be able to escape drastic assaults on their welfare states but may have to reconsider many of their policies in this period of capitalist changes.

Notes

1. See S.M. Miller and Donald Tamaskovic-Devey, *Recapitalizing America* (New York and London: Routledge & Kegan Paul, 1983).

2. The term 'passive intervention' was coined by Paul Starr and Esping-Andersen almost ten years later, but this second article sensed the concept which was beautifully developed by Starr and Esping-Andersen in 1979 in the journal *Working Papers*.

3. Piven and Cloward have criticised some Marxist analyses of the welfare state which emphasise the continuing importance of property rights in agitating the population; they contend that the welfare state, taken by many radicals as a major co-optator of unrest, has stimulated a concern with political rights and is leading to a new politics about the production and distribution of welfare state benefits. Frances Fox Piven and Richard Cloward, 'The American Road to Democratic Socialism', in *Democracy* 3, 3 (summer, 1983).

4. Peter Townsend, *Poverty in Britain* (London: Penguin Books, 1979).

16 THE EXPERIENCE OF THE DANISH WELFARE STATE

Jacob Vedel-Petersen

Denmark has a long history of welfare development, and the Danish welfare-state system is modelled on familiar Scandinavian lines. The welfare idea and its practical form are very similar in Denmark, Norway, Sweden and Finland.

We have a high standard of living, a high standard of education, a well-developed health system, a high housing standard and very little extreme poverty. Education is free — so is treatment of the sick. And there are various forms of housing subsidy for low-income families.

The social security system compensates for loss of earnings in the event of illness or unemployment and up to a level that is close to the individual's regular income. Financial support is available to people temporarily in need with a view to maintaining approximately the same standard of living. There are pensions for the elderly and for the disabled.

This development has implied certain consequences for the structure and economy of Danish society: a high level of taxation, a large section of the workforce employed in the public service and substantial public sector spending on social security and other public services.

As in the other Scandinavian countries, developments in Denmark were initiated primarily by strong Social Democrat governments. But I should hasten to emphasise that the general policy has enjoyed the broad support of parties on the right wing of the Danish *Folketing* (parliament) and that there has been no serious interruption of the trend during periods when Conservative and Liberal parties have held power. It is true that in the early 1970s a new party did emerge, drawing its support from protesters against the high rate of taxation. It has exerted some influence on the other parties but today it is on the wane.

Expansion of the social security system continued up until 1975, when it faltered — and in the past few years there has been a tendency, although moderate, to reduce spending in this sector.

Danes believe they have a good system, and until a few years ago they assumed it would continue to develop. Observers in less-developed countries looked on our system as something akin to paradise.

The Cost of Welfare

Then what was it that went wrong?

The welfare state has been criticised from many quarters and from different viewpoints, and criticism has occasionally had the nature of backlash. I shall start, however, with the factor that in my own opinion is the most forceful of them all: it looks as though we are unable to pay for the system. Denmark finds itself with a heavy balance-of-payments deficit and a serious budgetary deficit. These deficits are covered by foreign and domestic loans, the interest on which increases year by year. Interest payments are already a great burden, and if the process continues unabated, it is likely that within a few years interest will swallow up a very substantial part of the state's revenue. This will remove from below us the very basis of our social system.

The question is whether we should blame the welfare state for the predicament in which we find ourselves or whether the cause is to be sought elsewhere.

It is true that social spending has risen sharply. In Denmark the increase was 82 per cent from 1970-80. But half of this rise was due to demographic factors, in particular the relative increase in the number of old people in the population, and the effects of the economic crisis, in particular unemployment, which rose steeply during the 1970s. If, on top of this, it is considered that social benefits ought to stay abreast of the general development of welfare, i.e., the GNP, it is found that in fact the relative level of social benefits has risen by only 10 per cent during the ten-year period.

What I want to say is that in a situation with healthy employment and a second economy the welfare state can well afford an increase in the quality of its social security and services of 10-15 per cent over the course of a decade without bringing the country's economy to the brink of disaster. But in a period when the circle of persons entitled to assistance widens rapidly, the system falls apart.

It should also be borne in mind that many of these costs are not merely items of expenditure but also investments aimed at keeping the workforce intact; this is so, for example, in the case of money spent on the health service, for unemployment benefit, and for day-care institutions for children — not to mention the education system.

I point this out because our theme is the future of the welfare state, and I think it is an error to accuse this social system of contributing to an economic crisis that is international in character — nor should we condemn it for trying to preserve the human resources needed to lift the country out of the doldrums.

Slow Reaction to New Conditions

But these views must not cloud the fact that social costs have become very heavy and that Denmark is in an economic situation that requires urgent action. As I see it, however, the problem does not so much question the fundamental idea of the welfare state as it makes one wonder why it took this social system so long to react to new, external conditions — why the self-correcting forces are so slow in taking effect.

There are today certain indications that the man and woman in the street have begun to understand that changes are necessary. In labour-market negotiations on wage and working conditions in 1981, the trade unions tabled relatively modest demands, and prior to corresponding negotiations in 1983 the government was able to extract an undertaking from both sides that wage increases over the next two years would be kept within a very narrow limit. Moreover, the reins of government passed at new year from the Social Democrats to a Conservative–Liberal coalition. The new government is intent on pursuing an austerity policy. It does not have a parliamentary majority but it nevertheless enjoys so much popular backing that it is unlikely to be toppled in the very near future.

But it took six to eight years for the political situation to mature to the point where it was ready to grapple with the new problems. There are probably numerous explanatory factors. I shall try to pinpoint a few:

(1) In many parts of the population the view is still held that it is the affluent that bear the brunt of the tax burden. In other

words, a belief that incomes are equalised from rich to poor via taxation.

(2) Because the social system and welfare have been taken over by the state, the ordinary individual has no idea what they cost. In Denmark there is widespread acceptance of social benefits — even among people who do not receive them; and people pay their taxes largely without a murmur. But there is only a vague idea of the consequences of these benefits upon the national economy; this is precisely because the individual pays for them via taxation — and pays a good deal.

(3) The state, centralised, bureaucratic and professional welfare system has weakened local initiative and the activities of self-help organisations.

In the current situation, therefore, there is very little local preparedness for finding new solutions, and there is little more than a trace of the former tradition that all sectors in local society should pull together to solve problems, i.e. the business community, educational sector, banks, public administration, trade unions, etc.

The local, grass-roots forces in our society that used to be able to rectify problems on their own initiative have had their wings clipped.

(4) Denmark has a population of five million people. Of these, 850,000 are pensioners, 300,000 are unemployed, and 830,000 are civil servants. These groups do not vote in blocks at political elections but they do constitute solid groups which the political parties must take into consideration.

(5) The Social Democrats have for long stretches played a leading role in development of the welfare state. But the party seems to have had difficulty adjusting to the new situation. The trade-union movement has insisted that the party toe the traditional line — allowing the party little room for manoeuvre.

These are a few possible reasons as to why the welfare state is too ponderous in its reactions to the new economic order.

I would like to conclude with a few words on two subjects: first, an account for the policies of the new government; and second, one or two additions to the general criticism of the welfare state.

A Conservative–Liberal Policy

In the first six months that Denmark's new Conservative–Liberal government was in power, one of its first actions was to lay down a very narrow margin for wage increases over the next two years in both the public and the private sector — and also to suspend automatic indexation of wages and salaries. And for the time being it would appear that the decree is being respected. Next it halted all indexation of unemployment and sickness benefit. The effects will take some time to register but these are two very large areas of expenditure.

There have also been cutbacks in certain social areas. So far they have had only limited effect on the total social budget but they may be regarded as the forerunners for further cuts, as the government is still a long way off its aim of balancing the state budget.

Furthermore, the government has announced certain principles it intends following in the pursuit of its policies. For example, it is a firm believer in *privatisation*, i.e. the process of transferring certain functions from the public to the private sector — and these changes will envelop the social sector. In the long term, the government will also introduce measures that are more in the nature of *insurance*, in that people will have a greater individual knowledge of what they pay and what they get for their money. In addition, it wants to see more *business-type* operations in the public administration sector, combined with more freedom of decision in the different branches of government. And to a greater extent *charges* will be made for public services. The government is also planning to alter the block-grant system under which the state reimburses local authorities for certain services they provide; the idea is that local authorities should bear a greater degree of *economic responsibility* for the services they decide to offer their citizens. There are also plans to cancel and clear away many of the existing regulations, circulars, etc., in order to *limit central control to as little as possible.*

The government has also announced that it wants to create opportunities for innovation and experiment in many fields, ensuring that new thinking is not bogged down by restrictions and tight controls.

The government's policy is to improve competitiveness on the international market, stimulate production and reduce the size of the public sector. In the first instance it is the wage-earner who will foot the bill, together with the unemployed and recipients of certain social benefits. In the long term it is hoped to bring the economy into a state of balance and thereby improve the employment position. It is too early to forecast whether this target will be achieved. I have one or two remarks I would like to make about this situation:

(1) So far the fundamental elements in the Danish welfare-state system are not seriously impaired. We can see scattered signs of poverty among certain groups but the security of the elderly pensioner, the handicapped, the ill and those people sustaining a temporary loss of income remains. Within the next few years the government will presumably be forced to cut more deeply, and larger groups of the population will be hit. But we must acknowledge the fact today that it is possible to modify welfare policy without ruining its central aims.

(2) There are no serious indications yet that the new policy, which makes demands on the whole population, is a threat to political stability or the country's democratic institutions. There are no signs of chaos on the labour market and no demand for a strong man, i.e. a dictator.

(3) Despite a heavy burden of taxation and anxiety about the country's economy, there is still broad support in the Danish population for the welfare-state system with its cash benefits and costs. There are no political movements of any significance which want to make any radical changes in the system. But there are signs that the tax burden cannot be increased without a corresponding expansion of the underground economy and loopholes being found for avoiding tax.

Remarks on Criticism of the Welfare State

Finally, permit me to comment on some of the criticism levelled at the welfare state. This criticism is being universally debated, and many of the points have been referred to in the background paper to this conference.

Viewed from the Danish standpoint, much of the criticism is unjustified, some of it is exaggerated, and some of it is important and forward-looking. These are some of the points of criticism that do not apply to the situation in Denmark:

(1) A distinction must be drawn between those problems rooted in the economic crisis and those which may be attributed to the way the welfare state works.
(2) It is an illusion to believe the heavy public spending of the welfare state can be avoided. The money is spent on tasks that need doing whether they are performed by public or private bodies — if the stability, continuity and productivity of society are to be maintained.
(3) It is not correct that the Danish welfare state is inefficient. Productivity has risen sharply all the while the welfare state has been developing. The productive apparatus has been expanded considerably, and the national product was on the increase until the crisis occurred. It should also be borne in mind that there are many welfare states in the exclusive club of highly affluent countries.
(4) It is also claimed that the gap between rich and poor has widened. This is unlikely in Denmark. The difference between the highest-paid workers and the lowest-paid has shrunk, and the difference between the wages of male and female workers has also decreased. The gap was closing up until 1975 — at which point it became static.

The exaggerated points of criticism include the following:

(1) It is claimed that the welfare state has developed a colossal bureaucracy. This is exaggerated. In a welfare state many people are in public employment — but most of them are teachers, hospital and nursing-home staff, postal employees, etc. In other words, the majority are not bureaucrats but people doing a job that has to be done whether on public or private initiative.

Private administration may conceivably be cheaper than public but the difference is not as great as critics would have us believe.
(2) It is said that the welfare state is experiencing a change in the nature of democracy, and reference is made to the many extra-parliamentary activity groups. This is true — but we should remember at the same time that many of these groups have

had their claims channelled into the democratic institutions — claims which are in complete conformity with the idea of the welfare state. For instance, the Women's Lib movement, the Green movement, activist groups for the mentally handicapped, etc. Their fight has borne fruit, and can be considered as confirmation of the democratic strength of the welfare state.

Finally, there is a criticism that I believe looks forward. It is the criticism that complains of the welfare state having taken away the initiative and self-confidence of the individual, limiting his opportunities for solving his own problems, and alienating him from the political process. The usual answer to this is that both in the totalitarian state and under a totally liberal market economy the broad section of the public is even worse off in this respect. That is true but it is nevertheless a defect in the welfare state which threatens its very existence.

This criticism of the welfare state is voiced on both the right and left wings of the political spectrum. The underlying motives point in their respective directions: towards a free market economy on the one hand and further democratisation and social equality on the other.

Although, on the face of it, these approaches bear some resemblance to each other, they are probably incompatible when it comes to practical politics. On the other hand, the answer could well lie in some kind of compromise between the two.

Social Democratic policies have run into difficulty but a testing time is ahead for the new Conservative–Liberal government. It has demanded and received money from the public at large in return for a promise to bring order to the national economy. But even if it succeeds with this project, it will soon find itself facing the classic problem of the welfare state: balancing its budgets.

The solution could lie in different forms of social contracts, decentralisation and further democratisation in order that popular participation in the political processes can secure the flexibility and adaptability that the welfare state lacks. If a new and closer relationship can be struck between authorities and local, private forces, it is possible that a bridge could be built which would join the welfare citizen's conflicting interests between, on the one hand, a taxpayer-ego and, on the other, a recipient-ego of public services.

17 FAMILY POLICY IN FRANCE

Nicole Questiaux

In any discussion of the 'welfare state', it is very easy to make comparisons between the experiences of various cultures in different parts of the world. I am among those who beg permission to be cautious about international comparisons because, in our media-oriented societies, any idea can take like wildfire and then be misused in the very narrow confrontation of ideas that dominates our modern world. I have, therefore, decided to avoid comparing the French experience in family policy to the experience of other countries. The following anecdote illustrates why.

The first time I went to the United States, during the 1970s, I was invited by a private group of affluent citizens to attend a meeting in the Waldorf Astoria Hotel in Manhattan. The purpose of this meeting was to discuss whether the system of family allowances should be adopted in the United States. During this visit, I felt as if I was discovering America. I was astonished by the vitality of that society. And here I was standing up in the lobby of this famous hotel and speaking with great pride of how we in France had had family allowances for more than 25 years. Now I am not among those who think that America is not a welfare state but, to my astonishment, we spent three days discussing whether family allowances would be a disincentive to work. And I remember a black lady wearing a white hat who had looked disinterested throughout most of the conference and who, at the end of the discussions, opened one eye and said, 'Do you really think that for your miserable three dollars I will have another child?'

Many years later, I served as a minister in the government of François Mitterand after a very important change in French politics. The very first thing that we did was to increase family allowances. In a system which is considered to be the leader in the field of family policy, we increased family allowances immediately and significantly, a gesture which is all the more interesting when you realise that the family commitment bridges our well-known political divisions. Here, then, was a left-wing government spectacularly committed to a family policy which originated under the most conservative governments France has ever had. But whatever the government, the family policy has carried on all through French political life.

This leads us to understanding some of the complexities of welfare problems. We are living in a world of competition between economies, between organised industrial systems, and between cultures, which makes evaluation and problem-solving all the more difficult.

If one looks at the figures and compares family policy to other welfare expenses, the picture in France is one of continual reduction of the commitment to family policy. Looking back, it becomes clear that, during the last 30 years, the real share of family among other social expenses has been reduced by almost half. This is not true of the percentage in GNP because growth has carried all social expenses, but there has been a whittling away of the relative expenditure on family. And yet, when I meet with representatives of other countries and compare notes, I find that France is still among the leaders in the area of family policy. Simultaneously, more and more countries have become interested in family policy and when they have been able to refrain from spending in other areas, such as health, they have diverted a higher percentage to family policy. This is the case in Great Britain.

Family policy is involved in a severe competition with all of the other forms of welfare, and it is in this field that people will economise if they are unable to do so in other areas. Why? Because the natural growth of the pension system and the consumers' world of the health services weigh in favour of these expenses. In order to make way for family policy, there must be a conscious decision to do so. And we must go on deciding to do so. What we decide about family policy, therefore, is extremely significant as an indication of how we perceive the welfare state as a whole. I argue that if we do decide to continue having a welfare state, we shall. And if we decide not to have a welfare state, we shall not. Family policy is vulnerable. And if it is vulnerable in a climate of strong economic pressure, it will only be supported if it is felt to be legitimate. I have tried to build my argument around this idea of legitimacy. Why and when does a society strongly committed to family policy feel it is legitimate?

One of the most compelling arguments for the legitimacy of family policy is that it expresses society's commitment to children. In France, this is certainly the case. Over a long period of time, it is true that an organised family policy does show a relative shift of consumer income to families with children, which covers all sectors of the population. If one combines an overall family allowance with the country's families, a system of tax rebates and several forms of selective intervention related to different problems of the family (childcare, housing, education), it can be seen that a part of the country's activity is directed to the well-being of its children.

Data on the efficiency of the French scheme shows that it does redistribute towards families of two or three children. You may say that this is evident, but it is worthwhile to be sure of your stand, since the welfare state is being criticised for not doing what it was intended to do. As far as its commitment to young people is concerned, family policy is doing what it was expected to do. And I consider that together with the educational system, it is the only form of commitment to young people that may resist the ever-increasing bias toward the elderly that exists in the modern welfare state.

Another interesting fact is that the family policy has explored some of the needs of the family in a manner more adequate than the open market would have done. (It is surprising that nobody in France feels like opposing an intervention that is in the form of money which the family can spend as it likes or of actions that are specifically directed to childcare or education.) I believe, through long experience, that these various forms of assistance are not substitutes for one another, but rather combine in an answer to society's needs. We have examples in the French scene: action toward childcare carried out in money and kind under previous governments which resulted in a gain of several points in the infancy mortality rates through a policy directed towards certain priority families. It is interesting to note how the debate on childcare has moved away from ideological controversy — we do not oppose care in the home and the 'creches' as much as before. In the field of housing, contracts are now signed with the housing authorities as to how they will provide for the child in the city.

The second item to point out is that these programmes have not been a disincentive to work. I will not expand on this. However, the relationship between developing family policy and the increasing trend of women entering the workforce, is receiving more and more attention as an indicator of this point. The numerical growth of working women is far more important in this regard than the effects of family policy on single-parent families. It is true in the test case. This means that tested actions can provide a disincentive to work, when the mother is unable to get a significant salary in the job market, but I argue that, on the whole, in a country where more and more mothers of one or two children are in the workforce, the fact that they are entitled to family benefits is not a disincentive to work.

The third problem is the relationship between family policy and redistribution of wealth. Here things get less clear. In France, we do three things at the same time: we distribute allowances equally to all children, we have a system of tax rebates proportional to income, and we have set up a few allowances which are selectively aimed at lower income families. This is a paradox. There is one population segment that no political group wants to inconvenience — the middle class. In the 1970s it was discovered that this group, the middle class, was receiving relatively less than its share of benefits. A higher ceiling of means-tested allowances was therefore implemented to direct benefits towards this middle-income group. The socialists, although committed to overall equality, have continued in this direction. And in the recent freeze of incomes and wages, we have allowed the means-tested allowance to increase somewhat more quickly than the more equalising benefits, which was contrary to our principles, but which shows what kind of problems lie behind welfare policy.

Some sectors of opinion worry that our system does not redistribute income properly. Even those who are strongly committed to the egalitarian aspect of welfare have had to contend within their own ranks with the pressure to build some kind of anti-poverty plan into the family policy.

This is the type of idea that we sometimes import from the United States 10 or 15 years after its inception, when the Americans have already forgotten it. There does exist the argument in France that we should reduce the importance of the welfare state in order to increase wages, so that the benefits could be channelled into honorary or non-paying forms of intervention. It is becoming a more means-tested approach. However, I myself believe that this involves a certain risk and a major change in the distribution of benefits. Family policy now benefits all sectors of society and, at a time when they are asked to pay more for welfare anyway, it is not certain that it is a good idea to exclude the more wealthy from the family benefits.

My fourth point has to do with the legitimacy of a population policy. France has always been worried about its birth rate and a concern for the need for state intervention in this field has often been expressed. Other Western nations are also becoming increasingly concerned with their birth rates. This is why there is continuous controversy over the size of the family which should be encouraged and why the level of benefits of the second or third child have been frequently adjusted. The effect of such incentives is uncertain. In the long run, it seems more a factor of coincidence in society trends than of cause and effect. People have fewer children as a kind of silent resistance to society. If they are dispirited with unemployment and other difficulties, they will resist by bearing no children. This is why family policy is so important. It is integrated into the atmosphere in which people organise their lives. It seems that in periods when the French were having more children, they happened also to have a supportive family policy. So we must create a stable atmosphere by supporting the welfare state in order to convince those who plan ahead with regard to family policy.

We have also discovered that income is not redistributed properly; that families with two wage earners pay too much for this system. There is an underlying contradiction here already referred to by Professor Abel-Smith and others: that the working mother, the one we would actually like to see having a second or third child, pays more than she should and yet is expected to bear children in addition.

Another question to be dealt with is the role of the family. We deliberately intervene to aid the 'normal, basic family', but this so-called 'normal' family is acting in a role which is impossible to describe without the welfare state. The ideology which advocates reducing the role of the welfare state and putting more of the burden on the individual family, does not take into account the basic consideration that this family is nowadays accustomed to free education, day-care, allowances, and other services of the welfare state. Some of the resources provided by the state for handicapped young and old people, for example, are not always sufficient to boost the capacity of individual families to cope. We seem to be striving to make these families capable in ways for which they may not yet be ready. The bourgeois family knew well how to shelter its children. I know of one nasty young man who demanded more pocket money from his parents on the argument that he entitled them to tax rebates. The richer families are able to protect their young from unemployment by sending them for an extended time to the university. But not all families, even if their action is seconded by a family policy, are able to play this protective role.

Economics

Regarding the economics of family policy, it is the French experience that the cost of such policy is at the heart of the turmoil. Intervention on behalf of the family is the easiest type of benefit for the economists to play upon. If they desire inflation, they institute more aid to the family. If they want deflation, they decrease aid to the family. If they prove to be unsuccessful, they can always lay the blame on the welfare policy. (This is, of course, a caricature, since I hold economists in high regard.) In France, where these allowances are paid through contributions on wages deducted via the employers, the family policy is at the heart of a shift of financing. The firms argue that these costs undermine their competitive ability and that the nation as a whole should pay for the family policy because it is a national commitment. This implies a shift from the system where contributions are levied on the firm to a system related to the income tax.

Nobody really knows who pays in the end for social security contributions, although there are cupboards full of studies on the issue. The employers account for those costs in a policy of wages and prices. More often than not, however, it is the consumer who pays. But when there exists a freeze of wages and prices, a battle ensues to determine who pays. And we do not yet know how the labour force will react to the change.

The final problem, then, is one of acceptance. Whether certain people want a programme or not, the real question is whether or not they will accept it. There are two kinds of reaction to this issue. Some believe that the welfare state is wearing itself out — that we have reached the stage where we are involving so many people in the costs that they do not react favourably any more to the benefits. The other group sees the welfare state in the way that many people see tap water: they don't like it much, but when it is turned off they realise that they cannot do without it.

There are a number of contradictions which deserve brief mention. A fundamental discrepancy exists between long-term benefits to society such as population equilibrium, the occupational revolution and urbanisation and the fact that modern societies are using welfare as an immediate form of economic intervention. Another worry exists because people need to know what they are paying for. As much as I admire the synthetic analysis induced by the Beveridge Plan, in which it was as understood that the inactive were entitled to draw on the income of the active, I am not sure that such a synthesis will be accepted in the present day in a context of massive unemployment where many perceive all welfare as a failure. I have no solution for this problem, but I think it has become necessary to distinguish the problems of unemployment from the other aspects of welfare and to provide different solutions and arguments so that long-term programmes such as family policy are not linked to this feeling of failure.

In the economic battle to standardise costs, we should be aware of what it may mean to standardise cultures. People should realise that economic consequences of the same policies may be different in weaker economies. I lack the knowledge required to deal with this problem of values and priorities that may differ in the weaker economies of the third world, but it is certainly a topic for discussion. Sometimes these countries have better systems for dealing with welfare problems than we have.

PART FIVE

THE CASE OF ISRAEL

18 WELFARE AND INTEGRATION IN ISRAEL

Rivka Bar-Yosef

> The trouble is that no way has been found of equating a
> man's value in the market, his value as a citizen and his
> value for himself
>
> Equality of opportunity, that great architect of inequality

T.H. Marshall, *The Right to Welfare*, p. 119.

Israeli social policy, from its very beginning, pivoted around two
axial principles: welfare and integration.

In the public consciousness and in political debates in Israel the
two concepts are used for different social objectives, albeit somewhat vaguely and often with the tacit assumption that welfare will
or that it should bring about social integration. In many historical
instances this assumption fed the political incentive for social legislation (Heidenheimer, Heclo and Teich, 1975; Rimlinger, 1971).

Social science literature does not provide us with agreed upon
definitions of welfare and integration as separate concepts. Integration is one of the central concepts of sociological models of
society, while welfare is dealt with mostly by students of social
policy and very seldom included in general sociological treatises.
Social policy studies have nearly always some normative orientations, which explains why, besides the core definition of welfare,
there are such wide variations in conceptions concerning its scope
and domain. Neither are there clear criteria about the usage of
such terms as social rights, social policy, social welfare and welfare
state. Nevertheless, the multitude of approaches and definitions
indicates interesting facets of the problem and reveals the underlying assumptions, theoretical or ideological.

Welfare is sometimes equated with social policy and sometimes
with social policy and the 'integrative system' (Boulding, 1967, p.
3), or seen as part of the citizen's social rights which range from
welfare and security to 'the life of a civilized being according to the
standards prevailing in society' (Marshall, 1963, p. 47).

Titmuss refers to a structural model of society and specifies
'need' as the principle of allocation. He expects that universalistic

247

welfare policy will result in better integration (Titmuss, 1973, p. 401).

Welfare might be seen as a way to ensure solidarity and social cohesion (Wilensky and Lebeaux, 1965) or as being a lofty complex of 'human dignity, equality, liberty democracy, security, solidarity and economic efficiency' (Furniss and Tilton, 1977, pp. x-xi).

The common elements in the above and many other definitions is the notion of allocation of benefits from the collectivity to its members through unilateral transfer or other non-market types of exchange. The benefits are geared to socially legitimate needs, although eligibility does not necessarily depend on the needs of the recipient. By definition, universal services and benefits provide for the needy and the affluent alike (Davis, 1978).

Welfare and integration have different foci and require contrary role orientations from the individuals involved. Welfare centres on the recipient, the needs of the eligible person. The institutional structure is built to answer the question of 'who gets what'. Integration concerns the collectivity, the needs of society; it is a demand from the members of the society. The role of the welfare recipient is passive while the integration is based on activity; it is the role of the participant.

Both concepts can be incorporated in the same model of society. As such, it is probably logical to assume that they are connected, but there is no need to see them as causally dependent. The prevailing opinion that these processes are connected can be turned into theoretical hypotheses by applying well accepted socio-phychological theories. Two types of linkages can be formulated:

(1) 'the fair exchange' hypothesis based on the assumption that people are guided by norms of equity in exchange; the commitment of society to a welfare policy would in return elicit commitment to the values and institutions of the society from its members;
(2) 'the participation need' hypothesis based on various need scales and alienation theories, according to which people feel the need to be involved and to participate in meaningful social action.

While these hypotheses should not be rejected, on a *prima facie* basis events seem to belie them. Naive observation of modern societies reveals that countries with extreme welfare legislation are suffering from crises of integration; and political parties which were responsible for building and expanding the modern welfare system are losing popular support, often of those who were the principal beneficiaries of it. Israel is one of several such cases. In spite of the many specifically local features, its analysis would probably allow some generalisations applicable to other societies.

Welfare in Pre-state Israel

From the historical perspective the 35 years of existence of Israel are but a negligible period. It is thus not surprising that despite the dramatic event of the establishment of the state, the pre-state codes and institutional forms continue to impress themselves on contemporary Israeli social structures.

The ideologies of welfare and of social integration were formulated in greater part in the pre-state period, some ideas and values being deeply rooted in historical and religious tradition.

Before the establishment of the state in 1948 one cannot speak about social policy as an institutionalised, centrally guided system. The British Mandatory government functioned mostly as a political and administrative force and did not interfere either positively or negatively, in the social life of the two communities, the Jewish and the Arab. Save for a small number of labour laws, it showed little interest and less readiness in allocating resources for the social needs of the communities. The Jewish population developed its own voluntary quasi-state organisation in which, by necessity and by ideological leanings, social policy was given much attention. In spite of the strength of these voluntary organisations, they were constrained by not having universal political authority. Therefore social policy was fragmented and sectorial (Eisenstadt, 1967, pp. 24-68; Lotan, 1973; Neipris, 1971).

Welfare policy was determined by this fragmentary structure. The three types of welfare organisation normally considered (charity, public assistance and social rights) were each within the domain of a different sector, having a different ideological basis, target population and administration.

The Integrated Systems

Charity was the traditional way of providing for the 'needy'. Jewish religious and cultural tradition is very explicit about the social and moral value of charity. The Hebrew term in itself points toward its importance: *Tzedakah*, charity, has the same root as *tzedek*, justice. Charity is a basic moral duty and its forms are treated extensively by the Bible and by the later religious literature. In the Jewish tradition, charity, although formally a unilateral transfer depending on the discretion of the giver, had a meaning of a quasi-exchange. In order to fulfill his duty of *tzedakah*, the giver needed receivers. In a way, the receiver gave service by providing the giver with the opportunity to be a righteous person. Being poor or needy in the traditional Jewish society was not as degrading a status as in the rigid class societies, or where the values of the Protestant ethnic were dominant. There were instances when neediness and living on charity became entirely irrelevant for the status of the person. Those who chose to spend part or all of their adult life in learning the religious literature enjoyed a prestige and status irrespective of their material circumstances, as did those who came to live in the 'holy' cities of Jerusalem, Safed and Tiberias, to learn, to pray and live a strictly religious life. Many among these had some kind of occupation, but their earnings were seldom adequate for maintaining their large families. In both cases the charitable foundations provided for their rather meagre livelihood. The major part of the charity was administered by a large number of organisations run by rabbis and other religious office bearers. There was little and often no contact between the giver and the receiver. Distribution was entirely discretionary, usually based on three criteria: (1) affiliation with a local organisation, a *yeshiva* (religious school) or a religious movement which was the patron of the foundation; (2) merit, measured mostly as talent and diligence in learning; and (3) need, mostly of the family. Within the traditional religious context, charity was not solely oriented to the needs of the individual. It fulfilled a major social integrative function, both for the giver and the receiver. The foundations and the religious mediators created a distance between giver and receiver. Thus the exchange was removed from the personal level and from the giving/receiving situation. Instead of the asymmetry of dependence characteristic to the charity situation in which the receiver was expected to be humble and grateful, traditional charity was seen as exchange for the mutual benefit of both parties. At the same time the act of charity was more than an interaction between persons: it was a service to the community and the community's system, hence its integrative potential.

Social rights — the early prototype for the present system of social insurance can be found in the 'mutual aid' system of the *Histadrut* (General Federation of Labour — founded in 1920). The *Histadrut* was not a trade union in the classical sense. From its inception it was intended to be a comprehensive organisation for all the employees of the country, according to a socialist conception of people and society.

The idea of equality of all work and all workers led to the definition of 'worker' for all wage and salary earners and to the pre-state experiment of differences in renumeration being based on the number of dependents in the earner's family. It was the avowed aim of the *Histadrut* to be a 'socialist society', within the political and economic structure of a capitalist or mixed system. This was the justification for developing its three functional branches: (1) the entrepreneurial economy, which provided its economic power; (2) the trade union branch, which represented the rights of workers-employees; and (3) the social services branch, known as the mutual aid system. The entrepreneurial and producer activities of the *Histadrut* were given justification by the idea of 'class ownership' of the means of production. The equal value of all work was a comfortable ideological basis for an umbrella-type trade union which tried to accommodate both blue- and white-collar occupations.

As a trade union, the *Histadrut* had to support the struggle of different occupations for the maintenance of the relative differentials between them in spite of its ideology of 'all work is of equal value'.

The 'mutual aid' function of the *Histadrut* consisted of a complex of social services and financial benefits: a comprehensive health care system, old-age and survivors pensions, unemployment funds and special rate options in day-care centres and other educational and vocational training services. The service sector was an integral part of the complex of rights to which members of the *Histadrut* and their families were entitled by paying an income-linked progressive membership fee. According to the *Histadrut* conception, the fee was akin to an income tax paid voluntarily by the 'citizens' of the 'workers' society'.

The most complete model of the integrated socialist welfare principle was realised in the *kibbutz* movement. Here the principles of equality, democratic participation and welfare rights were meshed into a tightly structured complex. Welfare rights are an unconditional consequence of membership, wholly detached from performance or contribution (Katz and Golomb, 1974-5).

Unlike the *Histadrut*, the *kibbutz* was not a model for society as a whole. It was, and is, a select community for committed members. But both the *Histadrut* and the *kibbutz* developed a secular value system in which welfare, by right, was both one of the means toward solidarity and the end, as part of the social ideal of mutuality and collective responsibility in caring for individual needs. This secular ideal had an element of protest against the traditional Jewish community and its values of learning and charity. Charity was labelled as 'parasitism' and the virtues of a secular working community extolled compared with those of a learning community. The principles of mutuality and universality of members' rights were emphasised in contradistinction to the particularistic, discretionary pattern of 'giving' customary in the traditional community.

Integrative factors — in spite of the salient ideological-organisational differences between the secular-socialist and the orthodox-religious patterns, they were somewhat similar in some general features in a way that seems relevant to their integrative potential. Both systems were rooted in well-defined ideological commitment by their way of life. Mutual responsibility for the welfare of the members was part of the basic tenets. The 'givers' were not in power positions, nor were the 'receivers' stigmatised as either failures or morally inferior. But the same attributes which reinforce or even produce the integrative capacity of these models limit their integrative potential to certain types of communities. Membership therein demands strong entry conditions, which by definition must exclude large (and often the most problematic) groups. Neither the secular nor the religious community could provide welfare solutions for the non-committed, or the non-integrated. Integration was not the outcome of welfare; it was the necessary, preliminary condition: '... in the social pioneering ideology, there was no place for social cases or problems. All these were meant to be taken care of by the full implementation of the ideology. Hence, also the policy which was based on the assumption of "total" absorption could paradoxically not easily provide for different needs of immigrant groups' (Eisenstadt, 1967; p. 210).

The workers' movement could not cope with social deviance or 'traditional' poverty. In its ideology, people were responsible for their fate and the mutual aid system helped them to overcome crises which were deemed to be caused by ungovernable forces of the labour market or nature. In this framework there was no place for the concept of poverty: people were unemployed if there was no work available, they had a low income because the employers exploited them, or because they voluntarily accepted deprivation in order to fulfill some social calling.

The religious community was no more tolerant towards deviance. Though it did believe in transcendental control of human fate, it also presupposed that humans did have the freedom of moral choice; hence while poverty comes from heaven, conformity to norms depends on the person.

Public Assistance — Welfare for the 'Marginals'

The two major welfare systems were important safeguards against poverty, starvation and destitution of their membership, but because of their selectivity, many of those groups who are at present the main clientele of public assistance were excluded. These groups were taken care of, in a rather haphazard way, by various charities having primarily a religious or secular philanthropic orientation not connected with structured ideologies or social philosophy. Integration was neither a condition of eligibility nor the expected consequence, while in the socialist and religious aid systems a person in need rightfully expected to be taken care of without being stigmatised; public assistance was linked to the concept of failure. The recipient and the providing organisation were not part of the same community. The recipient was marginal and the organisation was the establishment. There was no mutuality which would redeem this type of welfare from stigma.

Welfare in the State of Israel

Israel gained its independence in 1948. It might be seen as a symbolic coincidence that this was the year in which the Beveridge Plan was first implemented in Great Britain and in which the

United Nations promulgated the Declaration of Human Rights, with articles 22 and 25 specifying far-reaching and comprehensive social-welfare rights. Probably these two events had some influence on strengthening the policy-makers in their tendency to shape the new Israel into a welfare state. But even without these external influences, Israel would have become a welfare state by reason of the ideology of the governing Labour Party, by the continuation of the pre-state voluntary institutional patterns and the necessity created by a mass immigration of unprecedented magnitude.

Already in 1949, before the cease-fire agreements with the Arab states, the new government appointed a committee to prepare the basic framework for welfare legislation. In 1953 the National Insurance Law was enacted (Salzberger, 1973, pp. 555-6). The law also established the National Insurance Institute, as an independent public authority operating under the parliamentary supervision of the Ministry of Labour. The NII became responsible for a comprehensive package of benefits and transfers based on compulsory insurance, which emphasised the idea of rights acquired by contribution — hence exchange and unilateral transfer.

In spite of its innovations, this was not a new beginning and elements of the pre-state patterns were firmly embedded in the new system. The former systems continued to exist and to provide additional or alternative welfare benefits to their members, though they were affected by the emergence of a governmental welfare policy.

The religious charities are now, as before, an important element of the integrative forces of the religious community. They symbolise the distinctiveness and the togetherness of the group. At the same time, they are used intentionally as a means of control over the members of the community and as inducements to attract new converts. They have an ambivalent instrumental relationship with the governments, rejecting its norms and control but using the political clout of the religious parties for obtaining substantial resources from the government.

The welfare complex of the *Histadrut* developed in a different direction. Through the governing Labour Party, the *Histadrut* became an integral part of the state welfare plan. Several functions were transferred from the realm of the *Histadrut* to that of the state (e.g. the employment offices and a large part of the educational network, unemployment payments etc.).

The NII did not replace the *Histadrut,* but established a partnership. The NII provided a universal, flat-rate, old-age pension, while the *Histadrut,* acting as a trade union, continued to be responsible for the wage-connected retirement plans of a large number of occupations (in addition to the rather meagre universal pension paid by the NII). The *Histadrut* remained the main provider of the curative health services. The incorporation of the *Histadrut* in the national welfare scheme was one of the main factors in changing the concept of membership.

At the time of its foundation, the membership of the *Histadrut* constituted a scant 11 per cent of the population, which grew to 40 per cent by 1958 and, at present, it is about 75 per cent. Much of this growth was not due to ideological or organisational commitment, but to the attractivenes of its 'mutual aid' system.

The transformation of a voluntary, ideologically committed, relatively selective organisation into a large, open, ideologically nearly-neutral corporation resulted in the drastic reduction of its integrative potential. The feeble efforts of the leadership to reiterate from time to time the original *Histadrut* principles raised resentment among those who joined the *Histadrut* in order to obtain its services (Lissak, 1970).

Public policy attitudes and the organisational pattern show a marked continuity with the pre-state practice. Public assistance was not made part of the National Insurance Institute. This fact in itself symbolised the difference in approach toward the formalised, legally well-defined welfare plan to be carried out by the NII and the rather vague, ambivalent basis on which the policy toward public assistance was based.

The status of public assistance was influenced by the 'work ideology' of the majority of the population and by patterns of traditional charity. These two approaches created an intrinsic contradiction which only strengthened the aura of stigma surrounding the programmes and activities of the Ministry of Welfare.

The Social Welfare Law of 1958 lagged behind the NII legislation not only in time but in innovativeness, clarity and precision. The law does not establish either the right to assistance or the criteria for eligibility (Shlonsky, 1971, pp. 24-8). In principle and in practice, the particularistic system of the traditional charity was continued on the level of state bureaucracy.

The Ministry of Welfare developed a particularistic ideology, as against the universalistic approach on which the NII was built. This

parallel ideology extolled the importance of the personal relationship, the discretionary ability to help according to specific individual needs. In essence, this was a secular statement of the Jewish
charity philosophy, which was reinforced by the case-study method
of the professional social worker. But unlike the charity in the traditional Jewish community, public assistance was not an integral
part of a total social conception: it did not assume a common value
system or express norms of mutuality between givers and receivers.

Ideologies of Compensation and Integration

The types of welfare institutions described draw their legitimacy
from the two major ideologies consented to in a welfare state: (a)
welfare as the consumption rights of the members of a community,
state, nation, etc., which is part and parcel of their social and political rights; and (b) welfare as an alternative way of satisfying the
consumption needs of those who are unable to provide for themselves through the market mechanism or the informal helping
system of their primary groups.

In addition, two non-welfare ideologies provide legitimacy for
several important welfare programmes: the ideology of 'moral
debt' and the ideology of absorption and integration. Both ideologies are linked to the concept of national identity and not to the
social conception of welfare.

The moral debt ideology contends that the nation is indebted to
those who, by voluntary action or as victims, suffered and sacri-
ficed on its behalf or in its interest. Casualties of the wars of Israel
and of terrorist attacks, the victims of Nazi concentration camps
and of anti-Jewish and anti-Zionist persecution in various countries are entitled to special welfare benefits, seen as repayment
earned as representatives of the nation. By according them a
special status, the concept of national unity is emphasised
(Shamgar, 1981).

The absorption ideology concerns society's 'duty' towards new
immigrants. It assigns to society the responsibility for creating
propitious conditions for the integration of new immigrants. The
welfare package to which the new immigrants are entitled is
intended to soften the shock of migration and to facilitate integration preventing or at least mitigating downward mobility.

Both plans emphasise the rights of the recipients and the

importance of their contribution to the collectivity, and as such they symbolise the cohesion and mutual responsibility of the nation.

The Functions of the Welfare System

In Israel, as in other modern welfare states, the system is intended to fulfil at least two functions, which theoretically at least, should have a strong positive impact on integration.

The 'minimum welfare' function is the modern realisation of the traditional idea of charity according to which the members of the community are to be provided with a 'socially acceptable minimum of subsistence'. Historical analysis of policy debates and decisions shows the influence of ideology concerning such concepts as the 'necessary minimum' and the 'socially acceptable minimum', and whether the reference group chosen for comparison was destitution or the established working class. The more egalitarian the ideology the stronger the leaning towards defining the average standard as the 'acceptable'. However, even the egalitarian approach was hampered by the puritanical strains of the pioneering period.

Acceptability being a function of the evaluators' reference norms, each of the relevant groups (the policy-makers and bureaucrats, the mediating professionals and the indigent population) has different standards. This difference in conception is one of the bases of conflict between the government and the social workers, and both of these and the recipients.

The universal benefits and services programmes were intended to provide at least the minimum acceptable welfare for all the Israelis without supplementary selective programmes. This intention was not realised and, even for the elimination of absolute poverty, selective programmes were necessary.

Housing is perhaps the most emotionally loaded issue. Besides its instrumental importance for the material well-being of individuals and their families housing is a key status element. Homes are crucial for feelings of integration, and they acquire additional significance for immigrants by symbolising stability and security (Bar-Yosef, 1968; 1970).

The opportunities for acquiring housing entirely by private means are not favourable. Housing programmes are selective, eligibility being based on a collection of heterogenous criteria: slum-clearing for sub-standard and overcrowded dwellings — known as 'the three plus' measure: young couples' rights, immigrants' rights, development areas and others. For each eligible group there are different kinds of benefits and different standards of housing. The standards also change with time, being adapted to the rise in the general standard of living. Those, then, who acquired their dwellings with the help of public funds early in the history of the state, are much worse off than the recent beneficiaries. The 'minimum welfare' of the present day Israel would have been luxury level in its early days. This development contrasts with expectations and concepts of fairness, which link length of stay in the country with rise in the standard of living.

The Status Maintenance Function

Three major welfare programmes aim at maintaining the status of the recipients irrespective of their socio-economic status: child allowance, unemployment benefits and benefits for immigrants. These are by definition non-egalitarian, not being geared to eliminate status differences but to maintain the position of the recipients in a stratified society. The underlying principle is one of acceptance of the model of a stratified society and recognition that the stability of achieved status is part of the complex of welfare rights safeguarded through a policy of collective responsibility. In a society like Israel's, with strong leanings toward egalitarianism, welfare policy which is so obviously non-egalitarian needs reinforcing legitimation and this is achieved by invoking some of the major consensual value principles.

Child allowance started as insurance for large families, large meaning more than two children. Now it covers all children under 18 (Rodgers, 1979, pp. 122-3). Israel is a child-centred familistic society. Children are considered important for the happiness and self-fulfilment of the individual and as assets of the society. As in many immigrant societies, the native-born children represent integration in the new society and are idealised. They are equally important in the traditional religious society of Jews and of Muslims. Universal child allowances are congruent with the general value system which overrides the cultural differences of various population groups. Governmental policy was led by natalistic tendencies, by considerations for the welfare of large families, and also by the universalistic postulate that maintenance of children is not the sole responsibility of their family. Children are seen as members of the society with welfare rights as individuals, hence the economic status of the family is irrelevant to eligibility for child allowances.

Unemployment insurance is another example of legitimation of income and status inequality. The unemployed have the right to claim payment or to be offered 'suitable work', which is defined as work similar to their former occupation or work which fits their level of education, training, skill and income.

The rationale of the law is obviously one of status maintenance, although this is mitigated by certain limitations of the linkage between the size of former earnings and by the relatively short period of eligibility (175 days for each 180 days of paid insurance). The 'suitable work' concept provides the legitimation of such status elements as remuneration, education and kind of work.

The justification for this approach is formulated in terms of personal needs, social ability and responsibility. By unemployment insurance the individual is relieved from full responsibility for unemployment. Social status is recognised as a person's rightful asset, the loss of which results in a critical impairment of one's basic well-being. Such a crisis of downward mobility is assumed to jeopardise the claimants' potential for contribution to and integration in the normal functioning of the society.

Benefits for the immigrants are somewhat similar in principle to those of unemployment insurance. Here also individual welfare considerations, social responsibility and social utility serve as justification for unequal treatment. Benefits vary mainly according to two criteria: the pre-migration occupational status of the immigrants and the prevailing standard of living in Israel.

For both principles Israeli society serves as a reference group. Occupational-educational position is one of the main bases of socio-economic status in Israel. Therefore, it is considered just, equitable and socially useful to treat the immigrants in accordance with the Israeli stratification system. In this way it is expected to conserve the human resources of the immigrants and to facilitate their absorption in the existing social structure. Linking the standard of the benefits to some concept of the 'average life-style' in Israel seems morally justifiable and a symbol of society's full acceptance of the new immigrants as fully-fledged members.

While undoubtedly this approach facilitates the integration of the privileged, it also creates a situation of relative deprivation (Runciman, 1966) for immigrants with lower education and less prestigious occupations. Because of the continuously rising standard of living in Israel, it also discriminates the earlier immigrants compared with more recent arrivals. By coincidence, a large number of the earlier immigrants were of lesser education and originally from countries with ascriptive systems of stratification. The feelings of relative deprivation of these immigrants is aggravated by loss of status when migrating from an ascriptive society to one favouring occupational achievement, and by comparing the standard of immigrants' benefits at the time of their arrival with the improved standard of the more affluent recent periods.

Conclusions

The typical definitions of welfare include the assumption that welfare policy will result in reducing human suffering, lessen inequalities and therefore furthering and strengthening social integration. By analysing some facets of Israeli welfare policy, I tried to show:

(a) that the meaning and the effect of welfare depend on the social context in which it is embedded;
(b) that elements of integration are not necessarily overlapping;
(c) that there is an intrinsic contradiction between egalitarianism and programmes aimed at status maintenance;
(d) and lastly, that welfare policy and egalitarian ideology generate expectations which by definition cannot be met, thus eliciting disintegrative sentiments, alienation and, in some instances, protesting behaviour.

References

Bar-Yosef, R., 'The Moroccans — Background to the Problem', 419-28, in *Integration and Development in Israel*, Eisenstadt, S.N., Bar-Yosef, R. and C. Alder (eds.), Israel Universities Press, Jerusalem, 1970.
Bar-Yosef, R., 'Desocialization and Resocialization: The Adjustment Process of Immigrants', *International Migration Review*, 3: 27-45, 1968.
Boulding, K., 'The Boundaries of Social Policy', *Social Work*, 12, 1: 3-11, January 1967.

Davis, B., *Universality, Selectivity and Effectiveness in Social Policy*, Heinemann, London, 1978.

Eisenstadt, S.N., *Israeli Society*, Weidenfeld and Nicolson, London, 1967.

Furniss, N. and Tilton, T., *The Case for the Welfare State: From Social Security to Social Equality*, Indiana University Press, Bloomington, 1977.

Heidenheimer, H.J., Heclo, H. and Teich, C., *Comparative Public Policy: The Politics of Social Choice in Europe and America*, St. Martin's Press, New York, 1955.

Katz, D. and Golomb, N., 'Integration, Effectiveness and Adaptation in Social Systems: A Comparative Analysis of Kibbutzim Communities', *Administration and Society*, 6 (3): 283-315, 1974; 6 (4): 389-421, 1975.

Lissak, M., 'Patterns of Change in Ideology and Class Structure in Israel', in *Integration and Development in Israel*, pp. 141-61, 1970.

Lotan, G., *Towards a Welfare State: Social Policy in Israel in the 70s*, Am Oved, Tel Aviv, 1973 (Hebrew).

Marshall, T.H., *The Right to Welfare*, Heinemann, London, 1981.

Neipris, J., 'Social Services in Israel', *Journal of Jewish Communal Services*, 14, XLVII, 4, Summer 1971.

Rodgers, B. with Doron, A. and Jones, M., *The Study of Social Policy: A Comparative Approach*, George Allen & Unwin, London, 1979.

Rimlinger, G.V., *Welfare Policy and Industrialization in Europe, America and Russia*, Wiley, New York, 1971.

Runciman, W.G., *Relative Deprivation and Social Justice*, Routledge and Kegan Paul, 1966.

Salzberger, Lotte and Shnitt, D., 'Social Welfare Legislation in Israel', *The Israel Law Review*, 8, 4: 550-79, October 1973.

Shamgar-Handelman, L., 'Administering to War Widows in Israel: The Birth of a Social Category', *Social Analysis*, 9, 3: 24-120, December 1981.

Shlonsky, H., *Welfare in Israel in a Comparative Perspective*, The University of Chicago, Chicago, 1971.

Titmus, R.M., 'Keynote Address' in *Developing Social Policy in Conditions of Rapid Change Role of Social Welfare*, Proceedings of the XVIth International Conference on Social Welfare, The Hague, Netherlands, pp. 33-43, 1972; Columbia University Press, New York, 1973.

United Nations Universal Declaration of Human Rights, 1948.

Wilensky, H.L. and Lebeaux, C.N., *Industrial Sociology and Social Welfare*, The Free Press, New York, 1965.

19 SOCIAL SERVICES: AT WHAT COSTS?

Yair Aharoni

From its inception, Israel followed the principle of the state's responsibility for the central and universal supply of a host of social services. The belief was that adequate level of these services would help close the gap between the 'old-timers' and new immigrants and create an almost egalitarian society. Although enormous strides have been made towards achieving these aims, expectations of social programmes have increased and dissatisfaction with their level continues. Today, many would like to reduce the objectives and thus reduce the resources needed to meet them since they feel that the state cannot continue to allocate more funds for social goals.

I

The huge influx of immigrants to Israel in the 1950s provided reinforcement to the basic egalitarian ideology. The majority of the new-comers came from Moslem countries, changing the demographic, social and cultural composition of the state, 'Thus the inequality that could be tolerated or even legitimized on the basis of achievement-oriented meritocratic values becomes illegitimate because of its linkage to an ascribed, seeming stratification' (Bar-Yosef, 1977, p. 112). This problem could have been solved only by massive efforts of the public sector, thus increasing the importance of that sector. Studies showing a gap between Jewish immigrants from Moslem countries and the European settlers who preceded them to Israel, were a reason for concern and even alarm because of their perceived meaning for the success in absorbing immigrants (see, for example, Patinkin, 1965, p. 63). Indeed, any perceived increase of income and wealth inequality caused public outcries. Within five years, two separate prestigious expert public commissions were established to examine income distribution developments and to ensure that the government was moving towards reducing inequality. In 1966, the first committee reported

262

that differences in income distribution in Israel were significantly lower than in other countries, and even more so when the influence of income tax was taken into account (Israel, Committee on Income Distribution and Social Inequality, 1966, p. 3). The second committee reported a further reduction in inequality among salaried urban Jewish families. It found 'inequality in 1970 was lower than in 1963/4', and 'an improvement in the relative position of the lower income brackets' (Israel, Committee on Income Distribution and Social Inequality, 1971, p. 4).

While Israel's ideology emphasised the egalitarian society, pervasive economic pressures for differentiation existed. Attempting to absorb into its economy large numbers of immigrants, Israel opted for a policy of rapid economic growth and industrialisation which increased the need for scarce technical and managerial skills. Contradictions resulted between the official ideology of equality and economic realities which pressured for differentiation.

One result has been that many increases in salaries were in the form of benefits not reported as income in the income surveys (Israel, Committee on Income Tax Reform, 1975, pp. 193-281). The reliability of the income surveys as a measure of inequality was also questioned because it was alleged that 'moonlighting' may have increased, while the income was rarely reported, in order to evade income tax.

These problems are one example of the difficulty of assessing total social costs and their distribution. Many of the costs are not registered in the national accounts, and the distribution of the benefits and the incidence of costs are not fully known. Yet, a general consensus existed in Israel that the state has to supply and finance a whole spectrum of social services, and that taxes should be used to redistribute income. To be sure, there were debates among experts whether services should be supplied universally or at the discretion of the social worker, whether subsidies should be granted to the needy or to the commodity. There were also disagreements on the amount of basic assistance needed. Still, the ideals were of an egalitarian society, and the major goal — to provide services to all and to close the gap between African–Asian and Western Jews — was implemented through governmental policies which increased the scope and the types of social services rendered. However, despite all efforts, there are still gaps in Israeli society and immigrants of Asian or African origin had, on the average, less income, worse dwelling conditions, and fewer years of education than their counterparts from Europe–America (Central Bureau of Statistics, 1982). The economic constraints on further increasing welfare type programmes have also been felt.

II

The costs of social services have grown considerably in all Western democracies in the last few decades. Social transfer payments have been rising much faster than the Gross Domestic Product. In Israel, too, these costs have been rising rapidly. Up to the mid 1970s, the increased costs were taken for granted as an integral part of the ideology. In fact, in the first three decades of Israel's existence, social services costs increased and expanded rapidly. Expenditures on social security, for example, grew from 4.6 per cent of GNP in 1950 to 7.4 per cent in 1960, to 8.6 per cent of GDP in 1970 and 11.6 per cent in 1974. Real expenditures on public health services increased during the 1960s at an annual rate of 18-20 per cent. National expenditures on education have grown from 6.0 per cent of GNP in 1962/3 to 7.5 per cent in 1972/3. There was expansion, too, in indexation schemes to protect the elderly and the needy against inflation and in protected institutions for the retarded, elderly or children in boarding schools.

The anticipation that defence expenditures in the budget and income would continue to decrease, gave momentum to the installation (and expansion) of many social welfare programmes. The years that defence costs as a percentage of GNP decreased (from 25 per cent in 1970 to 23 per cent in 1971/2) were also years of expansion of a variety of social services. However, after 1973 the cost of Israel's defence zoomed to a level of 27 to 29 per cent of GNP. Since 1973, the growth of GNP was arrested and the dependence on capital imports increased.

A committee on social welfare recommended in 1975 a change in the welfare philosophy from a universal supply of services to a sort of 'reverse discrimination' to increase benefits to those in need and to allow them to raise their living standards to levels similar to those of the Ashkenazi population.

Yet, the costs of social services continued to increase: expenditures on social security reached a peak of 17.0 per cent of GDP in 1977 and decreased to 15.8 per cent in 1980. National expenditures on education grew to 9.0 per cent in 1978/9. Health outlays reached 7.7 per cent of GNP in 1979/80.

There seems to be a tendency to use social services not only to help those in need, but also to create employment in these services. Between 1978 and 1981, 46.0 per cent of additional employed persons swelled the number of employees in education, health services, welfare and other public and community services. Only 21 per cent went to work in agriculture, industry, electricity, water and construction.

One result has been a very high tax burden: taxation has reached 54 per cent of GNP, and both internal and external debts zoomed. Total public civilian consumption also increased — from 10.3 per cent of GNP in 1970 to 12.4 per cent in 1981. These figures exclude, by definition, the transfer payments. These, plus direct subsidies, were 19 per cent of the GNP in the period 1970-4 and grew to 28 per cent of GNP in 1981. The consumption of education, health and other public welfare services (including non-profit organisations) increased in real terms at an annual average of 8.5 per cent in the period 1969-72; 5.9 per cent in 1972-4; 5.6 per cent in 1974-6; 5.0 per cent in 1976-8 and 3.4 per cent in 1978-81. Although the rate of increase was lower than before, it was still for most of the period higher than the increase in the GNP.

The increase in both defence costs and social expenditures was partially possible because the rate of investment was much lower: In 1974-7 annual gross investment decreased on the average by 7.9 per cent; in 1978 and 1979 there were increases, but in 1980 it dropped by 16.3 per cent; and in 1981 by 5.4 per cent.

At the same time that growing costs of governmental programmes caused dissatisfaction, citizens demanded continuation and expansion of these services. The backlash against the welfare state reported in other countries has not happened in Israel; to provide citizens with minimum income, nutrition, health and housing and assure them employment has been and continues to be an accepted tenet of Israeli policy. Moreover, it seems that with the increasing standard of living, there has been a growing impatience and less tolerance for gaps in income and dwelling conditions.

The combined burden of defence costs, welfare expenditures and payments of past debts has now reached very high proportions. Its continuation depends, in the short run, on the ability of the country to continue to secure foreign loans and grants and other types of aid. Whereas in the past Israel was able to mobilise its human capital and its high rate of savings to direct a large percentage of its resources to investment and growth, in the last few years, both savings and investments dwindled and productivity lagged. In order to ensure employment, low growth industries were not abandoned, and much additional employment was created in the public services. In the long run, however, a viable welfare state can be possible only by increasing productivity and the gross product.

III

The welfare state concept that the government assures a minimum standard of social services for everyone does not require that it supply all services directly. Although the ideal of egalitarian society has never been reached, taxes and the social security system did redistribute income. Certain social services were supplied directly by government, others were required by law or encouraged by incentives (e.g. pensions, employees' payment to health insurance or housing subsidies). The impact of these incentives on income distribution is less known, since the level of 'the expenditures' is not calculated. Many other services in Israel are voluntarily supplied by the private sector or by the *Histadrut* (Labour Federation); some are free of charge, others are supplied on the basis of compulsory insurance, and for others direct payment is made. In the last two decades, the rapid rise in both the size and scope of the public sector can no longer be explained away as the legitimate functions of a welfare state. We have instead an 'insurance' state, where citizens are protected against an array of risks by shifting the burden of their consequences to a larger group or the whole community or simply by eliminating them. We are insured against a variety of mishaps including natural disasters, poor health, unemployment, and the infirmities of old age. Workplace safety and working hours are regulated, ailing firms are supported, research and development subsidised, quality is controlled, social insurance is supplied, foreign competition is checked and even social status protected. The movement is away from a reliance on the rational individual as a decision-maker and bearer of the risks of his or her choice, to a socially determined allocation and distribution of resources, much of which is designed to shift the responsibility for both new and existing risks from individuals to society.

The more services are supplied by government expenditures or through transfers, the higher, *ceteris paribus*, is the tax burden. In Israel, the burden of individual income taxes reached a level that was perceived as intolerable. As a result, an increasing proportion of income to wage earners was paid through all sorts of fringe benefits. It was also widely felt that the proportion of undeclared income has been on the rise and despite a total tax reform executed in the mid-1970s income tax levels are still extremely high, affecting the willingness to work, and apparently continuing tax evasion and avoidance.

Social scientists prefer to study measurable phenomena, which they can quantify. When the growth of the public sector is discussed, they turn to data on governmental revenues and expenditures as a percentage of GNP, or distribution of these expenditures among different functions such as defence, welfare, heath, education and housing. Important as these measurements might be, however, they often miss the real issue. Public policy encompasses more than expenditures or revenues because most policy goals are implemented not through direct budget allocation, but through a combination of regulations, laws, changes in institutional setting. Many of the social costs are invisible — not registered in the national accounts. It appears that over the last two decades the invisible government has grown faster than its visible counterpart. This growth came about not only because of administrative and ideological factors. Many believe that using the market mechanisms, even if it is distorted by governmental directives, is a superior allocation mechanism than direct supply by government.

One example is the housing sector. The government used to build houses for the poor; today though it uses other methods, there is no significant aspect of the housing market in Israel that is not affected by government action. Indeed, it is almost impossible to untangle the maze of cost-increasing regulations on the one hand, and subsidies on the other. The government owns houses and through state-owned enterprises leases them to certain segments of the population at highly subsidised rents. The government also builds houses for sale, sometimes through state-owned enterprises, sometimes through private contractors. In other cases, the contractor may be granted a special permit to build on a higher percentage of the lot than permitted under the building code to enable the sale of some apartments at a lower rate for young couples. The government is also involved in the housing market by giving mortgages at subsidised rates and through its tax, labour and credit policies.

This maze of direct and indirect aid makes it more difficult to assess the size of the total costs and the distribution of benefits of the housing programmes. For example, the subsidies on low rent apartments is the difference between the rent paid and the economic rent, but these subsidies are not even calculated. It is not clear which classes have been the major beneficiaries of these costs, most of which are not registered.

It is even more difficult to assess indirect costs of housing programmes. When admission to public housing is based on a means test and when the projects are designed for the very poor, monotonous, architecturally ugly neighbourhoods that often perpetuate slum conditions can be created. Low rental housing projects limited to low income groups have been transformed into poverty enclaves. On the other hand, interest rate subsidies seem to have benefited mainly the upper middle class, and have also provided the recipients with the greatest possible range of options in housing type and location. It may well be that a policy of charging economic rents for public housing and giving rent subsidies to the poor would have created better housing conditions. It would certainly have made costs of the programme more visible.

In the real and incomplete world of information, institutional constraints and unequal distribution of talents, differences in organisational form are significant. First, they differ in the degree of visibility of information about the distribution of costs and benefits, and therefore of voters' awareness of this distribution. Secondly, since organisational forms differ in their efficiency and in the degree of discretion enjoyed by managers over such things as salaries and rules for distribution of benefits, different stakeholders will prefer different organisational forms. Thirdly, the use of certain organisational forms increases the quantity of services supplied and affects resource allocation at the expense of other costs. Fourthly, different forms of organisations differ in the perception of choice rendered to the users. Finally, reorganisation is sometimes used to disguise failure of a public policy to achieve its ends. A multitude of organisational forms are used by government: services can be supplied directly or through authorities, enterprises or wholly- or jointly-owned legal bodies, voluntary organisations, local authorities or invisible methods. We focus here on the major differences between direct supply of services, use of autonomous agencies and invisible methods.

Government involvement is usually prescribed when optimality cannot be achieved in the market or when market failure is shown. The non-existence of markets for bearing some risks reduces the well-being of those who prefer to transfer those risks to others at a certain price, as well as those who are willing to bear the risks at such a price. In unpredictable cases, not under the control of the individual decision-maker, the calls for such insurance comes quite early: subsidies to the blind, aid to the poor, or relief against suffering caused by natural disasters. With time, the demand for public insurance widens. Yet, risks cannot be eliminated by passing them on to the government. Risks that can be insured against by government entail costs, and a system for their distribution must be devised and agreed on. Unfortunately, such agreement is hard to reach, and the shifting of the problem to the public sector has not always been the optimal method.

Today, the aggregate demand for public insurance far exceeds the collective willingness to pay the 'premium'. Individuals trying to maximise their own utility attempt to tilt governmental benefits their own way and reduce costs to themselves. Yet, the costs of all new insurance programmes must be paid. In other words, as long as resources are scarce, they must be allocated. If market allocations are considered lacking, other allocation mechanisms must replace them. These may be based on power, rationing, or time spent in queues, when the first to come and those willing to wait in line will be served.

Each allocation mechanism involves certain problems, and each class in society would prefer a different distribution method. The rich would like distribution based on the market; the poor might prefer distribution based on time, which they have in relative abundance. Skilled persons would rather see distribution on the basis of skills, and the less skilled would prefer some equality of results. Since each individual wants certain things, one can easily catalogue contradictions, problems, and all sorts of disguised costs. For example, when services are supplied as a free good, the demand for them increases and the costs mount. Multifarious demands on services may eventually force the government to reduce the quality of the service. In other cases, it turns out that more is not necessarily better; more hospital beds do not ensure better medical services; they may be simply the result of an inefficient allocation mechanism which may increase the tendency to hospitalise people even when not necessary. Fewer pupils per teaching post may not result in better education, but only in increased education budget.

One way to reduce costs of public social services is to give those services free of charge only to the needy, and charge fees to those who can afford to pay. When 'means tests' are used, however, the incentive to earn more is drastically reduced, while the incentive to report less income than is really earned increases. Moreover, when more and more means tests are used, the effective marginal income tax may become prohibitive. Thus in 1975 (Aharoni, 1975), I demonstrated that different means tests for high school tuition fees, and for a variety of other services meant an effective marginal tax of more than 125 per cent in moving from poverty to low income!

There are many other costs that are never calculated: the outlays of the private sector in bookkeeping and accountants' salaries to satisfy government requirements for tax collection is a well-known example. By the same token, enormous costs and energy spent in avoiding tax is not registered anywhere.

Since resources are always scarce, and wants are apparently insatiable, the traditional class struggle has been replaced by conflict over the distribution of the tax burden and risk bearing, and the receipt of public benefits. Unable to satisfy all the public's wants or reduce the level of its expectations, governments simply satisfy some wants at the expense of others, and insofar as possible, in unseen ways. Contrary to popular belief, this redistribution has by no means always favoured the poor. What Boulding and Pfaff call 'implicit public grants' — special provisions of the tax law, public policy, or administrative practices — more often than not result in even greater inequalities.

Ever since the enactment of the Poor Laws in Elizabethan England, governments have felt compelled to add a 'distributional corrective' to soften the burden that market forces bring to some people. As many more groups in society acquired power, the distributional neutrality of competitive markets was further weakened as they succeeded in using that power to tilt benefits their way. By the twentieth century, social reforms were no longer expressions of *noblesse oblige*, but demands — backed by political power — of the more recently enfranchised for greater equality in income, opportunity and, quite often, results. Poverty and disease are no longer accepted simply as unfortunate manifestations of the natural order of things. Governments have stepped in to alleviate economic hardship, social problems and pressures, and to reduce risk. In the process they have been pushed into (at least) pledging to meet more and more demands, and to mitigate a growing number of risks by shifting them from individuals or groups to society at large.

In Israel, however, redistribution of income and increasing welfare costs have affected the nation's ability to achieve economic growth. A country may opt to increase productivity, promote innovation and reward work, or it can alternatively spend its energy arguing how to redistribute existing resources. But, an economic policy that invigorates growth will, in the final analysis, also enable better social services.

The challenge is not merely deciding on the level of resources spent, but to reach a consensus on objectives and how to implement them. Social services should not necessarily be supplied or financed by government alone; unobtainable objectives are not the best guide for public policy. Trying to alter basic patterns of individual behaviour is doomed to failure. The real challenge is to retain a sense of mutual obligation, despite the failed hopes that government can solve all problems.

References

Aharoni, Yair, 'Principles for reform in the direct tax system in Israel' (with A. Barnea and Y. Cohen), *Tax Quarterly*, vol. 9, nos. 35-6, August 1975, pp. 281-93, (in Hebrew).

Bank of Israel, 1981 Report.

Bar-Yosef, Rivka, 'Egalitarianism, participation and policy in Israel' in Erving Louis Horvitz, *Equity, Income and Policy: A Comparative Developmental Context*, Praeger, 1977, pp. 106-45.

Boulding, Kenneth E. and Pfaff, Martin (eds.), *Redistribution to the Rich and the Poor*, Belmont, California, Wadsworth, 1972, p. 2.

Central Bureau of Statistics, 1982.

Eisenstadt, Shmuel N., *Israel Society*, London, Weidenfeld and Nicolson, 1967.

Israel, Committee on Income Distribution and Social Inequality, 1966, 1971.

Israel, Committee on Income Tax Reform, 1975.

Patinkin, Don, *Israeli Economy: The First Decade*, Jerusalem, Falk Institute, March 1965.

Shapira, Yonathan, *The Organization of Power*, Tel Aviv, Am Oved, 1975.

20 SOCIAL WELFARE POLICY AND THE ADVANCEMENT OF THE DISADVANTAGED

Baruch Levy

Despite political differences among Israeli parties — right and left and among those of secular and religious orientation — a general consensus exists about the basic goals of Israeli social policy. Those of all political persuasions seem to share a broad ideological commitment to an improvement of the quality of life and the development and expansion of social equality, integration and solidarity. The basic aim of social welfare policy may then be seen as an attempt to maintain a reasonable standard of living for the entire population while lessening social deprivation and narrowing the socio-economic gaps which already exist.

The state of Israel is rightly considered as a Western society maintaining a life style that prevails in Eastern democratic countries. The foundation for this way of life was laid by the first leaders of the Zionist movement who immigrated to Palestine and assumed leadership in political and social areas. Ever since, the majority of the top echelons of any political or public office have been occupied by those of European and Anglo-Saxon backgrounds, known as Ashkenazi. Thus the absorption of new immigrants (mainly those who came from Asian and African countries) meant integration into an entirely different social and political framework while two main absorption policies prevailed. The first was the 'melting pot' which existed in the first ten to fifteen years of statehood, the second, the 'pluralism of cultures', emerged as a result of a re-evaluation of the first.

It should also be remembered that ever since the establishment of the new Jewish community in Palestine, defence and security issues dominated day-to-day life. This had a significant impact on social policies and programmes both in budgetary terms and in the general setting of national priorities.

Social Welfare Policy

Four major agencies in Israel play an instrumental role in the formulation and delivery of social welfare programmes:

(1) Government, through several ministries of social services, e.g. education, housing, health, labour, setting priorities and allocating budget to social agencies at the regional and local level.
(2) The Jewish Agency through social departments, e.g. education, youth aliyah, youth and pioneer settlement, mainly assisting in the settlement of Jewish new immigrants to the State of Israel.
(3) The Histadrut, the trade union federation of labour, responsible for planning and delivery of services on a national level, e.g. medical insurance (*Kupat Holim*), vocational and educational training and a wide network of community social services.
(4) Other public voluntary organisations, among which are WIZO, Na'Amat, Hadassah, etc., that are responsible for a rather wide network of social welfare facilities, e.g. day nurseries, family consultation centres, community centres and the like.

This situation presents some difficulties to the social planners at the national level who are faced with problems of co-ordination and setting of priorities by different organisations without having any authority, budgetary or otherwise, to maintain comprehensive policies.

Ever since the beginning of the establishment of the Jewish community in Palestine the social ideology was supportive of what is known as the 'universal approach' in social policies. This approach, according to which each and every one of the country's citizens is entited to a certain standard of social services and income maintenance, is rightly regarded as most advanced. In a heterogenic society, however, and in a country that is still in a process of immigration and integration, trying to absorb people from dozens of different countries, cultures and traditions, this can present a major problem of 'social gap'. This is because the point of departure for the various groups of citizens is not common and the advancement to a Western way of life is different for each of them. Thus, some could make better use of the universal approach in the social programmes and advance rapidly, while others were left behind.

In the course of time and in the wake of the large waves of immigration, it was necessary to introduce differentiation within the 'universal approach'. This was done in order to give preference to selected groups and regions in the country and to enrich them to be able to make better use of the provisions of the social services. The major methods in this context were enrichment programmes, development of human potential plans and additional special educational and social programmes for the disadvantaged.

The Compulsory Military Service Act requires all citizens to serve in the military framework for a relatively substantial period of two to three years. At the same time the state has been taking positive advantage of this national service using the military framework as an instrumental social and educational tool. This was done through a wide network of pre-military vocational and educational training, taking advantage of the disciplined and efficient framework to give another opportunity to those who as youngsters were low achievers in the normal way of schooling. In the course of time special programmes have been developed for disadvantaged youth aiming at their enhancement to become eligible for the national service and to be able for them to live in the country as productive citizens.

Other Characteristics of Israeli Society

Three aspects of dualism are suggested to have been in existence in Israeli Jewish society. The first is the division into Ashkenazi and Sephardic sectors. Ashkenazim is a general term for Jewish people coming from the European and American countries, brought up mainly in Western-oriented society, in what we call an 'open and free democratic society'. Sephardim is used as a general term for Jewish people coming from African and Asian societies, Arab-speaking countries and, in some cases, from less developed non-technological societies. The second aspect of dualism exists in the state of Israel between the Jewish community and the Arab community. These are two different cultures maintaining in most cases different religions, traditions and ways of life. The third relevant aspect of dualism is related to the continuing demanding defence and security situation versus the social welfare needs. The dualism in these three respects presented more difficulties for social planners and, in the course of time, could be detected as major factors for social deprivation and widening of the social gap among some of the groups in both Jewish and Arab sectors.

It is given that in any society there are and there have always been marginal people, low-class groups and poor citizens, all of whom would come today under the category of disadvantaged people. It is, however, suggested that we distinguish between two major aspects of social deprivation and disadvantage: the objective and the subjective. The objective deprivation is determined in accordance with agreed upon social standards of living. Normally these standards can be defined and measured and they vary from one society to another. The selected criteria for measurement of objective deprivation are housing, income and education; and their levels would have to be decided in accordance with the standard of living of the society. Generally speaking, the objective deprivation can more easily be tackled through government and public social programmes offering the appropriate services to those who are in need of them. Thus, an answer for shortage of housing or crowded housing could be given by public housing programmes, taking into consideration the needs, availability of resources and the general settlement policies. The same would be the case in the area of education and even more so in the income maintenance issues.

The Subjective deprivation is rather more complicated and is not easily solved. It is basically generated from emotions, beliefs and, sometimes, prejudice. It has not always to do with any concrete objective shortage. In other words, it is not necessarily true that a person should feel, at the same time, deprived both objectively and subjectively. There could be many cases in which many people don't have any objective reason to feel deprived: mainly they enjoy a good standard of living, good education, high income, and yet they subjectively feel deprived. Sometimes it is because of place of origin, sometimes it is because of a different colour or different tradition, culture, folklore. The solutions to problems of subjective deprivation are rather difficult and can not be assured automatically by the introduction of government and public social programmes in the conservative areas of education, housing, etc.

The situation in the state of Israel in this respect is even more dangerous because of the high correlation of objective deprivation and place of origin. According to the prime minister's report on youth in distress, 94 per cent of those who suffer from objective deprivation belong to the Sephardim origin. This presents yet another dangerous social phenomenon to the Israeli social policy-maker.

Social Policy Guidelines

As has been mentioned above, the differentiation within the 'universal approach' is a necessary guideline in planning social programmes. This principle will set the appropriate priorities for those segments of the society and/or areas in the country that need such emphasis in certain social services. Thus, sometimes a priority should be given to day nurseries and day-care centres in one neighbourhood while vocational training centres and family consultation stations should be emphasised in another, all based on the composition of the community and the neighbourhood, aiming at strengthening the weak points and enhancing them to reach a common point of departure with other segments of the society.

Advancement of disadvantaged people should not always be left to the special social and educational framework established for them as distinguished from the regular social administrations. In many cases the use of the 'normal' framework, such as regular schools, community centres, vocational training centres, youth movements, trade unions, etc. can reach a higher level of achievement. This is because the 'normal' institutions preclude the stigmatisation of the special social services and allow the disadvantaged to develop a better self-image while participating in general 'normal' society. In order not to hamper regular social institutions, appropriate apportioning should be observed in the composition of the educational units, i.e. children from disadvantaged neighbourhoods should not exceed (approximately) more than 25 per cent of class size. This system would allow the disadvantaged to integrate more easily into the community while developing their own individual fortes.

Use of Unique Social Frameworks

Using a combination of necessity and ideology, the IDF (Israeli Defence Force) has been maintaining a fine, relatively wide system of pre-military educational and vocational training. Thousands of youngsters of high school age (14-18) receive their education and professional training under the auspices of the military units while preparing themselves for national compulsory military service (beginning at age 18). The IDF maintains the principles of the 'normal' social framework and, in addition, offers the candidates from disadvantaged communities a sense of belonging within the prestigious and useful national service. While undergoing training candidates wear the same uniforms as soldiers in other units, including elite units, and they are educated by officers and non-commissioned officers wearing military uniforms. This serves as an incentive to their joining the ranks of the pre-military system.

The kibbutz is a unique socialistic Israeli creation which presents another fine framework for better integration and absorption of disadvantaged youth. Observing the principles of the 'normal' framework and differentiation, groups of disadvantaged youngsters joining the kibbutz for educational and vocational training, find themselves in a supportive atmosphere. As disadvantaged youth they were vulnerable to being ostracised from the main strain stream of society. By joining a kibbutz they are able to be rehabilitated and learn how to contribute to productive society.

Development towns are an innovative, recent Israeli social creation established in the 1950s to help absorb the large waves of newcomers and to settle rural parts of the country. In the light of the principles of sound integration of old-timers and newcomers, the development town system proved the success of the social integration process. This system can simultaneously serve as another unique framework for advancement of disadvantaged youth by accepting groups of them to live and work in the co-operative industrial framework. This approach led to the establishment of industrial schools and apprenticeship centres for young people in association with large plants and leading factories located in development towns.

Social Integration Principles

Legislation: It is questionable whether an approach similar to the 'affirmative action' regulations maintained in the United States would be appropriate to the state of Israel. This is because, when dealing with the disadvantaged in Israel, we have to bear in mind the high correlation between the disadvantaged and the place of origin. In other words, we are no longer dealing with minorities but rather with people from the Sephardic origin, who, in demographic distribution, form the majority of the population in the state of Israel. Therefore, it is doubtful whether an enactment *per se* could bring about any real solution to the pressing problem of advancement of the disadvantaged. The following, however, would be more sound principles to be observed and maintained.

Openness and awareness: The awareness on the part of the country's leadership as well as the general public to the problems of social integration and absorption of the disadvantaged is of high priority. The government and all other public organisations should do their utmost to educate the general public in all possible ways toward a better understanding of the national need for advancement of deprived segments of the society. The openness of the 'haves' to give a helping hand and to be willing to assist in any way the 'have-nots' is of crucial importance. In the state of Israel it appears that there have been signs of a beginning of that openness and awareness following the social uneasiness at the beginning of the 1970s. It is highly recommended, therefore, that this should be strengthened and maintained.

Active involvement: At the same time it is most important to encourage deprived members of society and the disadvantaged to play a more active role in the process of their advancement. Social programmes as well as educational institutions should aim at educating needy members of society to take advantage of available facilities and to train themselves to be as independent as possible by equipping themselves with skills and higher or advanced education. There should always be a public finger on the pulse of this process in order not to lose control and hence develop a rather passive and parasitic dependent segment of the society.

Summary

Deprivation within Israeli society has some unique and rather troublesome characteristics: the high correlation between the deprived segment of society and place of origin presents a dangerous social phenomenon. A thorough study of the factors that brought this situation about and analysis of proposals for rectifying it are of high national priority. While absorbing large waves of newcomers into the social framework founded by Western-oriented leaders, many obstacles had to be overcome. In the course of time several approaches in social welfare policies were employed and tested. Thus, while a huge social process has been taking place in creating a new Israeli society, a few mistakes have been detected and are yet to be rectified.

It is suggested that in the corrective process the use of 'normal' educational frameworks and those unique to the Israeli community be employed. Advancement of deprived people within such frameworks will bring about a twofold solution: enhancing their personal qualifications and thus bringing them back to the productive mainstream, and simultaneously strengthening their self-image through their joint activities and integration with general social and educational institutions.

21 WELFARE POLICY IN ISRAEL: THE DOMAIN OF EDUCATION

Elad Peled

Welfare Policies: Definitions

Of the many definitions of 'welfare policy', the one which is most appropriate for my purpose is the following:

> Welfare policy is a policy 'that provides economic security and social services for certain categories or all of its citizens; that redistributes its resources from the wealthier to the poorer; that takes responsibility for the basic well-being of all of its citizens' (Franz Xavier Kaufman, 1983). A policy that 'provides rights of access and does little or nothing to promote greater equality in terms of outcomes' (Abel-Smith, 1983).

This definition is the one which guides our selection of criteria to examine Israel's educational policy as a specific domain of its national welfare policy.

Criteria for Examining Educational Policy

All definitions of welfare policy consider educational services to be a major element in the general welfare services. We suggest four criteria to examine and evaluate its success or failure: access, allocation of resources, selection and assignment, and provision of self-image and social prestige. These criteria will be used in examining educational policies in regard to different target populations. The preference or deprivation of different target populations will express 'who wins — who loses' (Rivlin, 1971), or 'who gets what, when, how' (Lasswell, 1958). Specifically, the preference of one group of people above the others will express the politics of educational policy.

In a formal schematic way, our model shows the following:

Criteria for Examining Educational Policy as a Welfare Policy

1. The Criteria	2. Alternative Policies	3. Target Populations defined by:
1.1 Access to Education	2.1 Equal Opportunities	3.1 Race
1.2 Selection and Assignment	2.2 Differential Opportunities	3.2 Nationality
1.3 Allocation of Resources		3.3 Ethnicity
1.4 Provision of self-image and prestige/status		3.4 Religion
		3.5 Class
		3.6 Regional Geography

Welfare policy, in general, is not the outcome of a compassion for the poor, the weak or the disadvantaged, or a policy of benefaction. It is, rather, the outcome of the combination of an interaction between two factors: the political power of the target population and the dominant groups, and the ideological perceptions of social norms and values, such as equality and justice. In our context, 'values' are the 'norms and principles which people apply in decision making, the criteria they use in choosing which of the alternative courses of action to follow or whether to make no decisions at all'. (Jacob, 1971, p. 251).

The Israeli case-study illustrates and substantiates our hypothesis. This study is limited only to education of disadvantaged Jewish children whose origins are from Mid-eastern and North African countries (Sephardim–Oriental Jews).

Israel's Educational Policy and its Implementation Target Populations

Welfare policy is characterised by, among other things, a preference for deprived and underprivileged groups, in order to provide them with equal opportunities compared to other privileged groups (Perlman, 1981, p. 15). This preference, as well as ideological and political constellations, are expressed already by the definitition of the target population.

One aspect of educational policy is its ability to cope with 'pupils characterized by the syndrome of deprivation and disadvantage' (Minkowitz, 1969, pp. 17-40; Passow, 1970). This syndrome is experienced by: (a) low learning achievements, below the standard norms; (b) learning difficulties, primarily in understanding, making linkages, applications and conceptualisation; (c) low motivation for learning and for intellectual interest. Educational policy is a set of government decisions (local or national) enhancing 'allocation of values' (material and non-material) and formation of plans (goals, means and methods) for education (Easton, 1953; Dahl, 1963; Lasswell and Kaplan, 1950; Dye, 1972).

Policy is aimed at a group of people, characterised by distinct traits. The preference of one group over others shows 'who gets what, when, how' (Lasswell, 1958). Subsequently, by looking at the definitions of target population one may deduce the political priorities and preferences of the ruling groups.

Looking at the changing definitions of the target populations for educational policy in Israel, one may discern a clear political trend (Peled, 1983). In the 1940s, it is perceived as a marginal group, called 'street children' — children who dropped out of schools. The criterion is school attendance. In the 1950s it is perceived and defined as 'immigrant children'. The criterion is immigration.

In the early 1960s, it is more specific: Sephardim–Oriental children (attributing countries of origin to immigration). In the late 1960s, the 1970s and early 1980s, it is 'Teunei Tipuach' (the Hebrew expression for 'needing to be nurtured and fostered').

The hidden trait is ethnic. It concerns primarily (80 per cent and more) Jews of Sephardic and Oriental (Mid-Eastern and North African) origin. In our further analysis, we are using ethnic origins to evaluate Israel's educational policies according to four criteria: access to the school system, including their different levels (elementary, secondary, higher); selection and assignment of children to schools and within schools, following socio-political criteria; allocation of resources to the different target populations; provision of self-image and prestige to the different ethnic groups (dominant and subordinate).

Access

Two basic laws underlie Israel's policy of access to education. One is the law of compulsory education (1949), which imposes on children and parents the obligation of school attendance between the ages of 5 and 16 and declares the state's responsibility to finance this education. Below the age of 5, education is heavily subsidised by the government. Secondary education for the ages of 17 to 18 is free but not compulsory. The law of state education (1953) opens to parents a free choice between state-religious and state-secular schools. Consequently, these laws made access to schools free and equal for all. The figures shown in Table 21.1 illustrate this argument.

Selection and Assignment

There is no social selection and assignment of children to schools (elementary and junior high) other than geographical zoning and religious/secular choice (Stanner, 1966, pp. 119, 139-42). Beyond the tenth grade, a system of selection and assignment is operating, based upon merit-achievement criteria (Bentwich, 1965, pp. 86-93).

A barrier of selection separates secondary education from higher education, based upon merit-achievement criteria. An inner-school selection and assignment operates on the same criteria, resulting in a tracking system within schools, the result of which is that most of the lowest tracks are composed of Sephardi–Oriental children, whereas most of the highest tracks are composed of Ashkenasi children.

Allocation of Resources

One of the most common criteria for examining policy is by seeing how resources are allocated, who gains and who loses, who gets what, when and how. Looking at Israel's allocation of resources to the various target populations, one gets the impression that affirmative action is implemented significantly (Raziel, 1978, 64-5): in 1973 (about ten years after the beginning of the educational compensatory policy) schools whose children were predominantly disadvantaged showed 55 per cent more teaching hours per pupil

Table 21.1: Formal Years of Schooling (percentage, selected years)

Years in School	1961[a]		1975[b]		1980[c]					TOTAL
	Born Asia-Africa	Born Europe-America	Born Asia-Africa	Born Europe-America	Born Asia-Africa	Born Europe-America	Israeli Born As-Af	Born to Father Born Eu-Am	Born to Father Born Israel	
0	31.5	3.2	21.6	2.6	19.4	2.6	1.0	0.4	0.6	0.8
1-4	10.1	7.6	6.6	5.9	6.0	6.0	0.9	0.4	1.0	0.7
5-8	36.2	37.9	33.3	28.0	30.8	25.6	17.2	4.6	10.6	11.2
9-12	19.2	38.5	31.5	40.0	34.9	39.2	70.3	54.1	64.9	63.2
13+	3.0	12.8	7.0	22.9	8.9	26.6	10.6	40.5	22.9	24.1
TOTAL	100.0	100.0	100.0	100.0	100.0	100.0	100.0	100.0	100.0	100.0

Sources: a. 1961 — CBS, Population and Housing Census (1961), Table 28. b. 1975 — CBS, St. Abstract of Israel 27 (1976), p. 589. c. 1980 — CBS, St. Abstract of Israel 32 (1981), p. 608, Tab. XXII/I

than regular schools. In 1948, this figure increased to 91 per cent more hours. (Teaching hours compose 77 per cent of per-pupil cost.) This is only one indicator of an affirmative action allocation policy.

Provision of Self-image and Prestige

Group identity is the first step toward high self-image and ethnic resurgence in order to generate more political power (Ensman, 1977, p. 388; Weingrod, 1929. p. 60). The development of ethnic culture by ethnic groups is instrumental in that process.

Israel's cultural policy and its ethnic culture aspect encouraged a uniform culture, emanating from the dominant-group culture (Ashkenasim) in the 1940s to the early 1960s, through encouragement of ethnic folklore in the late 1960s through the middle 1970s, to fostering and developing Sephardim–Oriental culture and heritage since the late 1970s (Peled, 1984).

Ideological Perceptions of Educational Policy

Reiterating and reinforcing the above-mentioned definitions of 'ideological values', we would like to emphasise that 'ideologies thus become guides to the selective perception and recall of information' (K. Deutsch, 1970, p. 9). Ideological values in their 'operative' meaning (Seliger, 1970) are principal guides of policy.

The concept of 'equality' is one of the major principal guides of Israel's social policies. It is, therefore, interesting to look at the dynamic operative change of this concept during the last several decades. In the thirties and the forties, 'equalities' had an almost magic power. It was a dominant super-value, expressed in the extreme by the kibbutz way of life and an egalitarian-ascetic lifestyle. Its culture rejects competitive achievement as a leading educational concept.

In the 1950s, facing massive immigration, 'equality' in education means 'formal' equality, i.e. all children get, formally, the same resources and treatment. The outcome is, obviously, a growing gap between the privileged and the underprivileged children.

In the 1960s, 'formal equality' is substituted by the concept of 'equal educational opportunities', which leads subsequently to 'affirmative action' in regard to the disadvantaged children, who happen to be, mainly, Sephardim—Oriental Jews.

Political Power of Sephardim—Oriental Jews

Political power of a group may be measured by its electoral potential, indicated by its demographic size and by its political representation in the 'key' political bodies. As for the first indicator, the percentage of Sephardim—Orientals went from 23 per cent in 1949 to 52.5 per cent in 1982.

As for political representation, notwithstanding a large gap between Ashkenazi and Sephardi representations, there is an increase in Sephardi political representations (Smooha, 1978, pp. 197-8) (see Table 21.2). Consequently, their impact on policy became stronger.

Table 21.2: Sephardi Political Representation

Position	1955 %	1973 %
Knesset (parliament) members	8.8	16.7
Heads of local authorities	11.5	33.7
Local councillors	23.6	44.3

Policy Outcomes

Whether we are minimalists, defining educational (welfare) policy as providing only basic educational services to all of our citizens, or maximalists, regarding educational (welfare) policy as aiming at narrowing the educational gaps between children according to socio-economic or ethnic traits, we have to admit the following facts in evaluating Israel's welfare policy in education:

(a) access to schooling has been open and it is now free and non-discriminating according to any ascriptive or socio-economic criteria;
(b) selection and assignment within the school systems, following

merit and learning-achievement criteria ultimately becomes, to some extent, *ipso facto* ethnic differentiating;

(c) allocation of resources has attempted to compensate under-privileged groups of children;

(d) educational policy encouraged and promoted the self-image and prestige of the Sephardim–Orientals by fostering their ethnic culture and tradition.

However, based on ethnic characteristics, one may observe that equality between Sephardim–Oriental and Ashkenazi children has not been achieved. Moreover, even the educational gaps have not been narrowed significantly (Levy and Chen, 1976, p. 50). But if a welfare policy provides rights of access and does little or nothing to promote greater equality in terms of outcomes (Abel-Smith, 1983), Israel's educational policy is a classic, successful welfare policy.

References

Abel-Smith, Brian, 1983, 'The Major Problems of the Welfare State: defining the issues', in a conference on 'The Welfare State and its Aftermath', Jerusalem, 1983.

Bentwich, Joseph S., 1965, *Education in Israel*, Routledge & Kegan Paul, London.

Dahl, Robert A., 1963-76, *Modern Political Analysis*, 3rd edition, Prentice-Hall, Englewood Cliffs.

Deutsch, Karl W., 1970, *Politics and Government*, Houghton Mifflin Comp., Boston.

Dye, Thomas R., 1972, *Understanding Public Policy*, Prentice-Hall, Englewood Cliffs.

Easton, David, 1953, *The Political System*, Alfred A. Knopf, New York.

Ensman, Milton J. (ed.), 1977, *Ethnic Conflict in the Western World*, Cornell University Press, Ithaca.

Jacob, Philip E., 1971, 'Leaders' Values and the Dynamics of Community Integration: A Four-Nation Community Study' in Bonjean, Charles M., Clark, Terry N. and Leneberry, Robert L., *Community Politics*, The Free Press, New York, Collier-Macmillan, London.

Lasswell, Harold D., 1958, *Politics: Who Gets What, When, How*, A Meridian Book, New York.

Lasswell, Harold D. and Kaplan, Abraham, 1950, *Power and Society*, Yale University Press, New Haven and London.

Lewy Arie and Chen Michael, 1976, 'Closing or Widening of the Achievement Gap', *Studies in Educational Administration* (Hebrew), no. 4, Fall, Haifa.

Minkowitz, Abraham, 1969, *The Disadvantaged Child*, The School of Education, The Hebrew University, Jerusalem.

Passow, A. Harry (ed.), 1970, *Deprivation and Disadvantage*, Unesco Institute for Education, Hamburg.

Peled, Elad, 1983, 'Ideology and Political Power — Determinants of Educational Policy' in *Megamot*, December (Hebrew), Jerusalem.

Peled, Elad, 1984, 'Ethnic Culture as a Political Resource', to be published.

Perlman, Robert, 1981, *The Welfare State Under Stress: How will it Cope?*, Paul Berwald School of Social Work, The Hebrew University of Jerusalem, Jerusalem.

Raz-el Ofra, 1978, *Compensation and Welfare — For Whom? A Re-evaluation of Resources Allocation in Elementary Education*, Ministry of Education and Culture, Jerusalem.

Rivlin, Alice, 1971, *Systematic Thinking for Social Action*, The Brookings Institution, Washington D.C.

Seliger, Martin, 1970, 'Fundamental and Operative Ideology: The Two Principal Dimension of Political Argumentation', in *Policy Sciences*, 1, 325-38.

Smooha, Sami, 1978, *Israel: Pluralism and Conflict*, University of California Press, Berkeley and Los Angeles.

Stanner, Ruth, 1966, *Education Laws*, Jerusalem.

Weingrod, Alex, 1979, 'Recent Trends in Israeli Ethnicity', *Ethnic and Racial Studies*, vol. 2, no. 1, January, 55-65.

Xavier-Kaufman, Franz, 1983, 'The Emergence of the Welfare-State — Challenges and Responses', in the Conference on 'The Welfare State and its Aftermath', Jerusalem.

22 THE PROTEST OF A DISADVANTAGED POPULATION IN A WELFARE STATE

Yael Azmon

Introduction

The expansion of social welfare policy in Israel has not been accompanied by very much social thought. No serious attempt has been made on the basis either of a social-democratic or liberal-conservative ideology to examine social developments and to assess their desirability. Thought in the realm of social policy it seems has come to a halt. The various parties have not displayed interest in this field. Nevertheless, social developments sprang up all the time as 'facts on the ground', as the cumulative consequences of various social welfare programmes and of wage agreements that bear the imprint of the power position of the groups of workers involved in them. This combination created an open field for the presentation of new ideas by protest groups.

Signs seem to indicate that protest group activities, which first emerged as an accepted phenomenon in Israel in the late 1960s and early 1970s, are becoming a regular feature of Israeli politics in the 1980s as well. By protest groups I mean groups using collective action that is outside the institutionalised channels supplied by government or by political parties for influencing the selection of governmental personnel and/or policies. In dealing with protest groups, it is a common practice to distinguish between two main groups — those that develop in the middle class and those that spring up among the lower class, the disadvantaged population as I prefer to call it. (The term 'disadvantaged population', which is used in Israel in place of 'lower class' is defined by social service agencies on the basis of two economic criteria — the income and housing density — and by an educational criterion — years of father's schooling.) The characterisation of the participation of the poor, as in one way or another different from that of the middle class, is an accepted thesis in studies of protest activity (Frances Fox Piven and Richard A. Cloward, 1977).

289

In this paper I will discuss various aspects of protest activity, concentrating on the disadvantaged population in Israel. I will examine the features that characterise protest groups and the conditions that enabled them to emerge. In particular, I will point out some new conceptions of social welfare that have developed in Israeli politics in wake of the activities of these groups; all these in the light of the question of whether protest activity among the middle class and that which develops in the disadvantaged population exhibit different or similar patterns.

Protest political activity in the groups of the middle class in Israel is not an alternative to conventional political activity; nor is protest an activity typical of those who are outside the political party frameworks, or the preserve of citizens who are denied the opportunity of action within the usual frameworks. That is to say, protest activity is not a substitute for conventional activity but is a supplement to it, a different means used along with others to achieve specific goals. This phenomenon — the instrumental use of protest in combination with conventional political activity — is not unique to the middle class in Israel. We find a similar tendency among the middle class in Western countries — in Europe and America. Such findings emerged once again from a comprehensive comparative study recently conducted by Samuel Barnes and Max Kasse and reported in their book *Political Action* (1980). Israel also resembles those countries in the increase in the level of protest activity among the middle class. Where Israel differs from those Western countries is in the emergence of protest activity in combination with conventional political activity among the disadvantaged population. Such combined activity was not found in the lower class movements in the Western countries examined by Barnes and Kasse.

The protest activity of the disadvantaged population, which in the 1950s was infrequent and sporadic, intensified and came to be used in a much more directed and calculating manner that combines it with conventional political activity.

The participation patterns of the disadvantaged population and of the middle class thus appear to have converged with respect to three aspects: the intensification of protest activity, the instrumental use of protest, and its combination with conventional political activity.

The protest groups which developed in these different strata are similar in another two respects. Protest among the disadvantaged strata in Israel is not revolutionary activity aimed at effecting change in the social order; rather, it is an attempt to influence specific portions of social policy within the existing system. In this respect, too, the protest groups of the disadvantaged population do not differ from those of the middle class.

The protest groups of the different classes also resemble one another in their controlled use of means: each protest group sets for itself clear limitations and lines beyond which it will not go. Those lines differ for the different groups. For one, it may be refraining from any illegal actions, another may allow assaults on private and public property but not on persons, another may tolerate a certain measure of violence but bars the use of weapons.

I

We will describe two protest movements among the disadvantaged urban population active in Jerusalem, the Ohalim ('tents') and Dai ('enough'). The hard core of each of these groups includes only a few score individuals, but each of them is capable of mobilising hundreds of people in the neighbourhood.

Ohalim and Dai are movements of young people of similar background. The people who are at the core of these two groups are characterised, to some extent or other, by rejection from military service, irregular employment and police records. The ties among the members of these groups were built up in a similar manner: by growing up together and participating in the neighbourhood gangs. The activity of Dai is more recent than that of the Ohalim. It began about two years ago, following a surge of political organisation in the community as a result of the introduction into the neighbourhood of new resources through 'Project Renewal'.

The formation of the Ohalim group can be traced back to 1972 and the initiative of a lawyer of North African origin who, after immigrating to the country, shifted the focus of his activity and began working with a street gang in Jerusalem's Gonen quarter. In the early stages of his activity, he launched protest theatre in the neighbourhoods, and in the late 1970s, in conjunction with street gang leaders, organised a neighbourhood group called Ohel Yosef. The name Ohel Yosef was taken from the title of a play presented by the group called 'Joseph Went Down to Gonen'.

Ohalim formed ties with other disadvantaged neighbourhoods

in Jerusalem and encouraged the establishment of similar bodies, which joined together in an umbrella organisation. This city-wide group organised as a legal body and set as its objective the social struggle to improve education, culture and housing in Jerusalem's disadvantaged neighbourhoods.

From the time of the earliest stages of its organisation, this group was not averse to accepting financial and organisational aid from the Jerusalem Municipality and the Jerusalem Fund, even as it conducted demonstrations and squat-ins.

In order to gain public attention, Ohalim carried out media-attracting actions, the best known of which was the establishment of a 'settlement' called Ohel Moreh. In August 1980, a number of families from the Gonen quarter squatted on land near Malha, in Jerusalem, land owned by the Israel Land Authority. In this action, Ohalim succeeded in involving the mayor of Jerusalem, his assistants, and the minister of the interior in the negotiations for their eviction. The leaders of the group even had a meeting with the prime minister. The initiators of the action also managed to get the deputy mayor to serve as a mediator who acted to block their forcible eviction by the police. They received a promise of the mayor's help in obtaining public lands for the establishment of a co-operative urban neighbourhood for a group of young families in the neighbourhood whose housing situation was bad. We shall present this plan in a more elaborate light later on.

Along with these protest activities, the group of organisers succeeded in gaining leadership positions on the steering committee of 'Project Renewal' in the neighbourhood. ('Project Renewal' is a national undertaking and is the major welfare programme in Israel in the 1980s.) Their members joined the committee and their leader was elected chairman. It should be noted that to achieve this position, the members threatened violence against residents of the neighbourhood and against representatives of the institutions operating within the framework of the project. As a result, the group obtained legitimate powers within the institutionalised system of the steering committee, which provided it with new opportunities for using the public resources of the project to gain supporters in the community.

In the creation of the power base of this protest group, we witness a combination of threats of violence, the authority of office and manipulative use of public resources. These indicate the acquisition of a high level of political know-how. It is expressed in the shift from means in the domain of conventional activity to unconventional means, as well as in the very use of a broad range of means to amass power. What is more, the competition and squabbling between various government bodies, which often is an obstacle for needy groups in their attempts to solve their problems, was exploited skilfully by the leaders of the neighbourhood groups to their own benefit. It should be noted that these political skills were created in the weakest groups within the disadvantaged neighbourhoods themselves.

Considering that the protest groups among the disadvantaged population in urban neighbourhoods have a marked 'Oriental' country-of-origin colouring, it is noteworthy that the leadership of these groups imposed limitations on itself in the use of country-of-origin polarisation as a means of struggle. This can perhaps be explained by the deep-rooted awareness in Israel that fully fledged conflict along country-of-origin lines is an excessively grave danger for a country in a state of protracted war with its neighbours. To employ such means would not be compatible with the principle accepted by all groups that the unity of the Jewish people must be preserved, and the destruction of that unity by separatism or country-of-origin conflict must be avoided. (See S. Hasson, *International Journal of Urban and Regional Research*, forthcoming.)

II

The convergence of the patterns of action of the disadvantaged population with those of the middle class has its roots in a process of learning in the disadvantaged groups, effected by the flow of information and guidance from community workers and volunteers, and the receipt of funding assistance for activities from various establishment bodies, such as the Jerusalem Municipality and the Jewish Agency.

The similarity between the activities of these groups and those of the middle-class protest groups is also a result of imitation and attempts at organised co-operation between the movements. What was called a 'settlement' in the Malha quarter was meant as an imitation of the kind of activity carried out by Gush Emunim; the term 'settlement' adopted with intentional mimicry. The influence of the other middle-class group, 'Peace Now', is conveyed directly in attempts at co-operation between it and the Ohalim movement.

The aim of the co-operation, as far as Peace Now is concerned, is to translate objectives at the level of individual and neighbourhood deprivation into a matter of national priorities. A measure of success in achieving that objective was reflected in the adoption, by various groups among the disadvantaged population, of the slogan 'Invest in the neighbourhoods, not in the [West Bank] settlements'. For Peace Now, this co-operation has a twofold objective: in the short run, to create pressure on the government on the issue of settlements, and in the long run, to undermine support for the Likud government among groups of citizens who are considered to be its staunchest supporters. It should be noted that Peace Now achieved only limited success in this latter objective: those who accepted that slogan were not prepared to regard it as criticism of Prime Minister Begin's leadership or as expressing dissociation from Likud policy in general, but only as an attempt to exert influence on the specific issue of increasing the flow of economic resources to the disadvantaged neighbourhoods.

The members of the Ohalim movement are very cautious about establishing a permanent or binding tie with other political groups, not to mention with political parties. They want to receive support from all parties and all political bodies, but not to be a part of them, and particularly, not to be dominated or directed by them. They are prepared, as they say, 'to be political but not party political', a slogan which is taken from the lexicon of protest groups among the middle class.

The leadership of the Ohalim group has so far succeeded in walking the tightrope of collaboration in order to receive aid from political parties while preserving autonomy. This achievement required more than a small measure of political skill, which, as we have noted, was acquired by this protest movement over the last years.

The Israeli experience points to the fact that the lack of higher education among the lower class does not prevent it from adopting patterns of activity that are very similar to those of the middle class: patterns of activity which combine protest activity with conventional activity. While activity of this sort requires political skill, that skill does not depend on higher education. Lower-class groups in Israel can also acquire political skills through trial and error, a process of learning which does not depend on higher education. Learning through trial and error depends on the receipt of reinforcement of the interaction between the protest group and the authorities. The reinforcement consists of success in influencing government policy in those areas in which the group does battle. Such successes do not necessarily stem from the group's control of large quantities of resources or from sophistication in the use of resources. The success may well derive from the vulnerability of the opposite side, namely the authorities, and their responsiveness (as a consequence of that) to the group's demands. The authorities are vulnerable because of their somewhat disadvantageous position *vis-à-vis* the protest group, especially when the group has recourse to violence. The coverage of such events by the mass media places the authorities in a situation in which they can not appear 'photogenic': if they put down the eruption of violence, they appear oppressive; if they do not put it down, they appear weak. For that reason, the authorities prefer not to be 'photographed' together with violence, and to prevent such events from occurring. The groups which sprang up among the disadvantaged strata are well aware of this and are expert in exploiting the situation in which the authorities are trapped. At times, the mere threat of carrying out an action of violent protest is a resource they command in negotiations with the authorities. Thus, the desire of the authorities (on the national level and on the local level) to avoid a frontal clash with groups from the disadvantaged population has, at times, induced them to make concessions to the protest groups, beyond what they had initially intended. This gave rise to successes, which provided the basis for the continuation of the trial and error learning process.

III

To illustrate new conceptions of welfare policy initiated by these protest groups, we may consider housing policy. It should be noted that the most important factor in the creation of economic disparity among the employed population is not wage differences. Rather, the great economic gap among the employed population is a result of the great difference in the value of the Israeli family's principal economic asset — its housing. The public investment given to populations of different background for the solution of housing problems contributed to the creation of this gap. When the public investment given to a large family with many children in a disadvantaged neighbourhood took the form of an apartment in that same neighbourhood in a high-rise — in which the other apartments were also occupied by large families — the value of that apartment declined over the years, or, at least, did not rise in real terms; that family's capital did not expand. By contrast, an investment of the same size given to a family in a quarter with a high standard of construction, in a suburb, led to a steep rise in a matter of years in the value of the family's holdings. A solution of the second sort was offered to families who were able to invest in the plot and the construction of the house.

Another phenomenon which must be taken into account is the fact that within the disadvantaged population less attention is paid to preserving the quality of life in the building and the neighbourhood, and that families in that population, especially those with many children, are unable to keep up or improve their apartments and surroundings. That, too, leads to a decline in the value of their apartments, especially when families of this sort are housed together. In other words, the characteristics of the families in the disadvantaged population themselves bring down the value of their apartments. That being the case, it may be asked whether public investment should set for itself the goal of 'compensating' the problematic families for their unattractive features as neighbours which lower the value of their apartments? Should the goal be the allocation of resources to the disadvantaged population, or at least to those portions within it that are relatively mobile, of a magnitude and under conditions that would enable them to participate in the construction of a prestigious neighbourhood heterogeneous in terms of the country of origin and class of its residents? That might be a way to overcome the problem of the gap between the different classes, and could be accomplished by allocating resources to potential residents in such magnitude so as also to attract a population of a different background, who would be offered, as it were, suitable monetary 'compensation' for the negative social value of the residents of the neighbourhood.

An initiative of this sort has recently been launched in two disadvantaged Jerusalem neighbourhoods by protest groups led by young people. The Ohalim movement in Gonen set up a body, which is registered as a formal association, whose declared purpose is the establishment of a co-operative urban settlement. It is demanding pubic funding in the form of a grant of a site near the city and a public loan large enough to enable the erection of one-family houses for young couples from the neighbourhood, as well

as from other neighbourhoods. The population of the new neighbourhood must include 'Ashkenazi' (Western) young couples of
what the Gonen group calls 'good' social background. Since the
group includes violent persons the expectation is clearly that the
public investment would be of such value as to counter their own
negative social value, and would make joining also worthwhile for
families from other segments of the population. The group expects
that if those who join from other parts of the population in fact
receive adequate 'compensation' for the negative characteristics of
this population, this solution may gain currency as a solution to the
problem of the social gap. The demand for economic compensation for vices which developed in these groups, on the grounds
that society at large is to be blamed for the emergence of such
vices, is a novelty in conceptions of welfare policy in Israel.

The other protest group, Dai, from another Jerusalem neighbourhood, Musrara, issued a contrary demand in the realm of
housing. In the beginning of 1983, representatives of the group
conducted a squat-in strike in a public shelter; their slogan was
'Musrara for the people of Musrara', by which they meant that
apartments in the neighbourhood should be allocated to those
born in the neighbourhood. While the Gonen group is fighting to
obtain housing outside the neighbourhood, and only outside it, the
Musrara group is insisting on housing in Musrara and nowhere
else. How is it that two groups sharing a similar problem are
fighting for the very opposite solutions?

The difference does not reflect a difference in social outlook; it
is the result, rather, of economic calculation as to the anticipated
future value of apartments in Musrara and Gonen. Since Musrara
is located at the heart of the city, along the seam that joins the
eastern and western halves, in an area where vacant sites for building are scarce, the assumption is that the value of property holdings in the neighbourhood will rise. The assumption concerning
Gonen, by contrast, a neighbourhood on the fringes of the city, is
that the value of properties there will not rise, and in those sections
which are densely populated it will even decline.

In setting objectives, the protest groups in each of the neighbourhoods are guided by their own economic logic. Each of them
also enlists a suitable myth in the presentation of its demands. The
people from Gonen base their demand for housing outside the
neighbourhood on the contention that only somewhere new can
they establish a settlement, which, while it is an urban neighbour-

hood, in the city, will also be a co-operative settlement in the best tradition of co-operative settlement in the country. The Musrara people claim that what they want, as natives of Musrara who are deeply attached to it, is to live their future life in the neighbourhood, and not have to roam to distant fields in order to obtain reasonable housing.

Thus, new solutions in the realm of social welfare policy spring from below, from the protest groups. These groups have a good deal of skill in combining protest with conventional means and are articulate in adopting the appropriate myths in Israeli society in presenting their demands. Starting from a very poor initial position — these groups developed among the weakest parts of the disadvantaged neighbourhoods — they built up a bargaining position in their relations with the governing bodies. The groups which stem from disadvantaged urban neighbourhoods have been raising demands anchored in a new social conception — that of 'compensation' for their own negative characteristics. The moral notion underlying this conception is the casting of blame for the presence of the negative traits, including crime and violence among some members of these groups, on society as a whole. Society is to blame, since social deprivation in the past is what caused the development of these traits, consequently, society is morally bound to compensate them for this past deprivation. These movements succeeded in translating the social moral conception of historical deprivation and society's responsibility to make amends for it into operative demands on the level of policy, the mobilisation of resources, and the use of them in a sophisticated and effective way to promote their demands. They employ effectively, a broad range of means, which includes, as we have noted, violence.

Discussion

Protest groups among the disadvantaged groups exhibit instrumental use of protest, and its combination with conventional political activity in a way which is both sophisticated and effective. This has blurred the distinction between middle-class and lower-class patterns of political participation.

Protest activity has important implications for the broader subject of participation among the poor. To begin with, since the Israeli sample shows that class divisions predict patterns of political protest less well than is usually assumed in the research literature, the meaning of the concept of poverty in this context should be elucidated.

It should be taken into account that the situation described as poverty is subject to change. As the overall standard of living rises, and the poverty line is drawn anew, the population defined as poor may come to include income groups whose standard of living in absolute terms is higher than that of the population that had been defined as poor in the past, even if the difference between the standards of living of the various groups remains constant. This change in poverty in absolute terms has great relevance to the issue of participation. Control by the poor of a greater quantity and variety of independent resources increases their possibilities for participation: The control of economic resources, education, information, leisure time and the like provide means for participation while their scarcity impeded political participation by the poor in the past.

The control of resources within a population defined as poor may also be increased by the injection of public resources and their allocation by citizen participation frameworks, which are usually community level frameworks. Such a policy of resource allocation by bodies in which the residents themselves take part in decision-making aims at neutralising the influence of the poor population's limited resources on its possibilities for influencing its life environment. It is doubtful, however, whether the poor population's balance of resources can be substantially changed by allocating resources on the community level, without a concomitant change in the marginal position of its inhabitants in the overall employment and economic system (Peter Marris, 1982).

Another source expanding the possibilities of resource use by the poor is related to a change in the cirucmstances that determine the worthwhileness of protest as a resource for influencing policy. A general social process of increasing legitimacy for protest activity as a political means reduces the danger of sanctions by the governing power, and thereby reduces the cost of protest activity. Given that the extent to which protest is actually used is based on considerations of the gains it is likely to bring and the cost to be paid by the protesting group (William A. Gamson, 1975), a reduction in the cost of using protest creates conditions conducive to its use. Furthermore, since there is a general lack of resources in the poor population, and since protest, unlike economic resources and education is a resource that always exists potentially, an increase in its worthwhileness and thus of its actual use leads to enlargement of the overall quantity of resources controlled by a poor population.

An increase in the overall command of resources, whatever its source, increases the poor population's possibilities for participation. Moreover, it may be that the possibility of combining resources from different sources is itself of importance. Thus, the use of protest as a resource for political action may be influenced by the extent of control of resources from other sources. That is because the worthwhileness of employing protest, and consequently its availability as a resource, may be influenced by the extent to which cessation of the group's normal activity is a sanction for other groups or for the governing power — because of the latter's dependence on services or goods that the group supplies (William A. Gamson, 1975).

In other words, it appears that apart from the cumulative value of the control by the poor of a greater quantity of resources from various sources as a factor influencing the possibilities for participation, the combination, in different ways, of these resources is itself of special value.

The value of the combination of resources from different sources touches on a probem we have not dealt with so far, and which shall only be mentioned here — that is, the problem of the lack of autonomy in the activity of the citizen participation frameworks in relation to the governing power bodies that have a bearing on that activity. By lack of autonomy is meant a situation in which decision-making in the participation frameworks is directed by governing power bodies external to them. This problem, as Gittel notes (Marilyn Gittell, 1980), is especially acute among poor populations, where the organisational frameworks on the neighbourhood level, and local leadership are dependent on external sources of public money. The dependence of the leadership of such participation frameworks on the governing power bodies that provide the resources puts the value of these frameworks into question and is liable to make a fiction of citizen participation.

When participation in conventional community frameworks is combined with the planned use of protest — a combination which in our case was the result of penetration of the conventional participation framework in the underpriviledged neighbourhoods by protest groups — the chances are greater that the participation by groups from among the poor population will be autonomous. This combination enables use to be made of the public resources provided in conventional frameworks, while keeping the dependence on the governing power bodies that provide the resources in balance. This is accomplished by the application of counter-pressure on those governing power bodies by means of protest activity, or the threat to use protest. In any event, the problem of the extent of the autonomy of the political activity of groups from among the poor, and the conditions conducive to it, is a separate subject deserving study in and of itself.

References

Avizohar, Meir, *Money to All*, Tel-Aviv, Hadar, 1978 (in Hebrew).

Azmon Yael, 'The 1981 Elections and the Changing Fortunes of the Israeli Labour Party', *Government and Opposition*, vol. 16, no. 4, 1981, pp. 432-46.

Barnes, Samuel H. & Max Kaase, *Political Action*, London, Sage, 1979.

Bell, Daniel, *The End of Ideology*, NY, Free Press, 1967.

Gamson, William A., *The Strategy of Social Protest*, Homewood, Illinois, Dorsey, 1975.

Gittell, Marilyn, *Limits to Citizen Participation*, Beverley Hills, California, Sage, 1980.

Hasson, Shlomo, 'The Emergence of an Urban Social Movement in Israeli Society — An Integrated Approach', *International Journal of Urban and Regional Research*, forthcoming.

Marris, Peter, *Community Planning and Conceptions of Change*, London, Kegan Paul, 1982.

Marshall, T.H., *Essays: Class, Citizenship and Social Development*, Westfort, Connecticut, Greenwood Press, 1976.

O'Brien, David J., *Neighbourhood Organization and Interest-Group Processes*, Princeton, Princeton University Press, 1975.

Piven, Frances Fox and Richard A. Cloward, *Poor People's Movements*, NY, Pantheon, 1977.

Thompson, D.F., *The Democratic Citizen*, Cambridge, Cambridge University Press, 1970.

23 SOME FORMS OF RESISTANCE TO THE WELFARE STATE

Dan Bavly

I would like to outline some forms of resistance to the welfare state and to the regulated economy as seen through the eyes of a practicing CPA whose personal experience as well as that of his *confrères* add an empirical dimension to the discussion.

There seem to be four more overt forms of resistance by free enterprise societies to attempts to regulate economies in general and to the welfare state in particular: (1) the 'subterranean economy', in which the individual or corporate entrepreneur and businessman opts out of the recorded economy; (2) the decision of large elements of the labour force to lower their productivity or to work shorter hours; (3) the increasing industrial unrest and strikes in the more advanced social welfare democracies; (4) emigration in search of economic opportunities (a subject of special sensitivity in Israel) despite the objective advantages of the welfare state.

Though some of these phenomena antedate the rise of the welfare state, their distinctive features were crystallised and are still dominating some of the reactions relating to the practices, if not the theories, of the welfare state. It seems to be axiomatic that unless virtually all of society agrees to the system and complies with it voluntarily, the effectiveness and efficacy of the social welfare state is impaired. What is, however, less generally realised is that actual opposition has today reached threatening proportions.

1. The Subterranean Economy

The 'subterranean economy' (or 'hidden economy' or 'black economy' as it was baptized by O. Blauer and R. Pauley respectively) is the most salient reaction to the growing interference of democratic governments in the economic process. Common to craftsmen and successful businessmen, it counteracts the strains and restraints put on the economy by regulations, taxations and subsidies. Although difficult to be quantitatively measured, this type of economy created a whole structure of a free enterprise economy in which the market asserts itself through tax avoidance and evasion; this operates not only on the fringes of the law but often beyond it. Gaining in strength, it is creating a new type of moral attitude while eroding the means on which the welfare state is based.

In many ways, this new type of resistance to regulated economy vindicates the theories of the older classical economists. It is a reaction to the new-Keynesian demand economists, who suggested that greater government intervention in the economy and the contribution to the gross national product would help resolve economic maladies.

I certainly believe that, as in all social welfare states and regulated economies with their high rates of taxation, so also the government in Israel has been waging a losing war against the growing mass of tax avoiders and evaders for the past dozen years or so.

For as long as: the state of the economy is shaky; the tax rates remain as high as they are; the tax code is verbose in form and cumbersome in content; and the civil service continues to be overworked and, all too often, ineffectual; then there is no chance that the standards of taxpayer compliance will improve. Furthermore, the fact that the courts of law have repeatedly ruled that paying taxes is purely a legal question and that, within the limits of legality, tax avoidance is a socially acceptable norm, has led the enterprising, creative, wealthy businessman to retain increasingly expensive tax consultants. These specialists advise him as to tax shelters and point out paths, at times quite simple, to tax evasion.

2. Enterprise Investment and Productivity

I will not go into details in describing how welfare policies have influenced reduced productivity as this phenomenon was discussed by others in this volume. But I would like to point out that economic welfare is more dependent upon the readiness of the society to invest its resources and by 1960, in some of the post-Second World War democracies, the pace of new investment had come close to a complete standstill. At the same time, the labour force augmented its salary demands despite lowered productivity. As a result, the growth of the gross national product (GNP) has gradually slowed down and, at times in some countries, even contracted. I would like to argue that social welfare ideology, with the emphasis on the optimal equitable distribution of resources, pays far too little attention to GNP growth and when the capital on which taxes have been avoided opts for the tax haven, it not only immediately erodes the wealth of the national economy, it also affects its future growth prospects by not being invested within the country and by failing to create opportunities for labour to be better or more competitive.

3. Institutional Labour Unrest

It remains debatable as to whether social services have actually been improved by governmental supervision. One can hardly argue that the average level of education has improved (although it has had other beneficial effects) since the systems became compulsory. Or on a different level: it is often heard from senior medical doctors that the progress of the medical profession in the more advanced social welfare states is considerably slower than in those democracies in which doctors and hospitals can, at least some of the time, charge reasonable market prices. Yet it seems to me that an increased governmental supervision of services generally leads to more strikes and labour unrest.

A particular characteristic of the welfare state system is the rather paradoxical disenchantment of the state employees — from postman to teacher to doctor — with the system that employs them. This was at the root of the 1983 strike by almost the entire Israel medical hospitalisation system; while Israeli doctors were not very interested in the social implications of their strike, they were expressing their general frustration with the cumbersome system, characterised by its heavily bureaucratised and impersonal structure which rested heavily upon their shoulders.

4. Emigration in Search of Economic Opportunities

I would like to stress one final point which to my mind can be best portrayed in Israel: namely emigration as another expression of dissatisfaction with the system.

Israel, like some other countries, provides a wider range of services than the countries the Israeli emigrants choose in their effort to improve their condition, opting in their search for better economic opportunities. The majority of the Israeli population is more dependent upon the state than the citizens of most other democracies. This dependence has possiby affected the entrepreneurial efforts of the Israelis to an extent that is impossible to quantify but which can certainly provoke more than speculation.

One way to try to assess the nature of this influence is to compare the behaviour of the Israelis in their country with communities of a similar social background overseas (such as the Israeli expatriates now living in the Jewish community in Israel), or members of the Moroccan Jewish community who, in the 1950s left Morocco for France and neighbouring Western European countries, rather than for Israel.

It is common knowledge that the Moroccan immigrants in Israel have had more absorption problems than most other groups. However, in contrast to their difficulties in Israel, their cousins in Europe have completely shed their ties with their past history and are now in the process of achieving an impressive record of successful settlement and prosperity. Some of them have created niches for themselves in the worlds of academic and political life.

Moreover, studies of the ethnic groups which emigrated to the United States after the Second World War, show that those coming from Israel have shown a higher sociometric status than immigrants from other countries, often setting up their businesses from scratch, be they small retail stores, cab ownership or high technology enterprises. It is of special interest that the majority of these people, before they left Israel, had not attempted to set up any sort of enterprise of their own.

There is little doubt that the social welfare services offered by the State of Israel to its citizens, whether born in the country or immigrants, are more extensive than those offered in the United States to immigrants from Israel or those which Moroccan expatriates find in Europe. Yet both groups appear to have found greater opportunities and a climate in which they perform more impressively and enjoy as good or better a lifestyle than they would have had in Israel!

Thus, emigration is another form of personal opposition to the social welfare state. Israel would certainly have been a more prosperous, happier state with a stronger economy, had it been successful in persuading those who left it or never came in the first place to stake their claim here and do in Israel what they later did so successfully elsewhere.

PART SIX

CONCLUDING REMARKS

24 THE WELFARE STATE AND THE TRANSFORMATION OF THE MODERN SOCIAL ORDER

S.N Eisenstadt

I would like to make a few concluding observations about some of the major problems of the welfare state which have been discussed in this volume.

The central problem to which I shall address myself relates to the ways in which the welfare state, in combination with what is usually called 'late capitalism', has transformed modern society in general and modern democracies in particular. (Some of these transformations have also taken place in non-democratic countries as well, above all in some totalitarian societies, but these are beyond the province of our discussion.)

I will not recapitulate here the points made in the introductory statement but, rather, I will use that as a point of departure, taking for granted those changes in class structure, patterns of political participation, etc. which have been enumerated there.

A very useful starting point for such an analysis is Karl Polanyi's famous work on the 'Great Transformation', in which he distinguished between three types of economic systems. The first, found mainly in relatively primitive societies, he called a system of reciprocity. He called the second, found in ancient kingdoms and empires, the redistributive system, in which the centre absorbs revenues in different forms and redistributes them according to different social and political criteria. The third and last one is the market system, which emerged with capitalism in the modern world and which, according to Polanyi, almost entirely superseded the former ones.

A crucial aspect of the welfare state is that it consitutes a reinstallation of redistributive principles which is evident throughout the whole set of social services, allocations and transfers which have been widely analysed in discussions of the welfare state and, of course, in this volume as well.

But the creation of the welfare state was not simply a reinstallation or reconstitution of the redistributive principle. The type of society which was created through this system, in conjunction with the new type of economic policies (primarily Keynsian), differed in three crucial aspects from the redistributive systems of ancient times.

First, it did not do away with the market mechanism and the ideology of economic growth, which constituted a basic part of its own values. Accordingly, it did not even put these market mechanisms into a subsidiary role, as was the case in most ancient kingdoms and empires. Rather, it instituted the new redistributive system in close conjunction with various market mechanisms of the economy. It attempted to regulate these mechanisms, but certainly did not abolish them.

The second major difference between this new society, created by the welfare state and the new economic policies on the one hand, and the older redistributive system on the other, lies in the political dimension. Here a good starting point might indeed be a look at one of the historical roots of the welfare state: the provision of social services, especially to the poor and the needy. This, as we have seen, preceded the fully fledged welfare state. The recipients of social services have been usually defined as 'clients'.

But the modern democratic welfare state has greatly transformed the nature of both the clients and the relationship that existed between them and the providers of the services which they received. The modern clients are certainly no longer either the old type of recipients of philanthropic services, nor are they the sort of clients which developed in many of the ancient kingdoms or city-states. What has happened here is that this type of relationship became almost conterminus with citizenship. As the system developed, the demands for welfare, allocations, services or transfers were voiced more and more frequently in the name of the general rights of citizens and gradually were transformed from claims for specific services into demands for far-reaching entitlements, claims which were made in the name of either the universal right as citizen or in the name of some new overall criteria of distributive justice.

The third difference between these ancient redistributive systems and the modern welfare system is related to the various aspects of so-called post-industrial society, especially with regard to the growth of the service sectors and the growing importance of educational qualifications. The first is, to some degree at least, in line with the more traditional redistributive types of societies, but the second is, of course, something entirely new.

Thus, what has happened here is a truly astonishing combination of patrimonial distributive arrangements, with an emphasis on economic growth (mostly through capitalist market mechanisms) and of a technologically sophisticated economy and educated class together with a highly democratic, sometimes almost populist tendency.

It is these crucial transformations in some of the overall characteristics of the late modern society which lie behind the far-reaching changes in political participation and organisation, in the class structure and, above all, in the patterns of political and social participation on which we have commented in the introductory statement and which have been abundantly discussed in this book. It is impossible to understand the new aspects of social life without taking into account these transformations.

Thus, it is in this framework that we can fully understand the changes in the role of professions to which Professor Bourricaud has referred, as well as the need for a reassessment of potential contributions of social sciences and scientists in helping to ameliorate the working of the various welfare state agencies which Professor Janowitz has stressed in his discussion. Here, one of the central problems is the tension between the professionals who tend to appropriate for themselves the right to define the 'needs' of different sectors of the population and the growing demand of such sectors to define their own needs and to translate them into entitlements.

From all of these points of view, we witness today the emergence of a rather new type of social order, with new parameters, problems and crises which cannot be fully understood in terms of the older paradigms.

The preceding discussion also has some implications for the formulation of policy studies in general and as related to the problems of the welfare state in particular. Many such studies use very sophisticated methods of analysis in application to different economic or societal sectors, such as health, educational, environmental and economic policies. Yet, when they address themselves to the overall macro-societal framework, they do not usually examine the basic characteristics of this framework. They either assume, usually implicitly, that this general macro-societal framework is the sum total of the interrelations between the different sectors and/or that the basic characteristics of this framework are shaped by combination of welfare state and the classical, Keynsian economic policies with strong social-democratic assumptions. They do not, however, take into account that what has happened in most modern societies as a result of the institutionalisation of these features has not been just an expansion of services and technical arrangements, but rather some far-reaching, overall, macro-societal changes, whether those analysed above or some similar to them.

This is indeed connected with another aspect of policy studies, very closely related to some of the changes in democratic policies to which we have alluded before, namely that it is not aways clear to whom they address themselves. Quite often it is as if they saw themselves as providers of prescriptions for the powers that be, prescriptions that would show how to solve various acute social and economic problems.

But the experience of the last twenty years or so, as seen for instance in the fate of the Coleman Report, or in many other fields such as urban renewal and the like, has shown that it is not easy to give such prescriptions. This is so for several reasons. First, whatever advice can be given, should take into account the broader societal framework and not only the specific problem or sectorial framework to which it addresses itself. Second, the nature of social reality is always much more complex than most of these prescriptions envisage. Third, very often the very implementation of a policy change creates a new situation, which has to be continuously re-examined accordingly. There is, another very important aspect of this problem which has to be taken into account in this context: the nature of the public which makes demands on the policy-makers. Here it is important to recognise that policy scientists have greatly neglected what may be their most important function: education, the enlightening of the public and the assurance to them of their continuous enlightened participation in the formulation and execution of policies. This means, of course, that it is not enough to present prescriptions. It is also necessary to present the assumptions upon which the different recommendations are made and to point out the different alternatives and their respective costs.

This neglect has had a very deleterious effect on contemporary democratic societies, on the formation of public opinion and on the democratic political process. It seems to me that one of the major roles of the political scientists should be to remedy this situation. They should strive to do away with the negative effects, both in public and political life in contemporary democracies, of the highly specialised conceptual framework and jargon which have few common premises or shared commonsense assumptions, either between each other or between themselves and the wider public. It seems to me that without continuous interaction between scholars engaged in the study of modern political life in general and in policy studies in particular, and between the broader enlightened public and policy-makers, politicians and administrators alike, contemporary democratic societies, which are almost by definition also welfare-state societies, face very serious problems.

LIST OF CONTRIBUTORS

Professor Brian Abel-Smith, Department of Social Administration, London School of Economics and Political Sciences, London, England.

Professor Yair Aharoni, Faculty of Management, Tel Aviv University, Tel Aviv, Israel.

Dr Yael Azmon, Department of Sociology, The Hebrew University of Jerusalem, Jerusalem, Israel.

Professor Rivka Bar-Yosef, Department of Sociology, The Hebrew University of Jerusalem, Jerusalem, Israel.

Dan Bavly, C.P.A., author of *The Subterranean Economy*, McGraw-Hill, New York 1982.

Dr Raphaella Bilski Ben-Hur, Department of Political Sciences, The Hebrew University of Jerusalem, Jerusalem, Israel.

Professor Francois Bourricaud, Université de Paris-Sorbonne, Paris, France.

S.N. Eisenstadt, Department of Sociology, The Hebrew University of Jerusalem, Jerusalem, Israel.

Professor Peter Flora, Department of Sociology, University of Mannheim, Mannheim, Germany.

Professor Morris Janowitz, Department of Sociology, University of Chicago, Chicago, Illinois, USA.

Lars-Nørby Johansen, Labour Organisation Institute, Oslo, Norway.

Professor Franz-Xaver Kaufmann, Institute for Population Research and Social Policy, University of Bielefeld, Germany.

Dr Heinz Kienzl, Director General, Bank of Austria, Vienna, Austria.

Professor Jon Eivind Kolberg, Labour Organisation Institute, Oslo, Norway.

Professor Ralph M. Kramer, School of Social Welfare, University of California, Berkeley, California, USA.

Dr Baruch Levy, Director, Jacob Hiatt Institute, Brandeis University, Jerusalem, Israel.

Professor S.M. Miller, Department of Sociology, Boston University, Boston, Massachusetts, USA.

Dr Elad Peled, former Director-General, Ministry of Education and Culture, Department of Sociology and Anthropology, Ben-Gurion University of the Negev, Israel.

Dr Jacob Vedel-Petersen, The Danish Institute of Social Research, Copenhagen, Denmark.

Nicole Questiaux, former Minister of Welfare, France.

Professor Martin Rein, Faculty of Urban Studies and Planning, MIT and Harvard University, Cambridge, Massachusetts, USA.

Professor Walter Rüegg, Department of Sociology, University of Berne, Berne, Switzerland.

Arthur Seldon, Institute of Economic Affairs, London, England.

Professor Rei Shiratori, Director, Institute for Political Studies, Japan.

Shirley Williams, Chairperson of the Social Democratic Party, England.

INDEX